Monetary Policy and Central Banking

Monetary Policy and Central Banking

New Directions in Post-Keynesian Theory

Edited by

Louis-Philippe Rochon

Associate Professor and Director, International Economic Policy Institute, Laurentian University, Sudbury, Canada, Founding Co-editor, Review of Keynesian Economics

Salewa 'Yinka Olawoye

University of Missouri-Kansas City, USA

Edward Elgar

Cheltenham, UK • Northampton, MA, USA

Published by
Edward Elgar Publishing Limited
The Lypiatts
15 Lansdown Road
Cheltenham
Glos GL50 2JA
UK

Edward Elgar Publishing, Inc.
William Pratt House
9 Dewey Court
Northampton
Massachusetts 01060
USA

A catalogue record for this book
is available from the British Library

Library of Congress Control Number: 2012935281

MIX
Paper from
responsible sources
FSC
www.fsc.org   FSC® C018575

ISBN 978 1 84980 735 7 (cased)

Typeset by Servis Filmsetting Ltd, Stockport, Cheshire
Printed and bound by MPG Books Group, UK

Contents

Figures

Tables

Contributors

Angel Asensio is a lecturer at the University Paris 13, and researcher at the CEPN (Univ. Paris 13-CNRS, France). He is a member of ADEK (Association pour le Développement des Études Keynésiennes). He has recently published research papers on Post Keynesian theory, monetary and fiscal policy interactions, international interdependence and economic policy coordination.

Jörg Bibow is Associate Professor of Economics at Skidmore College, New York, and Research Associate at the Levy Economics Institute, Annandale-on-Hudson, New York, USA. Previously he held lecturing positions at the University of Cambridge, Hamburg University, and at Franklin College, Switzerland. He holds a PhD degree in economics from the University of Cambridge. He is the author of *Keynes on Monetary Policy, Finance and Uncertainty* (Routledge, 2009). He has published numerous articles and co-authored volumes in Europe and the US on European integration, central banking and global finance, including *Euroland and the World Economy: Global Player or Global Drag?* (Palgrave, 2007).

Robert Dimand is Professor of Economics at Brock University, St. Catharines, Ontario, Canada. Educated at McGill and Yale universities, he has written *The Origins of the Keynesian Revolution* (Edward Elgar and Stanford University Press, 1988) and more than 60 journal articles, and has edited 10 books.

Robert Guttmann is Professor of Economics at Hofstra University (New York) and, since 1993, also Visiting Professor at the Université Paris XIII (France). A specialist on monetary theory and financial instability, he has published widely in the United States, the European Union, and Latin America. Among his more noteworthy books are *How Credit-Money Shapes the Economy: The United States in a Global System* (M.E. Sharpe, 1994) and *Cybercash: The Coming Reign of Electronic Money* (Palgrave-Macmillan, 2003). His latest publication, co-authored with Dominique Plihon, is entitled 'Whither the euro?' for the Oxford University Press Handbook on Financial Crises.

Eric Kam is Associate Professor of Economics in the Department of Economics, Ryerson University, Toronto, Canada. He holds a PhD in economics from York University, and has previously taught at Huron University College, University of Western Ontario. His main research interests are in the fields of monetary theory, international monetary theory, microeconomic foundations of macroeconomics and the history of economic thought. He is the author/co-author of 20 academic publications in journals including the *Journal of Post Keynesian Economics, Economics Bulletin, Economics Letters*, the *Journal of Economic Studies, Economia Informa* and *Greek Economic Review*.

Robert Koehn is Lecturer in Economics at Brock University, St. Catharines, Ontario, was educated at McMaster University and the University of Toronto, Canada. He teaches labor economics, regional economics, and money and banking, and has published in the *Atlantic Economic Journal*, the *Forum for Social Economics*, the *Journal of Economic Asymmetries*, and the *Journal of Economic Issues*.

Marc Lavoie is Professor of Economics in the Department of Economics at the University of Ottawa, Canada, where he started teaching in 1979. Besides having published over 175 papers in refereed journals and book chapters, he has written a number of books, among which *Foundations of Post-Keynesian Economic Analysis* (Edward Elgar, 1992), *Introduction to Post-Keynesian Economics* (Palgrave/Macmillan, 2006) (with French, Spanish, Japanese and Chinese versions), as well as *Monetary Economics: An Integrated Approach to Money, Income, Production and Wealth* (Palgrave/Macmillan, 2007) with Wynne Godley. With Mario Seccareccia, he co-edited *Central Banking in the Modern World: Alternative Perspectives* (Edward Elgar, 2004). With Gennaro Zezza, he is editing the *Selected Writings of Wynne Godley* (2012).

Edwin Le Heron is Professor in Economics at the Bordeaux Institute of Political Studies, France, and researcher at CED (Centre Émile Durkheim). He is also President of ADEK (French Association for the Development of Keynesian Studies), which gathers French economists interested in Keynes and in Post Keynesian works. His research interests are monetary policy, Post Keynesian monetary theory, SFC modeling and the history of economic thought.

Noemi Levy-Orlik received her PhD in economics from the Universidad Nacional Autónoma de México (UNAM), Mexico City, in 1999. She is a professor in the Economics Department at UNAM. Her areas of research are in monetary economics, with particular attention to development issues of Latin American countries, with specific emphasis on finance and financial institutions in developing countries. She is presently coordinating the research project "Financial structures and finance for economic development", financed by DGAPA-UNAM. She is a member of the Mexican System of National Research (SNI-CONACYT). She has published two books, edited seven, coordinated journal issues and written multiple papers that have been published as book chapters and in journals.

Warren Mosler holds a BA in economics from the University of Connecticut, USA. He is founder and Principal of AVM, and founder of Illinois Income Investors. Over the years, he has held various positions in financial corporations in the USA. He is also the co-founder and Distinguished Research Associate of the Center for Full Employment and Price Stability at the University of Missouri in Kansas City. He is an Associate Fellow at the University of Newcastle, Australia.

Salewa 'Yinka Olawoye is a doctoral student at the University of Missouri, Kansas City (UMKC), USA. She holds bachelors' degrees in English language from the University of Lagos, Nigeria and in economics from Laurentian University, Canada. Her areas of specialization are international trade, central banking and development.

Louis-Philippe Rochon is Associate Professor of Economics at Laurentian University, Canada. He has authored over 85 journal and book articles, and has written or edited numerous books, including *Credit, Money and Production* (Edward Elgar, 2005), *Modern Theories of Money: The Nature and Role of Money in Capitalist Economies* (Edward Elgar, 2003, co-edited with Sergio Rossi), *Monetary and Exchange Rate Systems: A Global View of Financial Crises* (Edward Elgar, 2006, co-edited with Sergio Rossi), *Credit, Money and Macroeconomic Policy* (Edward Elgar, 2011, with Claude Gnos) and *Employment, Growth and Development* (Edward Elgar, 2012, with Claude Gnos and Domenica Tropeano). His papers have appeared in, for example, the *Review of Political Economy*, the *International Journal of Political Economy*, *Metroeconomica*, the *Journal of Economic Issues*, *Économie Appliquée*, and the *Journal of Post Keynesian Economics*. His research is on macroeconomic and monetary theory and policy, and Post Keynesian economics.

Mario Seccareccia is Professor of Economics at the University of Ottawa, Canada. He has also been a Visiting Professor at the University of Paris-Sud, the University of Bourgogne, and the National Autonomous University of Mexico, and a Lecturer at the Labour College of Canada, the Post Keynesian Summer School at the University of Missouri, and the Summer School of the Progressive Economics Forum in Canada. He has authored/co-authored or co-edited some 12 books or monographs, and some 90 scholarly articles and chapters of books in a wide variety of areas in economics, including monetary economics, macroeconomics, labor economics, the history of economic thought and economic history. He is also the editor of the *International Journal of Political Economy* and has edited or co-edited over 20 special issues of the journal since 2004.

Mark Setterfield is Professor of Economics in the Department of Economics at Trinity College, Hartford, Connecticut, USA, Associate Member of the Cambridge Centre for Economic and Public Policy at Cambridge University (UK), and Senior Research Associate at the International Economic Policy Institute, Laurentian University (Canada). His main research interests are macrodynamics and Post-Keynesian economics. He is the author of *Rapid Growth and Relative Decline: Modelling Macroeconomic Dynamics with Hysteresis* (Macmillan, 1997), the editor (or co-editor) of five volumes of essays, and has published in a variety of journals including the *Cambridge Journal of Economics*, *European Economic Review*, the *Journal of Post Keynesian Economics*, and *The Manchester School*.

John Smithin is Professor of Economics in the Department of Economics and the Schulich School of Business, York University, Toronto, Canada. He holds a PhD from McMaster University, and has previously taught at the University of Calgary, and Lanchester Polytechnic (now Coventry University) in England. His main research interests are in the fields of monetary theory and the philosophy of money and finance. He is the author/editor (co-author/co-editor) of *Keynes and Public Policy after Fifty Years* (1988), *Macroeconomics after Thatcher and Reagan* (1990), *Economic Integration between Unequal Partners* (1994), *Macroeconomic Policy and the Future of Capitalism* (1996), *Money, Financial Institutions and Macroeconomics* (1997), *What is Money?* (2000), *Globalization and Economic Growth* (2002), *Controversies in Monetary Economics* (1994, 2003), *Fundamentals of Economics for Business* (2006, 2009), and *Money, Enterprise and Income Distribution* (2009). He is currently working on a new book of with the provisional title, *Essays in the Fundamental Theory of Monetary Economics and Macroeconomics*, which aims at a definitive treatment of the issues in the these fields.

Domenica Tropeano is Associate Professor of Economics at the faculty of Economics of the University of Macerata, Italy. She has an MA from the University of Warwick and a doctorate from the European University Institute. She has studied and published in the fields of history of economic thought and history of macroeconomics, and is currently working on the issue of macroeconomic policies and globalization.

Kurt von Seekamm is a graduate of Trinity College, Hartford, Connecticut, USA, where he wrote his honors thesis on the effects of monetary and fiscal policy in a 3-equation New Keynesian model with a commercial banking sector. His research interests are in macroeconomics, particularly macroeconomic theory and policy, theories of endogenous money and depression economics.

Introduction

Louis-Philippe Rochon and Salewa 'Yinka Olawoye

The current – and ongoing – crisis has presented interesting challenges to policy makers as they scramble to propose a wide range of policies to deal with the continuing recession. Yet, policies proposed at the beginning of the crisis are radically different from those proposed currently, three years later. In a way, we are now back at square one: adopting pre-crisis policies post-crisis.

At the beginning of the crisis, shortly following the G20 meetings in Washington (November 15, 2008), many countries around the world, including Canada, the United States, Europe, and the UK, adopted an unprecedented degree of activist fiscal policies, ranging, among other policies, from bank and private sector bailouts to direct subsidies to households. This led some economists and pundits to claim aloud that the Master had returned, an obvious reference of course to Keynes (see Skidelsky, 2009). Further, at the Toronto G20 summit held in June 26–27, 2010, it was even recognized that "unprecedented and globally coordinated fiscal and monetary stimulus is playing a major role in helping to restore private demand and lending". Fiscal policy seemed to be an acceptable policy choice once again. For a while, it seemed that fiscal policy had regained much of its lost luster, dusted off the shelves, and accepted once again as a credible tool of macroeconomic stabilization.

Yet, to anyone with a memory span of more than a few years, these policies seemed somewhat oddly misplaced, given that until then, the consensus among economists and governments was for balanced budgets or even budget surpluses, what is now being referred to as "fiscal consolidation". Indeed, before the crisis, fiscal expansion was considered inflationary, and an ineffective way of stimulating output and growth. In fact, in new consensus models, fiscal policy is absent, and growth falls entirely on the ability of central banks to fine tune interest rates.

That was then. As the crisis progressed, policy makers did a U-turn and became convinced that the righteous path to growth was no longer through fiscal largess, but rather through fiscal restraints. Keynes was dead and governments reversed their position from about a year before. Indeed, governments now accepted the fact that austerity was the only means to prosperity. In Europe, perhaps more than anywhere else, austerity became well entrenched, to the detriment of all other possible objectives. The threat of a downgrade like the one that fell on the US was hanging over the heads of state like the sword of Damocles. The unemployed now became accepted casualties in the war against imaginary inflation and fiscal deficits. Countries such as Greece and Italy are being forced to accept draconian fiscal cutbacks in an attempt to clean their house – that is, to put their fiscal house in order. Fiscal consolidation is now a widely accepted policy prescription, dictated by credit agencies.

But at the onset of the crisis, things were quite different, and not only in terms of fiscal policy. Indeed, the Grand Keynesian experience seemed to have been extended to monetary policy as well, as central banks around the world turned to Keynesian-type policies, more specifically keeping interest rates at record low levels, and at near zero levels in the case of the United States, mimicking Keynes's proposal to, at least temporarily, euthanize the rentier class. Indeed, in Canada and the United States more notably, central bankers have even vowed to keep interest rates at near zero for a prolonged period.

Yet, setting interest rates close to its zero lower bound raises an interesting conundrum. With interest rates so low, what else can central banks do to stimulate the economy? Does this lower bound limit the central bank's ability to stimulate the economy? In a real way, the current crisis has thrust central bankers into a policy and intellectual void, not unlike the liquidity trap of the Keynesian era.

Indeed, in the past, in the old Keynesian incarnation of monetary theory, the liquidity trap represented the end of monetary stimulation: it was impossible for central banks to further increase the money supply and lower interest rates. Policy makers hence had no choice but to fall back on fiscal policy: monetary policy became ineffective.

Yet, there was always a mistrust of the effectiveness of fiscal policy among a great portion of the economic profession, which saw fiscal policy as inflationary and worse. In fact, even the theoretical framework of the new macroeconomic paradigm, the so-called "new consensus", now downplays the effectiveness or usefulness of fiscal policy. Monetary policy was always perceived as the only effective (or preferred) tool of expansionary policies. Fiscal policy was never considered an adequate substitute, although in times of a major recession or crisis, its usefulness was recognized. Indeed, fiscal policy appears nowhere in its three-equation model.

But with current rates so low, this called for ways of proving the effectiveness of monetary policy. In other words, modern-day Keynesians sought a solution to the so-called "liquidity trap situation". This is where quantitative easing or "Operation Twist" policies come in. Indeed, these policies were meant to be a solution to the liquidity trap: a way for central banks and monetary policy to remain relevant despite near-zero interest rates. To wit, the profession at large always sought ways to prove the usefulness of monetary policy even at low rates, going as far back as Alfred Pigou.

Of course, theoretical situations under the old Keynesian approach and the new consensus are different, certainly. Under the old Keynesian framework, interest rates were seen as endogenous and central banks were said to control the money supply, and increasing it no longer had an effect on interest rates. Under the new consensus, however, interest rates are seen as exogenous, similar to what Post Keynesians have been arguing for several decades now.

Yet, regardless of the exogenous or endogenous nature of interest rates, both situations share a similar conclusion: at near-zero rates, what can the central bank do to further stimulate the economy? Under the old Keynesian doctrine, the answer was "nothing" and we had to rely on fiscal policy. Now, central bankers are attempting new policies (some of which have been tried before, in fact) in an attempt to give relevance to monetary policy, despite low interest rates.

Whether these new policies will eventually have an impact on the macro-economy, however, remains to be seen. Federal Reserve Chairman Ben Bernanke, during testimony at the Joint Economic Committee on October 4, 2011, has already labeled Operation Twist as "Significant, but not a game changer". As for attempts to increase the liquidity of banks through quantitative easing, this was perhaps an ill-fated policy from the beginning. Increased liquidity does not lead to increased bank lending: banks lend because they have confidence in the ability of bank borrowers to repay their loans. This is consistent with the theory of endogenous money and the notion of a creditworthy bank borrower: banks are never constrained by the lack of deposits or liquidity.

Regardless of whether interest rates are near zero, Post Keynesians have always tended to downplay the importance of monetary policy in favor of fiscal policy, while rejecting the liquidity trap scenario alltogeher. This is not to say that monetary policy does not play an important role, but that it is rather an ineffective way of stimulating aggregate demand. Increasingly, Post Keynesians argue that central banks ought to keep interest rates at a low level and rely on fiscal policy to do the rest.

As of early 2012, many economies are still not on a guaranteed path toward growth. Indeed, unemployment seems stuck at relatively high levels and aggregate demand is, at best, anemic. As a result, there is increasing pressure on governments to continue spending. Yet, this appears increasingly less likely. The greater question, therefore, is the following: "where will the growth come from in the next decade?". After all, the household sector is overindebted and its attempt to lower its debt will be a drag on aggregate demand. The private sector, despite healthy profits, does not seem to be willing to invest, and banks are increasingly unwilling to lend. As for the possibility of an export-led growth strategy, the fear is that the pie is not big enough, given the fierce competition for those markets. This leaves only the government sector in the position to stimulate the economy sufficiently to lift it out of recession. But even this strategy seems unlikely as governments are now aggressively pursuing fiscal austerity measures in order to balance their books. In this sense, it is increasingly becoming business as usual, that is, policy makers and governments are turning to pre-crisis policies post-crisis, condemning us perhaps to another eventual crisis.

This raises interesting questions regarding the fate of Keynes after the crisis. Undoubtedly, the crisis shone a much-deserved spotlight on Keynes, no less than on or around the 75th anniversary of the publication of the *General Theory*. But this seems to be temporary. In fact, if the profession at large seems to have embraced Keynes during the crisis, they are just as quick to reject him once the crisis is over – whenever that may be. Indeed, even before the crisis is over, calls for austerity measures in the US as well as in England and the whole of Europe are becoming policy. This raises serious questions about the eventuality of another crisis, and the odds are high that we will go down a path of economic *déjà vu*.

Ultimately, one conclusion that seems to be emerging now is that monetary policy is broken. Its narrow focus on inflation has clearly led many critics to argue that monetary policy is misguided. Some Post Keynesians have recently emphasized this point and have insisted that the rate of interest is an income distributive variable that is best used to this end. Interest rates are not effective when used in a countercyclical manner and as such should be left at a low level ("parked" to use Rochon and Setterfield's expression) indefinitely. This would be in accordance with Keynes's expressed desire to euthanize the rentier class, whose "revenge" can be costly. In the end, we are back to where Keynes started: the use of fiscal policy to stimulate effective demand and to leave "monetary details in the background" – that is, keeping interest rates low.

This book is the result of a conference held in Toronto, Canada, on May 27–28, 2009, and financed generously by the Social Sciences and Humanities Research Council of Canada (SSHRC) and Laurentian University. Sponsored by the International Economic Policy Institute at Laurentian University, it brought together a number of leading Post Keynesians who discussed, on the one hand, the possible causes of the financial crisis, and on the other, and perhaps more importantly, the challenges the crisis posed for current monetary policy and central banking. It is but one of many such conferences financed by SSHRC, and one of many more to come.

We would very much like to thank all the participants for their involvement in the conference. The discussion was both stimulating and rewarding, and further emphasized the need to further discuss the role of monetary policy and its place within the greater macroeconomic policy framework.

REFERENCE

Skidelsky, R. (2009), *Keynes: The Return of the Master*, London: Allen Lane.

PART I

Central banking and monetary policy

1. Between the cup and the lip: on Post Keynesian interest rate rules and long-term interest rate management

Angel Asensio*

> If, however, we are tempted to assert that money is the drink which stimulates the system to activity, we must remind ourselves that there may be several slips between the cup and the lip. (Keynes, *General Theory*)

1 INTRODUCTION

Because the crisis-led financial institutions and banks hold huge amounts of bad debts, they lost confidence in one another and economic agents lost confidence in the stability of the financial system as well. Consequently, the banking crisis specter is still hovering, thereby discouraging firms and households from launching long-term productive and financial investments. Although central banks promptly reduced their intervention rate drastically and pumped high-powered money massively, they have not found much success as regards economic activity. The "transmission mechanisms" look to be broken.

The literature on monetary rules will be seriously shocken because of the renewed evidence that monetary policy is first concerned with confidence, for confidence is rarely referred to in that literature. This chapter emphasizes how powerful this concept is in explaining the monetary policy transmission, and how, as a matter of consequence, monetary policy should deal with it if the transmission mechanisms are to be recovered.

While the discussion will tackle various aspects of the subject, it will not focus specifically on the prudential aspects, to which much attention has been paid. Instead, our questioning will serve two purposes: first, to emphasize some requirements for the effective control over long-term interest rates; and second to deal with monetary policy in the context of the current crisis, which raises specific problems.

The Post Keynesian approach to monetary policy is exemplified by the various interest rate rules that have been proposed recently.[1] However, contrary to the mainstream, which is still concerned with the design of a mythical "optimal monetary rule", the Post Keynesian rules should not be thought of as automatic responses to any interest rate or output gap regarding a supposed "natural" position. Rather, they have to be considered as a device aimed at approaching normative, ideal objectives which perhaps will not be reached, depending on how strong uncertainty and the related "state of confidence" impact on monetary/financial decisions and, thereby, the monetary transmission channels.

Accordingly, this chapter is organized as follows. Section 2 emphasizes the positive contribution of these interest rate rules to the Post Keynesian modern theory of monetary policy. Section 3 considers several hindrances the rules may come up against. As we are not really concerned in this chapter with the ultimate policy objectives,[2] the discussion will mainly focus on the control authorities have on intermediary objectives, namely the short- and long-term interest rates. Section 4 focuses on the role of confidence. It starts from Keynes's definition of the interest rate as a conventional variable, subject to the changing "views about the future", and investigates how monetary authorities should attempt to move the market convention toward the desired level. The section also considers specific difficulties central banks are faced with in the current troubled situation. It is argued that a "cheap money" policy, along with an offensive fiscal policy, is much better adapted to the situation than inflation targeting and fiscal orthodoxy. Section 5 summarizes the main findings and concludes the chapter.

2 POST KEYNESIAN INTEREST RATE RULES AND THEIR OPERATING CHANNELS

Rochon and Setterfield (2007a) have proposed an enlightening classification of the Post Keynesian proposals in terms of "activist" and "parking it" rules. While both kinds of rules are aimed at taking advantage of the potential effects of monetary policy both in the short and long runs, the former focuses on policies which are aimed at operating through the short-run relation between the long-term interest rates and the effective demand (Fontana and Palacio-Vera, 2003, 2007; Atesoglu, 2007; Palley, 2007; Sawyer, 2007; Tily, 2009), while the latter focuses on policies which are aimed at operating through the relation between the "parked" (short/long-term) interest rates and the income distribution (Pasinetti, 1981; Lavoie, 1999; Rochon and Setterfield, 2007a,b, 2008; Smithin, 2007; Wray, 2007).[3]

Rules Operating through the Short-run Relation between the Long-term Interest Rate and the Level of Output

The rule proposed in Atesoglu (2007) is based on Keynes's definition of the "neutral rate" (1936: 243), the interest rate which is consistent with full employment. It is aimed at adjusting the central bank rate at a neutral level, that is, in such a way that the long-term interest rate is adjusted to its own neutral level as well. Although Atesoglu's proposal does not deal explicitly with the long-term effects of monetary policy, his approach does not deny these effects of course.

Tily (2007, 2009) advocates low long-term interest rates ("cheap money"). This general statement, however, does not seem to be concerned with the "parking it" type of rules, for two reasons: first, his proposal is not oriented toward any distributive objective, and, second, "cheap money" could involve different levels of interest rate, depending on the economic context.[4] The "cheap money" objectives actually consist in smoothing the economic cycle at a high level of employment and in reducing the related risk of debt inflation/debt deflation which is likely to be higher in "dear money" regimes (Tily, 2009, pp. 105–6).

The innovative proposal for a "flexible opportunistic approach" developed by Fontana and Palacio-Vera (2003, 2007) seeks explicitly to stimulate the growth rate of output and employment, besides stabilizing the output in the short run and achieving price stability in the long run (see also Sawyer, 2007).[5] In the standard opportunistic approach (Orphanides and Wilcox, 1996), it is suggested that, in order to be able to take advantage of a possible exogenous adjustment of the inflation rate towards the long-run target, the central bank should not adjust interest rates as long as the actual inflation rate remains within some predetermined upper and lower limits around the target. By contrast, the flexible opportunistic approach puts forward that the possible long-run effects of the monetary policy on the potential output is in favor of a policy loosening when the actual rate of inflation is below the target but above the predetermined lower bound. In a similar way, if the actual rate of inflation is above the target but below the predetermined upper bound, the flexible opportunistic approach states that the monetary policy should decrease the interest rate moderately, so as to take advantage of a possible positive effect on the potential output, which would subsequently offset possible inflationary pressures.

According to Palley (2007: 61), inflation targeting "biases decisions toward low inflation by obscuring the fact that policy also affects unemployment, real wages, and growth". Taking these effects into account, Palley calls for setting the rate of interest so as to balance the possible advantages that may follow from accepting an increased inflation rate with the advantage of low inflation. In his model, when unemployment is sufficiently high, the only cost to monetary stimulus is increased inflation. The authorities in that case may reduce the rate of interest so that unemployment decreases towards the MURI (minimum unemployment rate of inflation, beyond which further inflation increases might have a counterproductive effect on employment[6]). However, under certain conditions, a trade-off between employment and growth may arise as unemployment falls. Indeed, "lower unemployment raises economic growth if the economy is in the wage-led region [but] lowers growth if it is in the profit-led region" (ibid.: 75). Hence, if the economy becomes profit led while unemployment decreases (as the profit rate is negatively affected by unemployment), the trade-off arises.

This interesting feature of Palley's model suggests that the rate of interest should not be adjusted according to a rigid predetermined rule, for the economy may become wage or profit led depending on the level of unemployment, which affects the terms of the trade-off facing monetary policy.

Rules Operating through the Relation between the Rate of Interest and the Income Distribution

Rules that aim at operating through the relation between the interest rates and the income distribution do not deny that the interest rate policy impacts on the economy trajectory in the short and long runs, although they focus on the sharing of the income growth in a long-run perspective. Basically, it is asserted that owing to the many uncertainties in the transmission mechanism (Bateman, 2003; Wray, 2007), monetary policy can hardly get much success in the "activist" way of setting interest rates. It is therefore recommended that the interest rate is set so that undesirable distributive effects are avoided. The resulting "parking it" rules divide into short-term nominal rate and long-term real rate rules.

Let us first discuss the "fair rate" rule, understood in the spirit of Pasinetti (1981; see also Lavoie, 1999), and the "low real rate" proposed in Smithin (2007; see also Atesoglu and Smithin, 2006; Hein and Stockhammer, 2007). Both are real rate-based rules and share the normative purpose of providing economic policy with an "explicit distributional objective". The "fair rate" rule consists in equalizing the real interest rate with the productivity growth rate, so that the rentiers' share in the national income is constant. Smithin's rule, on the other hand, aims at setting the real interest rate at a low level (again a "cheap money" policy, but in the "parking it" approach this time). The distribution effect here differs essentially because

> [I]t does not . . . guarantee a share for *existing* wealth holders (as opposed to entrepreneurs or workers) in *current* productivity increases, as would the notion of the "fair" interest rate . . . This omission might be justified on the grounds that it is the latter, rather than the former, who are actually responsible for the productivity increases. (Smithin 2007: 116; original italics)

As Wray (2007: 120) also rejects "discretionary policy and doubt[s] the veracity of conventional views of central bank ability to achieve traditional goals such as robust growth, low inflation, or high employment", the "Kansas city" rule recommends a constant zero short-term nominal rate[7] which aims at returning "to Keynes's call for low interest rates and euthanasia of the rentier".[8]

Table 1.1 summarizes some central features of the "activist" and "parking it" rules.

3   UNCERTAIN TRANSMISSION MECHANISMS

The success of an interest rate rule rests on the condition that the transmission mechanisms really work, which, however, is questionable, whatever the rule is specified in terms of long-term rate or the policy instrument (or any short-turn rate strongly linked to the instrument).

Do Central Banks Control Long-term Interest Rates?

First, it is important to note that the central bank does not control directly the long-term interest rates, which are decided by banks (as far as bank loans are concerned) and by the market conditions as far as private loans are concerned. Of course, the central bank's refinancing policy influences both: when the central bank refinancing rate is increased, banks tend to pass on the difference more or less to the various credit rates they offer, and as credits become more expansive, borrowers tend to get finance in the non-bank sector, which transmits the long-term rate increase to that sector as well.

However, as stated in Keynes's liquidity preference theory, the central bank influence on the long-term rates is not the only force that determines their level. The point is that the shifting nature of the state of confidence has serious implications for the ability of monetary policy to control the long-term interest rate effectively, especially in the case of interest rate reductions. In order to make this clear within the Post Keynesian approach to endogenous money, let us suppose that the monetary base is increased as a result of a lower refinancing short-term rates policy, and that consequently, lower long-term bank rates start

Table 1.1   Post Keynesian interest rate rules and operating channels

Interest rate rule	Operating channel	
	Income distribution ("parking it" rules)	Output gap (activist rules)
Nominal interest rate (NIR)	(*Short-term nominal rate*) • "Kansas City rule" (Wray) NIR = 0, "Euthanasia of the rentier"	(*Long-term nominal rate*) • "Neutral rate" (Atesoglu) NIR adjusted to full employment • "Picks a quadruple"* (Palley) NIR adjusted to the MURI (or, if need be, to the trade-off employment/growth) • "Cheap money" (Tily) NIR set so that RIR is "low", investment is high and financial risk is low
Real interest rate (RIR)	(*Long-term real rate*) • "Fair rate" (Pasinetti/Lavoie) RIR = productivity growth • Smithin's rule RIR = 0	(*Long-term real rate*) • "Flexible opportunistic rule" (Fontana and Palacio-Vera) (decrease RIR even if inflation is slightly above the target, for it might increase the productivity growth) • Flexible "fair rate" (Sawyer) RIR adjusted so that its possible influence on the productivity growth is not overlooked

Note: * In Palley's model, "the monetary authority is picking a quadruple consisting of inflation, unemployment, real wages, and growth".

boosting the demand for credit. If, at the same time, the liquidity preference increases, banks may be able to sell more credit without reducing their interest rates substantially, for bonds and other non-bank loan rates tend to rise in this case in order to compensate for the increasing liquidity preference. Even if "the monetary authority were prepared to deal both ways on specified terms in debts of all maturities, and even more so if it were prepared to deal in debts of varying degree of risk", there would be "limitations on the ability of the monetary authority to establish any given complex of rates of interest for debts of different terms and risk" (Keynes 1936: 205, 207).

Some of these limitations (see ibid.: 207–8 for a detailed discussion) can be considered purely theoretical, insofar as they would arise only in extreme circumstances (virtually absolute liquidity preference when rates are considered too low; breakdown of stability in the rate of interest – owing to a flight from the currency or other financial crisis); but others apply in normal circumstances (the intermediate cost of bringing the borrower and the lender together, the allowance for risk required by the lender, including liquidity risk).[9]

Furthermore, changes in the liquidity preference may also be triggered by the central bank policy itself. For example, let us suppose that the cut in the short-term rate starts to have some effect on the long-term rate. According to Keynes's theory of interest, if the market belief is that the "conventional" long-term rate is higher than the actual, that is, if a future increase is expected, the liquidity preference increases as well (this point is discussed further in Section 4), thereby limiting or possibly preventing the reduction in the long-term rate.

Hence, while the Post Keynesian endogenous money approach is right when it states that banks do deliver the amount of credit money that is demanded at the current interest rate, and while it is also correct to say that the long-term rate is exogenous in the sense that it does not result from a market-clearing process, nevertheless it is not assured that the central bank has enough control as to set the rate at the level it decides (although it is often assumed).[10]

The point has obvious implications in the debate on interest rate rules. Whether long-term interest rates have to be adjusted with respect to the output gap or according to some distributional objective does not close the debate; it remains to deal with the delicate question of how to get the desired interest rate adjustment. The problem is even more difficult when the policy rule involves real rates, for it is assumed in this case that, provided the central bank is able to adjust the long-term nominal rate, it can also adjust the nominal rate to take account of the expected inflation rate. But this requires that the expected rate of inflation is independent of the nominal rate of interest, which is not self-evidently true. Even if authorities intend to anchor expectations by committing themselves to an inflation target, the official target would not anchor expectations if agents thought that the nominal interest rate was inconsistent with the target. Thus, either the central bank anchors the expected inflation but cannot set the nominal rate independently, or the central bank sets the interest rate but cannot anchor the expected inflation rate independently. In either case, the central bank can hardly be said to control the real interest rate.

Conflicting Objectives and the "Kansas City Rule" sustainability

If, as in the "Kansas City rule", the rule is specified in terms of the policy instrument, or in terms of a rate which is strongly related to the policy instrument, as in the Kansas City rule, things go differently. A zero short-term nominal interest rate may be recommendable in the context of economic depression, but it may also be questionable in other contexts.

The question of the feasibility of the rule here is not to be taken in the strict sense of the word, since the central bank can reasonably be said to have a good control over the short-term rates in general. It rather relies on both the relevance or sustainability of the rule and its effectiveness with respect to the "euthanasia of the rentier".

As for effectiveness, the transmission between the short-term interbank interest rate and the long-term interest rates of the economy is subject to the limitation discussed above. Sustainability on the other hand requires that no prior objectives could normally lead authorities to renounce implementing the rule. But there are recurrent forces in our economic systems which could give raise to such prior objectives. In the face of distributive tensions aimed, for example, at increasing the share of profits or wages, a zero refinancing rate would allow for monetary accommodation of the resulting inflationary pressures.[11] It is no doubt a good thing that the central bank accommodates banks when they need to refinance themselves as a result of the credit money they have created in response to viable activities, but when the demand for credit money results from the kind of distributive inflationary pressures mentioned above, the central bank faces a dilemma: either it accommodates inflation, so that unemployment does not rise, or it fights the distributive conflict by means of higher interest and unemployment rates.[12] Such a dilemma has no objective solution that could be picked out from economic theory, especially if inflationary pressures are strong and threaten the confidence in the purchasing power of money. It is a political decision, a matter for the community as a whole.

The dilemma would vanish if, as recommended in Setterfield (2007; see also Hein and Stockhammer, 2007; Rochon and Setterfield, 2007a,b; Setterfield and Lima, 2008), an incomes policy could harmonize the distribution of income. But even in that case, it is doubtful whether a zero-rate rule is really sustainable, for there are events which may prompt the central bank to adjust the overnight rate. For example, Wray (2007) points out the problem of exchange rate stabilization in fixed peg regimes, although his discussion then abstracts from the problem by assuming flexible exchange rates. Yet such an assumption does not really solve the problem, especially in the case of a large or medium-sized country. Such a country indeed cannot really have a totally independent interest rate policy even in the case of a flexible exchange rate, for there are negative externalities, some of which pass through the exchange rate variations (as in the case of "competitive depreciation"), which normally trigger interest rate policy responses in foreign countries; these are aimed at offsetting the externalities and the related exchange rate variations.[13] Hence, anticipating the foreign reaction, the policy of the home country may be to set the interest rate in accordance with a commonly "acceptable" exchange rate, instead of unilaterally implementing a "parking it" rule.

4   COPING WITH CONFIDENCE

Rochon and Setterfield's (2007b) comparative evaluation of the "parking it" variants corroborates the idea that interest rate rules that perform well in certain contexts may have lower performances in other contexts. This is also a noticeable feature of the "activist" rules discussed above. It is an advantage that Post Keynesians offer a range of policies from which the adequate one can be picked up in accordance with the context. The Post Keynesian approach in this perspective shows some flexibility in comparison to the mainstream. However, keeping this positive contribution in the background, we must now turn to the delicate point of setting long-term interest rates effectively in a system deprived of a natural anchor, where the liquidity preference and the demand for money are shifting variables.

As argued in the previous section, the long-term interest rate can hardly be considered a pure exogenous variable that monetary authorities could put at the desired level, although it does not result from any market-clearing forces either.[14] Keynes actually considered the rate of interest a "highly psychological phenomenon" whose level cannot diverge durably from the market convention. Consequently, the essential problem for the monetary policy is to influence on the market convention; this is a precondition for being able to adjust the long-term rate of interest toward the desired level.

The Long-term Interest Rate as a Convention

The idea that the success of monetary policy is never ensured is a recurring theme of Keynes's *General Theory*, especially in chapter 13 (section 3), chapter 15 (section 2), and chapter 19 (sections 2 and 3):

> [The rate of interest] is a highly conventional . . . phenomenon. For its actual value is largely governed by the prevailing view as to what its value is expected to be. *Any* level of interest which is accepted with sufficient conviction as *likely*

to be durable *will* be durable; subject, of course, in a changing society to fluctuations for all kinds of reasons round the expected normal. (Keynes, 1936: 203; original italics)

Therefore unemployment develops "because people want the moon" (ibid.: 235), that is, because the long-term equilibrium interest rate is not low enough when liquidity preference is too high, given the marginal efficiency of capital and the aggregate propensity to consume. According to this view, the challenge for monetary policy does not amount simply to putting the short-term rate at some desired level; it is also necessary to have some influence on the convention so that the long-term interest rate adjusts in a way which allows for full employment. The task is difficult because the state of confidence is volatile and makes the liquidity preference and inducement to invest shifting variables, with the result that both the control over the long-term interest rate and the final effect on effective demand are erratic.

Things turn out especially delicate when it is considered that the short-term interest rate variations themselves may influence the state of confidence as well, thereby producing shifts in the macroeconomic relationships and making uncertainty endogenous to the monetary policy itself. Successful policies therefore have to "take into account the unpredictable reactions of businessmen to those policies" (Bateman, 2003: 82). Quoting Keynes again, we are led to the conclusion that "a monetary policy which strikes public opinion as being experimental in character or easily liable to change may fail in its objective of greatly reducing the long-term rate of interest, because M_2 may tend to increase almost without limit in response to a reduction of r below a certain figure" (Keynes, 1936: 203).

Can Monetary Policy Change the Convention?

A prudent monetary policy, on the other hand, can take advantage of the conventional nature of the interest rate:

> if it appeals to public opinion as being reasonable and practicable and in the public interest, rooted in strong conviction, and promoted by an authority unlikely to be superseded . . . Public opinion can be fairly rapidly accustomed to a modest fall in the rate of interest and the conventional expectation of the future may be modified accordingly; thus preparing the way for a further movement – up to a point. The fall in the long-term rate of interest in Great Britain after her departure from the gold standard provides an interesting example of this; – the major movements were effected by a series of discontinuous jumps, as the liquidity function of the public, having become accustomed to each successive reduction, became ready to respond to some new incentive in the news or in the policy of the authorities. (Ibid.: 203–4)

Note that if the central bank acts to decrease the long-term interest rate gradually, the expected reductions may have a negative impact on the marginal efficiency of capital[15] and if, on the other hand, the central bank attempts a sharp adjustment in the long-term interest rate, the liquidity preference may rise and the marginal efficiency of capital may decrease.[16] Hence, there are conditions for the success of a monetary policy. The key element is that, at any time, the policy which is being implemented meets the market convention, so that pernicious effects on the liquidity preference and on the marginal efficiency of capital are avoided.

Although the way is narrow and success is not assured, four conditions for a successful monetary policy can be made explicit:[17]

1. As the variation in the long-term interest rate that authorities are seeking must correspond to the public opinion expectation, authorities should announce a long-term interest rate target in accordance with a normative objective on which public opinion has debated and agreed.
2. Logically, such a *conventional target* cannot be very distant from the current rate, otherwise it could not meet the convention, since it would require the short-term rate being adjusted immoderately (which would "strike the public"), or, if the short-term rate is moved gradually, the long-term rate would decrease gradually (which would be harmful for the marginal efficiency of capital).
3. Once the target is set, authorities should adjust the short-term rates they control gradually, so that it does not look "experimental or easily liable to change", and it allows for checking whether the policy is working well or not, if there are undesired outcomes, and so on, so that authorities may adapt their policy to the unforeseeable changing context.
4. Note that adjusting the short-term interest rates gradually does not mean slowly, for the long-term interest rate must adjust rapidly to the new convention rather than gradually, so the above-mentioned negative effect on the marginal efficiency of capital is avoided.

These conditions are probably harder to get in times of financial crisis, because of the various factors that weaken the state of the confidence, which is discussed below.

Why the "State of Confidence" Has Been Harmed for a Long Time

Prudential measures, even determined measures, are necessary conditions of the economic recovery, but they are not sufficient, for lots of bad debts are weakening the state of confidence and the monetary policy effectiveness. Several causes of concern will be lasting until bad debts have been massively reduced and the private and public sector balance sheets have been made safe:

1.   The current depression is damaging the public accounts both because of the expenditures that are automatically and/or deliberately triggered by the economic slump and because of the decrease in government fiscal revenues. This is impacting on the state of confidence both directly (for increases in public debts make economic agents expect possible future taxes and/or inflation[18] aimed at reducing the real value of the debt) and indirectly (for authorities' capacity to support the economic activity will be harmed by a higher public debt).

2.   As the financial situation of firms and households is being severely affected, debts which were safe in the context before the financial crash will become bad debts in the depressed context.

3.   The loss of confidence, in turn, tends to offset the ability of the central bank to get lower long-term interest rates and support the economic activity. As far as it is expected (and therefore agents do not trust the central bank capacity to support the economy), this enforces the market convention according to which long-term interest rates will remain at high levels.

4.   Important amounts of credit money have been created in exchange for private debts that cannot be recovered, as debtors have failed, or are going to fail. According to Fisher's identity, increases in the money quantity are concomitant with real income increases and stable prices in a safe economic context (given the velocity of money). In the current context, however, large amounts of money have been (endogenously) created which have no real counterpart (to which one can refer as "bad money"). Until now, no serious inflationary pressures have been observed because of the very strong decrease in the velocity of money (increase in the liquidity preference). But, when the depression ends, holders will seek to substitute real assets, financial assets and speculative commodities for money. The money velocity then will probably return to the pre-crisis level much more rapidly than the increase in real income, thereby allowing for nominal price inflation (unless the central banks rapidly get an improbable massive withdrawal of the excess money; see below).[19] As one can hardly imagine that the excess money will be allowed to feed a new financial bubble in a hurry (but who really knows?), it is the price of real assets and speculative goods (such as gold, oil, and so on), rather than financial assets, that is likely to be pushed up first, possibly followed by a wage-indexation effect.

5.   Banks have accumulated important reserves at low cost during the rescue episode. Although authorities claim that they will withdraw these liquidities in due time without any trouble, there is room for doubt, since a proportion of these liquidities have been pumped in exchange for bad debts that are likely to be irrecoverable. Central banks could therefore hardly withdraw the total amount of high-powered money they have injected without seriously harming the financial system again (remember that the US banking system collapsed in February 1933 owing to the problem of bad debts). The good thing is that banks will be able to create credit money at low rates when private agents start borrowing again to finance new projects; the thorn of the rose is that they will thereby accommodate the additional demand for money involved by the increasing factor cost when inflation develops.

These five "mechanisms' are self-enforcing, for they result from the financial crisis and, at the same time, make it more serious, insofar as they weaken the state of confidence (thereby pushing up the liquidity preference and long-term interest rates, and pushing down the expected return on capital and inducement to invest). In addition, they harm the capacity of authorities to deal successfully with the crisis, for, on the one hand, the central banks' control over long-term interest rates is made much more uncertain, and on the other, after the phase of depression, central banks will be faced with the hard choices we have mentioned regarding excess money and the related inflationary pressures. Of course, central banks technically have the capacity to remove inflationary pressures, but as argued above the social cost of such a policy could hardly be supported in a context of financial fragility and high unemployment.

To Strike at the Root of the Problem

The magnitude of the inflationary pressures will eventually depend on the effective capacity of authorities to withdraw the excess money that has been pumped in exchange for private bad debts. The optimistic scenario is that bad debts become good debts, thanks to a general economic recovery which would improve substantially the private financial situations. In this case, while bad debts become safe, authorities (including central banks, governments and the ad hoc institutions that have been created in order to withdraw and recycle bad debts) can withdraw liquidities, in exchange for the (finally not so bad) debts they hold, without hurting the financial system.[20]

Unfortunately, there is room for less optimistic views. The spontaneous response of the authorities to the financial crisis has been to collectivize the problem by means of money pumping, financial support, nationalizations and ad hoc institutions aimed at recycling bad debts. But these necessary decisions have transferred the problem to the public sector, in order to rescue the financial system. How then will authorities deal with the problem? As regards central banks, the collectivization process could develop along two different ways. The first one consists in letting the inflation process go on (rather than implementing an "income policy of fear"), until the real value of debts has depreciated enough so as to compensate for the value of the stock of irrecoverable debts (to the detriment of creditors). This solution would preserve the economic activity and employment, while the alternative solution of a monetary policy aimed at stabilizing the price index would put the burden of the collectivized losses on the unemployed (and the debtor, as the interest rate would increase).[21]

Along these lines, the process of collectivization of private losses itself would induce policy responses that would not support economic activity at all. Even if inflation were the chosen solution, it would only spare short-term interest rate increases. Economic recovery therefore requires offensive policies. In this perspective, "cheap money" should be welcomed provided that the credit money finances safe (non-inflationary) economic investments. The danger would rather be that a restricted credit policy would put the burden of past mistakes on current safe economic projects. However, as short-term interest rates have already been reduced close to the minimum, and as the monetary policy control over long-term rates will be difficult as long as the state of confidence has not recovered, an offensive fiscal policy, rather than a defensive one which would be aimed at limiting the public deficit, should be encouraged. In both cases public deficits have to reach historical peaks, but the former could stimulate recovery and allow some hope that a substantial amount of bad debts turn out to be recoverable, while the latter would work pro-cyclically and might therefore make the bad debt troubles still more serious.

5   CONCLUSION

Although the Post Keynesian interest rules discussed in this chapter may be feasible and sustainable in favorable circumstances, there is a difficulty in the setting of long-term interest rates. According to Keynes's theory of the rate of interest, the problem amounts basically to managing to influence the market convention; this is a precondition for being able to adjust the long-term rate of interest toward the desired level. It is a matter of confidence between markets and authorities.[22] As Keynes asserted, for a monetary policy to be effective, the variation in the long-term interest rate authorities are seeking must correspond to public expectations.

Authorities should therefore announce a long-term interest rate target in accordance with a normative objective that public opinion has debated and agreed on. We have argued that such a *conventional target* cannot be very distant from the current rate, and that authorities should adjust the short-term rates they control gradually, but not slowly, so that it does not appear to be "experimental or easily liable to change" and so that authorities can adapt their strategy according to the observed effectiveness and the unforeseeable changing context.

Moving the interest rate convention is harder to achieve in the context of the current crisis, because of the deleterious effects on private and public accounts that bad debts have had. To restore the "state of confidence", authorities will have to get rid of potentially irrecoverable debts without throwing the baby out with the bath water. In this perspective, there are strong arguments in favor of monetary accommodation and temporary public deficits (which is not to say permanent large deficits and inflationary policies), even though long-term interest rates do not respond significantly to the short-term impulses of central banks. Fortunately, this is how authorities started managing around the world, at odds with the obviously irrelevant and dangerous orthodox monetary and fiscal policies.

NOTES

* This chapter provides substantial developments of the ideas contained in a previous paper prepared for the Post Keynesian Economics Study Group workshop: "Inflation targeting: is there a credible alternative?" Balliol College, Oxford, 4 April 2008 (rewritten in association with M. Hayes and published as "Post Keynesian alternative to inflation targeting", *Intervention*, **6** (1): 67–81, 2009.

1. See *Journal of Post Keynesian Economics*, **30** (1), 2007 and *International Journal of Political Economy*, **37** (2), 2008 for a recent appraisal.

2. There is a consensus about the ultimate objectives of interest rules "in terms of their capacities to promote desirable (high growth, low inflation) macroeconomic outcomes and to assist the growth and inflation targeting objectives of the policy authorities" (Rochon and Setterfield, 2007b).

3. In Palley's model, income distribution also plays a role as far as the long-run consequences of the monetary policy are concerned, but the derived interest rate policy is not of the "parking it" type.

4. The author, however, does not discuss their point.

5. Sawyer (2007: 12–13) actually suggests a mixed rule based on Pasinetti's "fair" long-term real interest rate proposal (which is of the "parking it" type; see below) and on the recognition that the underlying trend, whose estimation is problematic, "may itself be influenced by demand policies" (which rejoins "activists" rules).

6. This is related to the backward-bending Phillips curve of the model: as real wage resistance increases as inflation increases, the "grease effect" on employment, which is associated with the negative effect of inflation on real wages, erodes as inflation increases. See Palley (2007) for details.

7. Câmara Neto and Vernengo (2004) also advocate a low interest rate policy so as to make it easier for the government to implement a sound countercyclical fiscal policy.

8. According to Keynes, "The social philosophy towards which the General Theory might lead" (Keynes, 1936: 374–7) focuses on our ability to manage the rate of interest so as to rise the inducement to invest to the level where, given the aggregate propensity to consume (including the state), full employment holds. Now, insofar as the accumulation of capital decreases the marginal efficiency of capital, a decrease in the long-term interest rate will be necessary in the long run. That is the essence of Keynes's prediction of the euthanasia of the rentier. According to his argument, the ideal policy is to adjust the long-term interest rate to the level that ensures full employment, given the marginal efficiency of capital and the aggregate propensity to consume. Whether a zero short-term interest rate would work that way remains to be discussed.

9. See, however, the optimistic views on the subject presented in Tily (2006, 2007).

10. See Smithin (1994: 172–3); Lavoie (1996: 277, 1999: 2, 7); Tily (2006: 657); Rochon and Setterfield (2008: 6). According to Lavoie (1999: 2), "monetary authorities have the ultimate say on the convention", but the author also pointed out that the spreads between the long-term rates and the overnight rate vary according to the liquidity preference of the commercial banks and the participants in the financial markets: "As Smithin (1996: 93) puts it, a role for Keynesian liquidity preference can be retained in this scenario, in that liquidity preference considerations may well periodically insert a wedge between those rates of interest which are more or less directly under the central bank control and rates elsewhere" (Lavoie 1999: 2).

11. Hein and Stockhammer (2007: 17), based on a cost-push argument, suggest that low real interest rates rather reduce inflationary pressures and that it is, on the contrary, high interest rates that fuel inflation. Although such a mechanism must of course be considered, there are many cost-push channels which could feed distribution conflict even when interest rates are low (as the mentioned wage or profit pressures, but also government taxes, oil and raw material), and in these cases, the monetary policy induced by the "parking it" rule would certainly allow for inflation.

12. This dilemma between inflation and what Davidson (2006) called "income policy of fear" shows that inflationary distributive tensions develop when the central bank allows for it, that is, when the central bank refinancing conditions do not remove inflation pressures completely, so that banks deliver the additional money demand that results from the rising nominal prices, wages. In this sense, it can be said that a monetary policy may feed inflation, even though the primary cause is an income distribution conflict.

13. This is not to say that the short-term nominal interest rate is the appropriate instrument for achieving a specific exchange rate target; it is just to say that monetary authorities may hardly disregard the effects that short-term rates may have on the exchange rate (through their effects on long-term rates, international capital flows, balance of payments, and so on).

14. Assuming an exogenous interest rate may make sense in the field of macroeconomic modeling, as conventions are necessarily considered exogenous for those models being tractable, but it should be recognized that such a simplification causes severe limitations to the model's conclusions, insofar as the possible interactions between the interest rate policy and the market convention is merely overlooked.

15. This is a second-order argument, where the expectation that future investment will be content with a lower yield (because of the expected falls in the future rate of interest) depresses the prospective yield of current investment (Keynes, 1936: 143). The argument is also developed in relation to expected money-wage decreases in Keynes (p. 263), where monetary policy also is considered.

16. "Just as a moderate increase in the quantity of money may exert an inadequate influence over the long-term rate of interest, whilst an immoderate increase may offset its other advantages by its disturbing effect on confidence" (Keynes, 1936: 266–7).

17. Although the discussion deals strictly with monetary policy, remember that authorities may also have some influence over the long-term interest rates by means of a debt management policy, as Tily (2006, 2007) put forward accurately.

18. The case for inflation is discussed below.

19. "Excess money" here does not refer to an excess of the supply over the demand for money which would be inconsistent with the Post Keynesian approach to endogenous money (where the money supply sticks to the demand); it refers to the notion of "bad money", as defined above. The mechanism of inflation in this case is similar to the one which is involved in financial bubbles, although real assets and speculative goods are concerned, rather than financial assets. Of course, at the macroeconomic level there must be an impact on the factor costs (capital goods, oil, indexed wages, and so on) if the production prices are to be increased.

20. In accordance with the discussion above, if the liquidity withdrawing process is not rapid enough to offset the decrease in liquidity preference, temporary inflationary pressures may develop until it is achieved.

21. This solution could also further damage the financial system, as discussed above.

22. See Le Héron (2006, 2007) for an analysis of Alan Greenspan's strategy in terms of confidence versus credibility.

REFERENCES

Atesoglu, H.S. (2007), "The neutral rate of interest and a new monetary policy rule", *Journal of Post Keynesian Economics*, **29**: 689–97.

Atesoglu, H.S. and Smithin, J. (2006), "Inflation targeting in a simple macroeconomic model", *Journal of Post Keynesian Economics*, **28**: 673–88.

Bateman, B.W. (2003), "The end of Keynes and philosophy?", in J. Runde and S. Mizuhara (eds), *The Philosophy of Keynes's Economics: Probability, Uncertainty, and Convention*, London and New York: Routledge, pp. 71–84.

Câmara Neto, A.F. and Vernengo, M. (2004), "Fiscal policy and the Washington Consensus: a Post Keynesian perspective", *Journal of Post Keynesian Economics*, **27**: 333–43.

Davidson, P. (2006), "Can, or should, a central bank inflation target?", *Journal of Post Keynesian Economics*, **28**: 689–703.

Fontana, G. and Palacio-Vera, A. (2003), "Is there an active role for monetary policy in the endogenous money approach?", *Journal of Economic Issues*, **37** (2): 511–17.

Fontana, G. and Palacio-Vera, A. (2007), "Are long-run price stability and short-run output stabilization all that monetary policy can aim for?", *Metroeconomica*, **58**: 269–98.

Hein, E. and Stockhammer, E. (2007), "Macroeconomic policy mix, employment and inflation in a Post-Keynesian alternative to the new consensus model", IMK Working Paper 10/2007, Düsseldorf: Macroeconomic Policy Institute (IMK), Hans Böckler Foundation.

Keynes, J.M. (1936), *The General Theory of Employment, Interest and Money*, London: Macmillan.

Lavoie, M. (1996), "Horizontalism, structuralism, liquidity preference and the principle of increasing risk", *Scottish Journal of Political Economy*, **43** (3): 275–300.

Lavoie, M. (1999), "Fair rates of interest and Post-Keynesian economics: the Canadian case", University of Ottawa, available at: http://aix1.uottawa.ca/~robinson/english/wp/fairratecla.pdf (accessed March 2008).

Le Héron, E. (2006), "Alan Greenspan, the confidence strategy", *Brazilian Journal of Political Economy*, **26**: 502–17.

Le Héron, E. (2007), "The new governance in monetary policy: a critical appraisal of the Fed and the ECB', in P. Arestis, E. Hein and E. Le Héron (eds), *Aspects of Modern Monetary and Macroeconomic Policies*, London: Palgrave Macmillan, pp. 146–71.

Orphanides, A. and Wilcox, D.W. (1996), *The Opportunistic Approach to Disinflation*, Washington, DC: Board of Governors of the Federal Reserve System.

Palley, T.I. (2007), "Macroeconomics and monetary policy: competing theoretical frameworks", *Journal of Post Keynesian Economics*, **30**: 61–78.

Pasinetti, L. (1981), *Structural Change and Economic Growth*, Cambridge: Cambridge University Press.

Rochon, L.P. and Setterfield, M. (2007a), "Interest rates, income distribution, and monetary policy dominance: Post Keynesians and the 'fair rate' of interest", *Journal of Post Keynesian Economics*, **30**: 13–42.

Rochon, L.P. and Setterfield, M. (2007b), "Post Keynesian interest rate rules and macroeconomic performance: a comparative evaluation", paper presented at the Eastern Economic Association Conference, New York, February.

Rochon, L.P. and Setterfield, M. (2008), "The political economy of interest-rate setting, inflation, and income distribution", *International Journal of Political Economy*, **37** (2): 5–25.

Sawyer, M. (2007), "Seeking to reformulate macroeconomic policies", paper presented at the 3rd bi-annual conference of the CEMF: "Post Keynesian Principles of Economic Policy", University of Burgundy, Dijon, December.

Setterfield, M. (2007), "Is inflation targeting inimical to employment?", available at: http://www.trincoll.edu/~setterfi/Is%20Inflation%20Targeting%20 Inimical%20to%20Employment%20-%20Cambs%20conf%20vol.pdf (accessed March 2008).

Setterfield, M. and Lima, G.T. (2008), "Inflation targeting and macroeconomic stability in a Post Keynesian economy", *Journal of Post Keynesian Economics*, **30**: 435–61.

Smithin, J. (1994), *Controversies in Monetary Economics*, Aldershot, UK and Brookfield, VT, USA: Edward Elgar.

Smithin, J. (1996), *Macroeconomic Policy and the Future of Capitalism: The Revenge of the Rentiers and the Threat to Prosperity*, Cheltenham, UK and Brookfield, VT, USA: Edward Elgar.

Smithin, J. (2007), "A real interest rate rule for monetary policy?", *Journal of Post Keynesian Economics*, **30**: 101–18.

Tily, G. (2006), "Keynes's theory of liquidity preference and his debt management and monetary policies", *Cambridge Journal of Economics*, **30**: 657–70.

Tily, G. (2007), *Keynes's General Theory, the Rate of Interest and "Keynesian" Economics*, Basingstoke: Palgrave Macmillan.

Tily, G. (2009), "The *General Theory* and monetary policy – investment versus inflation", *Intervention*, **6** (1): 97–118.

Wray, R. (2007), "A Post Keynesian view of central bank independence, policy targets, and the rules versus discretion debate", *Journal of Post Keynesian Economics*, **30**: 119–41.

2. Stabilization policy with an endogenous commercial bank*

Mark Setterfield and Kurt von Seekamm

1 INTRODUCTION

The three-equation New Keynesian or "new consensus" model is now a staple feature of monetary macroeconomics.[1] One common criticism of this model is that it retains pre-Keynesian notions of the workings of the real economy, as encapsulated in "natural" rates of interest and unemployment (Setterfield, 2004; Smithin, 2004; Lavoie, 2006). A second criticism is that in its eagerness to embrace the modern "science" of monetary policy, according to which the central bank manipulates the interest rate rather than the quantity of money in circulation, the new consensus has become divorced from the monetary theory of the private financial sector – in particular, the orthodox monetary base multiplier explanation of commercial banking, with which it is incompatible (Friedman, 2003).[2] The concern of this chapter is with the second of these criticisms.

Various methods of integrating an account of private financial behavior into the new consensus have already been proposed. Some seek to "recover" traditional LM analysis (see, for example, Tamborini, 2009). Others, however, provide accounts of the financial sector that are consistent with the tenets of endogenous money theory, in which the behavior of commercial banks and the loan-creation process are seen as the nexus of the monetary sector (see, for example, Howells, 2009). Indeed, drawing on this second approach and motivated by the recent financial crisis, several authors have already begun to study the significance of exogenous shocks emanating from the private financial sector as a source of macroeconomic instability in new consensus models (Lavoie, 2009; Weise and Barbera, 2009). In this chapter, we build on these latter contributions by *endogenizing* the behavior of the private financial sector. Specifically, we amend a popular variant of the new consensus model by introducing a commercial bank, which acts as an intermediary between the central bank and the non-bank private sector. Like the central bank, the commercial bank acts as a price maker, adding a premium or mark-up to the overnight rate set by the central bank to establish the commercial rate of interest at which households and firms borrow. This it does in accordance with an explicit reaction function. The key question that we address is: what if any effect does the behavior of this financial intermediary have on macroeconomic stabilization policy?

The remainder of the chapter is organized as follows. In Section 2, we outline the baseline new consensus model on which our analysis builds. Section 3 then specifies the behavior of the commercial bank that we introduce into this model. In Section 4, we study the implications of the resulting amended model for macroeconomic stabilization policy. Section 5 draws some conclusions.

2   A BASELINE NEW CONSENSUS MODEL

Our analysis is based on a variant of the new consensus model developed by Carlin and Soskice (2005). This variant suits our purposes well since it is designed to emphasize the behavior of the central bank in its pursuit of macroeconomic stabilization.

In the Carlin–Soskice (hereafter C–S) model, the private sector is modeled in terms of two familiar equations: a standard IS curve; and an inertial Phillips curve embodying the accelerationist hypothesis.[3] These equations can be stated as follows:

$$y_1 = A - ar_0 \tag{2.1}$$

$$\pi_1 = \pi_0 + \alpha(y_1 - y^e), \tag{2.2}$$

where y and y^e are the actual and "natural" levels of output, respectively, r is the real interest rate and π denotes the rate of inflation. The private sector achieves equilibrium when $\Delta\pi = 0$ which, from (2.2), implies that $y = y_e$. Substituting this result into equation (2.1) and rearranging, we obtain:

$$r_S = \frac{A - y^e}{a},$$

which Carlin and Soskice (2005, p. 3) interpret as "the so-called 'stabilizing' or Wicksellian (Woodford) rate of interest such that output is in equilibrium when $[r = r_S]$".[4]

The central bank, meanwhile, is modeled as a forward-looking social welfare maximizer with rational expectations. Without loss of generality (see ibid., pp. 3–13) the time horizon of the central bank is limited to one period ahead. Given this, and the fact that the underlying model of the private economy stated above is deterministic, the central bank can be described as possessing "myopic perfect foresight" (Flaschel et al., 1997). Formally, the central bank is described as engaging in the constrained optimization of a quadratic loss function. Its problem can be stated as:

$$\min_r L = (y_1 - y^e)^2 + \beta(\pi_1 - \pi^T)^2$$
$$\text{s.t. } y_1 = A - ar_0$$
$$\pi_1 = \pi_0 + \alpha(y_1 - y^e)$$

or:

$$\min_r L = (A - ar_0 - y^e)^2 + \beta[\pi_0 + \alpha(A - ar_0 - y^e) - \pi^T]^2.$$

The first-order condition of this problem is:

$$\frac{dL}{dr_0} = -2a(A - ar_0 - y^e) - 2a\alpha\beta[\pi_0 + \alpha(A - ar_0 - y^e) - \pi^T] = 0,$$

and solving this first-order condition for r_0 yields:

$$r_0 = r_S + \frac{\alpha\beta}{a(1 + \alpha^2\beta)}(\pi_0 - \pi^T). \qquad (2.3)$$

Equation (2.3) is the interest rate operating procedure (IROP) consistent with the objective of the central bank described above. Together with equations (2.1) and (2.2), it provides us with a full description of the workings of the economy in the C–S model.

It is straightforward to show by means of a conventional stability analysis that by following the IROP in (2.3), the central bank will succeed in leading the economy towards the equilibrium state described earlier (where output is at its natural rate and inflation achieves a steady state). Hence note that, assuming $\Delta\pi \approx \dot{\pi}$, equation (2.2) can be rewritten as:

$$\dot{\pi} = \alpha(y - y^e), \qquad (2.4)$$

while differentiating equations (2.1) and (2.3) with respect to time yields:[5]

$$\dot{y} = -a\dot{r}$$

and:

$$\dot{r} = \frac{\alpha\beta}{a(1 + \alpha^2\beta)}\dot{\pi}.$$

Substituting the second of these expressions into the first and then substituting equation (2.4) into the result gives us:

$$\dot{y} = \frac{-\alpha^2\beta}{(1 + \alpha^2\beta)}(y - y^e). \qquad (2.5)$$

Equations (2.4) and (2.5) provide two differential equations in two unknowns (y and π), which can be expressed in matrix form as:

$$\begin{bmatrix} \dot{y} \\ \dot{\pi} \end{bmatrix} = \begin{bmatrix} \dfrac{-\alpha^2\beta}{(1 + \alpha^2\beta)} & 0 \\ \alpha & 0 \end{bmatrix} \begin{bmatrix} y \\ \pi \end{bmatrix} + \begin{bmatrix} \dfrac{\alpha^2\beta}{(1 + \alpha^2\beta)} y^e \\ -\alpha y^e \end{bmatrix}. \qquad (2.6)$$

Inspection of (2.6) reveals that $\mathrm{Tr}\, J = -\alpha^2\beta/(1 + \alpha^2\beta) < 0$ and $|J| = 0$. The system is therefore stable but involves a zero root, which has implications for its equilibrium solution. More specifically, as is obvious from inspection of equations (2.4) and (2.5), imposition of the equilibrium conditions $\dot{y} = \dot{\pi} = 0$ yields a unique equilibrium value of output (y^e), but the corresponding equilibrium rate of inflation is indeterminate. It can therefore be noted in passing that the interest rate r_S is not *the* stabilizing interest rate consistent with $y = y^e$ (as is claimed by Carlin and Soskice, 2005, p. 3). Instead, as inspection of the IROP in (2.3) reveals (in light of the stability results derived above), there are *many* such stabilizing interest rates, depending on the precise steady-state rate of inflation (π^*) that the economy achieves, and hence the precise equilibrium value of the "inflation target gap" $\pi^* - \pi^T$ that will appear (in equilibrium) on the right-hand side of equation (2.3). What r_S in fact denotes is the unique "fully adjusted" value of the interest rate. In other words, it is the value that the interest rate attains when the economy reaches a "fully adjusted position": a position of equilibrium that is also consistent with the realization of the target values of all variables (in this case, the central bank's target rate of inflation). Once again this is made clear by inspection of equation (2.3), according to which the particular steady-state rate of inflation $\pi^* = \pi^T$ will yield $r = r_S$.

3   AN ENDOGENOUS COMMERCIAL BANK

The preceding analysis demonstrates that in the C–S model, a central bank that pursues monetary policy by adjusting the interest rate in accordance with equation (2.3) will succeed in stabilizing the economy in response to shocks. But an obvious shortcoming of this model is that it provides no description of the private financial sector. It is as if the central bank lends directly to households and firms – something that is very obviously at variance with reality. This is undesirable, not least because greater realism was part of the motivation for developing the new consensus model in the first place (see, for example, Romer, 2000).

We remedy this shortcoming by introducing into the C–S model a commercial bank, which acts as an intermediary between the central bank on the one hand and households and firms on the other. It does so by lending to creditworthy borrowers in the non-bank private sector at an interest rate of its own making, which is arrived at by marking up the overnight rate at which it can lend from the central bank.[6] Formally, we begin (following Lavoie, 2009 and Weise and Barbera, 2009) by writing:

$$r_0 = \varphi_0 + \theta_0, \tag{2.7}$$

where φ is the overnight interest rate set by the central bank, and θ is the mark-up that the commercial bank adds to this overnight rate to establish the commercial interest rate (r) faced by borrowers in the non-bank private sector. The commercial bank mark-up reflects both the term structure of the loans it makes (which we take as given) and other sources of lender's risk (see also Lavoie, 2009). However, unlike Lavoie and Barbera and Weise, who take the value of θ as exogenously given, we identify macroeconomic influences on the commercial bank's perception of lender's risk and hence model θ as an endogenous reaction to the state of the economy. Formally, we describe the commercial bank as setting its mark-up in accordance with a reaction function of the form:

$$\theta_0 = \theta(y_1^E, \pi_1^E, \varphi_0^E, \rho_0), \tag{2.8}$$

where an E superscript denotes the expected value of a variable and ρ is increasing in influences on the commercial bank's perception of lender's risk that are not captured by the other variables in (2.8) (including their animal spirits). Note that, like the central bank, the commercial bank is forward looking over a limited time horizon of one period, and has some information about the lag structure of the economy (understanding that once it has formed an expectation of φ_0, it can anticipate the value of y_1 and hence π_1). Furthermore, we assume that $\theta_y < 0$, $\theta_\pi > 0$, $\theta_\varphi < 0$, and $\theta_\rho > 0$. The sign of the last derivative is obvious from the definition of ρ, but the other derivatives merit some explanation.

First, we hypothesize that if commercial banks expect y to fall or π

to rise, they will interpret either event as signaling a deterioration in the general state of the economy which raises the prospect of default by borrowers and thus increases the lender's risk.[7] Hence the mark-up will rise in response to either a fall in expected output or a rise in expected inflation ($\theta_y < 0$, $\theta_\pi > 0$). Of course, to the extent that it issues loans at fixed interest rates, a rise in the rate of inflation will also diminish the real value of the commercial bank's existing loan portfolio, which may also provoke it to raise rates on new loans issued in response to higher expected inflation.[8] Second, we hypothesize that the commercial bank believes that an information asymmetry exists as between itself and the central bank – specifically, that the central bank has more and/or better information about the likely future state of the economy. Hence the commercial bank will raise its mark-up if the central bank cuts its overnight rate ($\theta_\varphi < 0$), because independently of its output expectations, the commercial bank will perceive a cut in φ to be an indication of weakness in the general state of the economy, and hence an increase in the risk of default and the associated lender's risk. This behavior is in keeping with empirical evidence which suggests that, in the US, the Federal Funds rate is negatively correlated with credit spreads (Weise and Barbera, 2009).

Our approach to modeling commercial bank behavior is similar to that of Palley (2008). Like Palley, we posit that θ is sensitive to real output and to the animal spirits of the commercial bank. Unlike Palley, however, we overlook the influence of asset prices and the volume of loans on θ, while taking into account the effects of inflation and the commercial bank's reaction to *central* bank behavior. Of the two omissions mentioned above, the first is explained by the fact that our model does not include an asset market, and the second by the fact that we abstract from structuralist concerns with the response of commercial interest rates to the expansion of commercial banks' loan portfolios (on which see, for example, Pollin, 1991). Further discussion of the first omission appears in the conclusion of our chapter.[9]

In order to incorporate commercial bank behavior into our model, we make the simplifying assumption that the mark-up rule in (2.8) is linear, which allows us to write:

$$\theta_0 = \varepsilon y_1^E + \gamma \pi_1^E + \eta \varphi_0^E + \mu \rho_0, \qquad (2.9)$$

where, in accordance with (2.8), ε, $\eta < 0$ and γ, $\mu > 0$. Finally, we assume that $x^E = x \; \forall \; x = y, \pi, \varphi$ in (2.9), so that the final version of our commercial bank reaction function can be written as:

$$\theta_0 = \varepsilon y_1 + \gamma \pi_1 + \eta \varphi_0 + \mu \rho_0. \qquad (2.10)$$

It could be argued that this last assumption is tantamount to assuming that (like the central bank) the commercial bank has myopic perfect foresight. This assumption sits uneasily with our model of commercial bank behavior and, in particular, our claim that the commercial bank reacts to changes in φ on the basis of a perceived information asymmetry between itself and the central bank – a perception that would be difficult to justify in the long run if the commercial bank repeatedly proved to be every bit as adept at forecasting output and inflation as the central bank. But an alternative interpretation is that we are simply abstracting from expectational error on the part of the private sector in the analysis that follows, in order to focus attention on other features of the model's adjustment dynamics – much as did Keynes (1936) in his exposition of the principle of effective demand in the *General Theory*. Relaxing our assumption about commercial bank expectations would potentially enrich the dynamics of our model, but would require that we specify exactly how these expectations are formed and (in the event that they are incorrect) updated. We leave this task to future research.[10]

We are now in a position to evaluate the consequences of commercial bank behavior for the central bank's macroeconomic stabilization policies. It is to this task that we now turn.

4 MACROECONOMIC STABILIZATION WITH AN ENDOGENOUS COMMERCIAL BANK

Our first objective is to derive anew the central bank's IROP, bearing in mind that the monetary policy operations of the central bank are now complicated by the behavior of the commercial bank as captured in (2.10). The easiest way of performing this task is to restate the central bank's decision-making problem from Section 2 in the manner in which it was originally formulated by Carlin and Soskice (2005, p. 13):[11]

$$\min_{y} L = (y_1 - y^e)^2 + \beta(\pi_1 - \pi^T)^2$$

$$\text{s.t. } \pi_1 = \pi_0 + \alpha(y_1 - y^e)$$

which, upon substitution, can be restated as:

$$\min_{y} L = (y_1 - y^e)^2 + \beta[\pi_0 + \alpha(y_1 - y^e) - \pi^T]^2.$$

The first-order condition of this decision problem is:

$$\frac{\partial L}{\partial y} = 2(y_1 - y^e) + 2\alpha\beta[\pi_0 + \alpha(y_1 - y^e) - \pi^T] = 0,$$

and solving this first-order condition for the output gap yields:

$$(y_1 - y^e) = \frac{-\alpha\beta}{1 + \alpha^2\beta}(\pi_0 - \pi^T). \tag{2.11}$$

Equation (2.11) captures what Carlin and Soskice (p. 13) term the "monetary rule". It describes the trade-off between future output and current inflation that is acceptable to the central bank (that is, consistent with the minimization of its loss function) given the constraints imposed by the structure of the private economy.

Now note that it follows from the IS curve in equation (2.1) that:

$$y^e = A - ar_S,$$

where r_S is the "fully adjusted" value of the interest rate, as described earlier. Subtracting this expression from equation (2.1) yields a second expression for the output gap of the form:

$$y_1 - y^e = -a(r_0 - r_S). \tag{2.12}$$

If, drawing on equation (2.7), we now write:

$$r_S = \varphi_S + \theta_S,$$

where $\theta_S = \varepsilon y^e + \gamma\pi^T + \eta\varphi_S + \mu\bar{\rho}$ and $\bar{\rho}$ represents the "normal" value of ρ, then by substituting this expression and equation (2.7) into equation (2.12), we arrive at:

$$y_1 - y^e = -a[(\varphi_0 - \varphi_S) + (\theta_0 - \theta_S)]. \tag{2.13}$$

Substituting into (2.13) for θ_0 and θ_S yields:

$$y_1 - y^e =$$
$$-a[(\varphi_0 - \varphi_S) + \varepsilon(y_1 - y^e) + \gamma(\pi_1 - \pi^T) + \eta(\varphi_0 - \varphi_S) + \mu(\rho_0 - \bar{\rho})],$$

and if we then substitute the Phillips curve in equation (2.2) into this last expression and solve for the output gap, we arrive at:

$$y_1 - y^e = \frac{-a}{1 + a(\varepsilon + \alpha\gamma)}[(1 + \eta)(\varphi_0 - \varphi_S) + \gamma(\pi_0 - \pi^T) + \mu(\rho_0 - \bar{\rho})].$$

Finally, substituting this last expression into the monetary rule derived earlier yields:

$$\frac{-\alpha\beta}{1 + \alpha^2\beta}(\pi_0 - \pi^T) =$$

$$\frac{-a}{1 + a(\varepsilon + \alpha\gamma)}[(1 + \eta)(\varphi_0 - \varphi_S) + \gamma(\pi_0 - \pi^T) + \mu(\rho_0 - \bar{\rho})],$$

and solving for φ_0, we get:

$$\varphi_0 = \varphi_S + \frac{1}{1 + \eta}\left[\frac{\alpha\beta(1 + a\varepsilon) - a\gamma}{a(1 + \alpha^2\beta)}(\pi_0 - \pi^T) + \mu(\rho_0 - \bar{\rho})\right]. \quad (2.14)$$

The expression in (2.14) is now the central bank's IROP.

Comparing equations (2.3) and (2.14), two observations regarding the implications of commercial bank behavior for central bank stabilization policy are immediately apparent. First, it is evident that, with an endogenous commercial bank, the central bank requires more information (specifically, knowledge of the parameters η, ε, γ, μ, and $\bar{\rho}$ together with the variable ρ_0) in order to conduct monetary policy in accordance with its objective function. Whether or not the central bank has access to this information is, of course, open to debate. Second, even if we assume that the central bank *does* possess the information demanded by equation (2.14), commercial bank activity will affect the *extent* to which the central bank needs to vary the overnight interest rate in order to stabilize the economy. In the first place, since $\varepsilon < 0$, we will observe $\alpha\beta(1 + a\varepsilon) - a\gamma < \alpha\beta$. Other things equal, this means that, in response to any given change in the rate of inflation, the variation in the overnight rate required by equation (2.14) is smaller than that required by (2.3). However, the fact that $\eta < 0$ means that, other things equal, the response of the overnight rate to any given change in the rate of inflation required by (2.14) is *larger* than that required by (2.3). Moreover, in equation (2.14), the central bank will need to vary the overnight rate in response to changes in ρ, a factor that is absent altogether from (2.3). These last two consequences of commercial bank activity, which demand (other things being equal) *greater* variation in the overnight rate, may pose problems for the central bank in light of the zero lower-bound constraint on the value of the nominal interest rate.

But these issues apart, what, if any, consequences does endogenous commercial bank activity have for the ability of the central bank to stabilize the economy? In order to answer this question, first note that if we combine equations (2.2), (2.7) and (2.10) and then substitute the result into equation (2.1), we arrive at the modified IS curve:

$$y_1 = \frac{1}{1 + a(\varepsilon + \alpha\gamma)}\{A - a[(1 + \eta)\varphi_0 + \gamma(\pi_0 - \alpha y^e) + \mu\rho_0]\}.$$

Assuming that $\rho_0 = \bar{\rho}$ and differentiating the modified IS curve with respect to time yields:

$$\dot{y} = \frac{-a}{1 + a(\varepsilon + \alpha\gamma)}[(1 + \eta)\dot{\varphi} + \gamma\dot{\pi}]. \tag{2.15}$$

Meanwhile, it follows from the IROP in (2.14) that:

$$\dot{\varphi} = \frac{\alpha\beta(1 + a\varepsilon) - a\gamma}{(1 + \eta)a(1 + \alpha^2\beta)}\dot{\pi}. \tag{2.16}$$

Finally, substituting (2.16) into (2.15) and then substituting equation (2.4) into the result yields:

$$\dot{y} = \frac{-\alpha^2\beta}{(1 + \alpha^2\beta)}(y - y^e).$$

It is immediately obvious that this last expression is exactly the same as the equation of motion in equation (2.5). In other words, despite the introduction of an endogenous commercial bank, the dynamics of the economy are still described by (2.6), and the system has exactly the same stability properties as the baseline model discussed in Section 2.

At first, this result may seem counterintuitive. But on second thoughts there is a straightforward explanation. Even though our model has been complicated by the introduction of an endogenous commercial bank, the central bank has rational expectations (specifically, myopic perfect foresight). As such, the central bank simply takes into account the complications introduced by commercial bank behavior, acts accordingly (with respect to its interest rate setting behavior), and the result is successful stabilization policy (in the event of a shock, the economy will be propelled back to its natural level of output and to a steady-state rate of inflation).

But what if the information demands placed on the central bank by equation (2.14) are excessive? In other words, what effect will commercial bank activity have on stabilization policy if the central bank suffers an incomplete understanding of commercial bank behavior? In order to address this question, consider the extreme case where the "true model" of the private sector is given by equations (2.1), (2.2), (2.7) and (2.10), but where the central bank's model of the economy comprises equations (2.1), (2.2), (2.7) and:

$$\theta = \bar{\theta}. \tag{2.10a}$$

In other words, the central bank is aware that the commercial bank acts as a financial intermediary and that it does so by marking up the overnight rate. But it is completely ignorant of the basis on which this mark-up is established and instead treats θ as a constant. In this scenario, the "true" dynamics of the private economy are once again summarized by equations (2.4) and (2.15). But by combining equations (2.1), (2.7) and (2.10), the central bank now believes that the IS curve of the economy can be written as:

$$y_1 = A - a(\varphi_0 - \bar{\theta}),$$

so that:

$$y^e = A - a(\varphi_S - \bar{\theta}).$$

Subtracting the second of these expressions from the first yields:

$$y_1 - y^e = -a(\varphi_0 - \varphi_S).$$

Finally, substituting this last expression into the central bank's monetary rule in equation (2.1) and solving for φ_0 yields:

$$\varphi_0 = \varphi_S + \frac{\alpha\beta}{a(1 + \alpha^2\beta)}(\pi_0 - \pi^T). \tag{2.17}$$

Equation (2.17) describes the central bank's IROP under conditions of complete central bank ignorance of commercial bank behavior. Perhaps not surprisingly, the IROP is essentially the same as that in equation (2.3) (that is, in the original C–S model, in which there is no commercial bank).

It follows from equation (2.17) that:

$$\dot{\varphi} = \frac{\alpha\beta}{a(1 + \alpha^2\beta)}\dot{\pi}.$$

Substituting this expression into equation (2.15), and then substituting equation (2.4) into the result yields:

$$\dot{y} = \frac{-\alpha[(1 + \eta)\alpha\beta + a\gamma(1 + \alpha^2\beta)]}{[1 + a(\varepsilon + \alpha\gamma)](1 + \alpha^2\beta)}(y - y^e). \tag{2.18}$$

The dynamics of the economy are now represented by equations (2.4) and (2.18), a system that can be summarized as:

$$\begin{bmatrix} \dot{y} \\ \dot{\pi} \end{bmatrix} = \begin{bmatrix} \Omega & 0 \\ \alpha & 0 \end{bmatrix} \begin{bmatrix} y \\ \pi \end{bmatrix} + \begin{bmatrix} \Omega y^e \\ -\alpha y^e \end{bmatrix}, \qquad (2.19)$$

where:

$$\Omega = \frac{-\alpha[(1 + \eta)\alpha\beta + a\gamma(1 + \alpha^2\beta)]}{[1 + a(\varepsilon + \alpha\gamma)](1 + \alpha^2\beta)}.$$

It is clear from the expression in (2.19) that $|J| = 0$ and $\mathrm{Tr}\, J = \Omega < 0$ if:

$$(1 + \eta)\alpha\beta + a\gamma(1 + \alpha^2\beta) > 0 \Rightarrow \eta > -\left[1 + \frac{a\gamma(1 + \alpha^2\beta)}{\alpha\beta}\right]$$

and:

$$1 + a(\varepsilon + \alpha\gamma) > 0 \Rightarrow \varepsilon > -\left[\frac{1}{a} + \alpha\gamma\right].$$

Although there are now stability conditions that must be met in order for the central bank's stabilization policy to be successful, both of these conditions are plausible. Hence the first condition requires only that the commercial bank's reaction to changes in the overnight rate not be "too large" (specifically, somewhat more than proportional). While this condition might be violated during a time of economic and financial crisis (as experienced from late 2007 through early 2009, for example), it otherwise appears reasonable. The second condition again requires only that the commercial bank's reaction to changes in output not be "too large". Given that the parameter a – the interest sensitivity of output – is often regarded as small by critics of the efficacy of monetary policy (see, for example, Arestis and Sawyer, 2004), it is likely that "too large" means, once again, somewhat more than proportional. And while, once again, this condition may be violated during a time of economic and financial crisis, it otherwise appears plausible.

The upshot of these results is that the stability of the economy is robust to the introduction of endogenous commercial bank behavior and (under certain – plausible – conditions) central bank ignorance of this behavior. In other words, apart from under special case conditions that would appear to most closely resemble "depression economics", central bank stabilization policy will succeed in restoring the economy to the natural level of output and to a steady-state rate of inflation following a macroeconomic shock, even if the monetary transmission mechanism is complicated by a commercial bank that responds endogenously to changes in the state of the economy and to central bank policy, and even if the central bank is ignorant of the precise behavior of the commercial bank in this regard.

5 CONCLUSION

On the face of it, the introduction of an endogenous commercial bank acting as an intermediary between the central bank and households and firms would appear to make effective stabilization policy more difficult to pursue. To some extent, this intuition is borne out by the results in this chapter. First, the amount of information that the central bank requires in order to conduct monetary policy in accordance with its objective function is increased – at least in principle. Second, the extent to which the central bank must vary the overnight interest rate in order to stabilize the economy may be increased, with the result that the zero lower-bound constraint on the value of the nominal interest rate is more likely to confound monetary policy.

And yet the analysis suggests that otherwise, the introduction of an endogenous commercial bank has little effect on the capacity of the central bank to stabilize the economy – even when it is fundamentally ignorant of commercial bank behavior, so that it falls foul of the first problem identified above. This last result does require that certain stability conditions hold. These conditions may not be satisfied in the event of acute financial distress, lending some credence to Goodhart's (2009) argument that the new consensus is a "fair weather" model. But in general the stability conditions required appear plausible, and we are left with the result that the standard new consensus model can be "stressed" to the extent contemplated in this chapter without it substantially affecting the prospects for a successful stabilization policy.

Two possible conclusions follow. The first is essentially pessimistic: the result reported above does not establish that a stabilization policy can survive any and all "stresses" emanating from private financial behavior, and the model developed in this chapter may simply lack the sophistication necessary to demonstrate this. We have already noted that the model abstracts from the dynamics of asset markets and their potential impact on borrowing and lending behavior (and aggregate demand formation) – although Palley (2008), whose model does include an asset market, does not stress asset prices as a significant destabilizing force. Another and potentially more important omission is the endogenous accumulation of stock-flow imbalances (such as increases in the debt–income ratio of households), which recent experience suggests may have large and discontinuous effects on commercial bank assessments of a lender's risk.

The second conclusion is optimistic: subject to the limitations noted above, the analysis demonstrates that policy makers need be far from omniscient in order to successfully stabilize the economy most of the time. In fact, the analysis towards the end of Section 4 incorporates a classic "Lucas (1976) critique" problem, in which the central bank's structural model of private sector behavior treats as parametric a variable (θ) that is endogenous to the central bank's own policy interventions. And yet, under plausible conditions, this has no effect on the efficacy of stabilization policy. The upshot of this result is that policy intervention can be beneficial even when its design and conduct is demonstrably imperfect.

NOTES

*   An earlier version of this chapter was presented at the IEPI conference "The Political Economy of Central banking", Toronto, Canada, May 2009. We are grateful to conference participants for their comments. Any remaining errors are our own.
1.   See, for example, Clarida et al. (1999) and Woodford (2003) for canonical descriptions of this model.
2.   In the new consensus, the quantity of money in circulation is a "residual", determined endogenously by the non-bank private sector's demand for loans and the willingness of commercial banks to issue loans to creditworthy households and firms at the ruling interest rate. This generates a demand for reserves on the part of commercial banks seeking to remain liquid as the loans they have created generate spending in the non-bank private sector, the receipts from which accrue as deposits in the banking sector. Hence the creation of broad money drives the creation of base money, rather than the other way around (as in the traditional monetary base multiplier story).
3.   In terms of the variables that appear in equation (2.2), this hypothesis states that $y \neq y_e \Rightarrow \Delta\pi \neq 0$. Note that by retaining this hypothesis throughout the analysis that follows, we are setting aside the first of the two criticisms of the new consensus model identified earlier in favor of exclusive focus on the second. Drawing on the earlier work of Setterfield (2004) and Lavoie (2006), it would be straightforward to extend the analysis in this chapter by either relaxing the accelerationist hypothesis or introducing hysteresis effects to replace the implicit assumption that the natural level of output is invariant with respect to the output gap. We leave such extensions to future research.
4.   A somewhat different interpretation of r_S is provided below.
5.   Note that, in converting to continuous time analysis, time subscripts are dropped from all variables both here and elsewhere in the chapter.
6.   Throughout the analysis that follows we implicitly assume that the commercial bank's standard for creditworthiness is constant, and focus attention on its manipulation of the mark-up and hence (given the central bank's overnight rate) the commercial interest rate. It is possible, of course, that commercial banks may be more inclined to alter their conventional standards for evaluating creditworthiness – and hence the proportion of loan applications they deem creditworthy – in response to the perceived sources of variation in lender's risk that we discuss below (see, for example, Rochon, 2006). We leave investigation of this possibility to future research, but see Fontana and Setterfield (2009) for a preliminary investigation based on exogenous variation in commercial banks' standards of creditworthiness.

7. A reduction in output and hence income will diminish the ability of debtors to service their loans, thus increasing the risk of default. Meanwhile, an increase in inflation may be interpreted by the commercial bank as an indicator of future interest rate hikes by the central bank (which will reduce income and thus increase the risk of default).

8. In addition, and despite the fact that (2.8) describes the determination of a *real* interest rate mark-up, the sign of θ_π can be interpreted as a psychological response resulting from lenders' deep aversion to inflation.

9. The second omission is of less significance for our purposes, since as shown by Palley (2008), its incorporation would result only in the possibility that $\theta_y > 0$. This would only serve to reinforce the results derived in Section 4 regarding the prospects for successful stabilization policy.

10. See, for example, Lima and Setterfield (2008) for a preliminary analysis, in the context of a macrodynamic model, of expectations formation by decision makers whose information about the future is deficient.

11. Note that the original IROP in equation (2.3) can also be derived in this fashion. See Carlin and Soskice (2005, p. 13).

REFERENCES

Arestis, P. and M. Sawyer (2004), "On the effectiveness of monetary policy and of fiscal policy", *Review of Social Economy*, **62**, 441–63.

Carlin, W. and D. Soskice (2005), "The 3-equation New Keynesian model: a graphical exposition", *Contributions to Macroeconomics*, **5**, Article 13.

Clarida, R., J. Galì and M. Gertler (1999), "The science of monetary policy: a new Keynesian perspective", *Journal of Economic Literature*, **37**, 1661–707.

Flaschel, P., R. Franke and W. Semmler (1997), *Dynamic Macroeconomics: Instability, Fluctuations and Growth in Monetary Economics*, Cambridge, MA: MIT Press.

Fontana, G. and M. Setterfield (2009), "A simple (and teachable) macroeconomic model with endogenous money", in G. Fontana and M. Setterfield (eds), *Macroeconomic Theory and Macroeconomic Pedagogy*, London: Palgrave Macmillan, pp. 144–68.

Friedman, B.M. (2003), "The *LM* curve: a not-so-fond farewell", NBER Working Paper 10123, Cambridge, MA.

Goodhart, C.A.E. (2009), "The continuing muddles of monetary theory: a steadfast refusal to face facts", *Economica*, **76**, 821–30.

Howells, P. (2009), "Money and banking in a realistic macro model", in G. Fontana and M. Setterfield (eds), *Macroeconomic Theory and Macroeconomic Pedagogy*, London: Palgrave Macmillan, pp. 169–88.

Keynes, J.M. (1936), *The General Theory of Employment, Interest and Money*, London: Macmillan.

Lavoie, M. (2006), "A post-Keynesian amendment to the new consensus on monetary policy", *Metroeconomica*, **57**, 165–92.

Lavoie, M. (2009), "Taming the new consensus: hysteresis and some other Post-Keynesian amendments", in G. Fontana and M. Setterfield (eds), *Macroeconomic Theory and Macroeconomic Pedagogy*, London: Palgrave Macmillan, pp. 191–213.

Lima, G.T. and M. Setterfield (2008), "Inflation targeting and macroeconomic stability in a Post Keynesian economy", *Journal of Post Keynesian Economics*, **30**, 435–61.

Lucas, R.E. (1976), "Econometric policy evaluation: a critique", *Carnegie-Rochester Conference Series on Public Policy*, **1**, 19–46.

Palley, T.I. (2008), "Macroeconomics without the LM: a Post-Keynesian perspective", IMK (Hans Böckler Foundation) Working Paper 13/2008, Düsseldorf.

Pollin, R. (1991), "Two theories of money supply endogeneity: some empirical evidence", *Journal of Post Keynesian Economics*, **13**, 366–96.

Rochon, L.-P. (2006), "Endogenous money, central banks and the banking system: Basil Moore and the supply of credit", in M. Setterfield (ed.), *Complexity, Endogenous Money and Macroeconomic Theory: Essays in Honour of Basil J. Moore*, Cheltenham, UK and Northampton, MA, USA: Edward Elgar, pp. 170–86.

Romer, D. (2000), "Keynesian macroeconomics without the *LM* curve", *Journal of Economic Perspectives*, **14**, 149–69.

Setterfield, M. (2004), "Central banking, stability and macroeconomic outcomes: a comparison of new consensus and Post-Keynesian monetary macroeconomics", in M. Lavoie and M. Seccareccia (eds), *Central Banking in the Modern World: Alternative Perspectives*, Cheltenham, UK and Northampton, MA, USA: Edward Elgar, pp. 35–56.

Smithin, J. (2004), "Interest rate operating procedures and income distribution", in M. Lavoie and M. Seccareccia (eds), *Central Banking in the Modern World: Alternative Perspectives*, Cheltenham, UK and Northampton, MA, USA: Edward Elgar, pp. 57–69.

Tamborini, R. (2009), "Rescuing the *LM* curve (and the money market) in a modern macro course", in G. Fontana and M. Setterfield (eds), *Macroeconomic Theory and Macroeconomic Pedagogy*, London: Palgrave Macmillan, pp. 76–99.

Weise, C.L. and R.J. Barbera (2009), "Minsky meets Wicksell: using the Wicksellian model to understand the twenty-first century business cycle", in G. Fontana and M. Setterfield (eds), *Macroeconomic Theory and Macroeconomic Pedagogy*, London: Palgrave Macmillan, pp. 214–33.

Woodford, M. (2003), *Interest and Prices: Foundations of a Theory of Monetary Policy*, Princeton, NJ: Princeton University Press.

3. Capitalism in one country? A re-examination of mercantilist systems from the financial point of view

Eric Kam and John Smithin*

1 INTRODUCTION

Kam and Smithin (2008) use the term "monetary mercantilism" not to refer to protectionism as such, but rather a general policy of stimulating aggregate demand, and hence full employment, economic growth, general prosperity, and so on, by various financial and monetary techniques. These might include, for example, a monetary policy that delivers low and stable real interest rates (Smithin, 2003, 2007, 2009), or Keynesian-type expansionary fiscal policy. We note that Humphrey (1998) also uses the expression "mercantilism" (without the qualifier) in a somewhat similar way, casting the entire history of economic thought as a contest between "mercantilism" and "classical economics", with figures such as John Law, James Steuart, Thomas Tooke, John Maynard Keynes and Nicholas Kaldor on the one side, and David Hume, Adam Smith, Henry Thornton, David Ricardo and Milton Friedman, on the other. According to Humphrey (1998: 2):

> This policy prescription [protectionism] was, of course, the mercantilist's main claim to fame. But the hallmark that secures them a permanent niche in the history of monetary doctrines was their contra- or anti-quantity theory of money.

As far as the international situation is concerned, the expectations of those pursuing such "mercantilist" strategies (as now defined) might well have been that along with higher growth they would also lead to a strong current account, and (perhaps most obviously under a system of floating exchange rates) the building up of a foreign *credit* position, rather than becoming indebted either to other nations or to international financial institutions.

Kam and Smithin (2008) have also suggested that historically, whether under flexible exchange rates or not (and whether or not the issues were fully understood/articulated by the relevant decision makers at the time), strategies that might be characterized this way were indeed employed by many nations that *did* succeed in achieving stronger economic growth, and hence a prominent global economic and political position in the "capitalisms" of their day.

In this chapter, moreover, it is shown that similar policy options continue to exist, even in modern conditions created by globalization, increasing economic integration, and increased capital mobility (Palley, 2004),[1] given certain preconditions. These are, first, the domestic political situation, specifically a certain type of domestic political "settlement" or bargain (Ingham, 2004; Kim, 2009), leading to the development of the necessary domestic financial and business infrastructure; second, an independent currency; and third; either floating exchange rates, or, with fixed nominal rates, the existence of sufficient residual frictions or (perceived) remaining currency risk such that the conditions of a "virtual" floating exchange rate system are replicated. This is the meaning of the expression "capitalism in one country" (a pun on Stalin's "socialism in one country").

However, it would not be correct to describe such an approach as a "beggar-thy-neighbor" policy, as some writers might be inclined to do. As shown below, if one country alone does pursue the type of policy suggested here and others do not, there may be circumstances in which it will be to the first mover's sole advantage. They may eventually gain a hegemonic position, as has been seen historically. However, we would also argue that the world economy is not in principle a zero-sum game. Even in such cases, if each nation (given the necessary socio-political preconditions) were to pursue similar policies simultaneously then (in that ideal set of circumstances) the result would simply be higher overall world growth with balance across both the current and capital accounts (Kam and Smithin, 2008). There are also other situations in which expansionary policies seem simply to improve domestic conditions, and have little or no effect on the real exchange rate or on the foreign credit position. There seems to be nothing, therefore, to preclude offering similar policy advice to each jurisdiction separately. It should still be emphasized, nonetheless, that the formal analyses undertaken below relate to only one jurisdiction acting alone with others taking no action.

The underlying premise of the chapter is a heterodox rather than a mainstream approach to monetary and financial issues, including, specifically, the concepts of endogenous money and the importance of credit/debt creation for the enterprise economy (Smithin, 2009, 2010). Also prominent is the key idea that *both* the real interest rate *and* the real exchange rate are *monetary* variables, rather than being determined by such things as time preference in the one case, or the barter terms of trade in the other (Smithin, 2003, 2006; Kam and Smithin, 2004, 2008; Kam, 2005). This chapter illustrates that policy views on international economics relations, quite as much as those on the domestic economy, will differ essentially depending on the underlying social ontology and the theory of money and finance adopted (Seccareccia, 2003/04; Bougrine and Seccareccia, 2008). In what follows, a formal macroeconomic model of the open economy is presented, examining such topics as the role of flexible versus fixed exchange rate regimes, changes in the general level of aggregate demand, changes in domestic monetary and fiscal policy, and innovations in productivity.

2 A SIMPLE MACROECONOMIC MODEL OF A SMALL OPEN ECONOMY WITH FLEXIBLE EXCHANGE RATES

Consider the following linear model of a small open economy with a separate currency and floating exchange rates, and which, as a result of domestic political conditions, is able to issue foreign debt denominated in the domestic currency:

$$y = [1/(1 + \varepsilon\eta + \gamma)]d - [(1 + \varepsilon)/(1 + \varepsilon\eta + \gamma)]t$$

$$- [(\alpha - \varepsilon\theta)/(1 + \varepsilon\eta + \gamma)]q + [\varepsilon/(1 + \varepsilon\eta + \gamma)][a - w_0 - r] \quad (3.1)$$

$$p = p_0 + t + w_0 - a - \theta q + \eta y \quad (3.2)$$

$$\delta b/\delta\tau = \alpha q + \gamma y + rb \quad (3.3)$$

$$\delta q/\delta\tau = r^* - r + \zeta b. \quad (3.4)$$

The endogenous variables are:

y = the growth rate of real domestic product (GDP);
p = the domestic inflation rate;
q = the logarithm of the real exchange rate (where the nominal exchange rate is defined as the foreign currency price of one unit of domestic currency); and
b = the real foreign debt position as a percentage of base-year real GDP, denominated in domestic currency.

The exogenous variables, including policy-determined variables, are:

d = autonomous demand as a percentage of GDP, equal to government spending as a percentage of GDP *plus* an intercept term from an investment function as a percentage of GDP – Keynes's (1964) "animal spirits" – *minus* the average propensity to save;

t = the average tax rate;

r = the domestic real interest as influenced (in particular) by the financial policies of the domestic central bank;

a = the log of labor productivity;

w_0 = the intercept in an after-tax target real wage equation (in logs), representing socio-political influences on the real wage bargain (the strength of labor unions, the state of labor law, and so on);

r^* = the foreign real interest rate; and

p_0 = the intercept in the inflation equation; this will depend on fixed parameters of the money demand and (endogenous) money-supply equations.

From among the exogenous variables r^*, p_0 and w_0 will be treated as constants for present purposes. Therefore, the chapter investigates changes in each of d, t, r, and a, respectively. The parameters of the system are:

ε = the sensitivity of aggregate investment as a percentage of GDP to changes in the average mark-up or "rate of surplus value" ($\varepsilon > 0$);

α = the sensitivity of the trade balance as a percentage of GDP to changes in the real exchange rate ($\alpha > 0$);

η = the sensitivity of the after-tax target real wage target (in logs) to an increase in real GDP growth ($\eta > 0$);

θ = the weight assigned to the price of imports (in terms of domestic currency) in calculating the price index used to determine the after-tax real wage target, ($\theta < \theta < 0$);

γ = the analog to the textbook Keynesian "propensity to import" ($0 < \gamma < 1$); and

ζ = the sensitivity of the currency risk premium to changes in the foreign debt position as a percentage of base-year real GDP ($\zeta > 0$).

The terms $\delta b/\delta \tau$ and $\delta q/\delta \tau$ are the time derivatives of the foreign debt position, and the (log of) the expected future real exchange rate, respectively. Note also that ($\alpha - \varepsilon\theta$) > 0. This term is taken to be positive by analogy to the "Marshall–Lerner conditions" from non-monetary international trade theory. For mathematical convenience, the foreign price level is normalized at $P^* = 1$, and the foreign inflation rate therefore, at $p^* = 0$.

3   STABILITY IN THE FLEXIBLE EXCHANGE RATE CASE

Setting all exogenous variables equal to zero the dynamic system reduces to:

$$\delta b / \delta \tau = \alpha q + \gamma y \qquad (3.5)$$

$$\delta q / \delta \tau = \zeta b. \qquad (3.6)$$

Also, note that from (3.1) we have:

$$y = -[(\alpha - \varepsilon \theta)/(1 + \varepsilon \eta + \gamma)]q. \qquad (3.7)$$

Therefore, the system can be written in matrix form as:

$$\begin{vmatrix} \delta b/\delta \tau \\ \delta q/\delta \tau \end{vmatrix} = \begin{vmatrix} 0 & [\alpha(1 + \varepsilon \eta) + \varepsilon \gamma \theta]/(1 + \varepsilon \eta + \gamma) \\ \zeta & 0 \end{vmatrix} \begin{vmatrix} b \\ q \end{vmatrix}. \qquad (3.8)$$

Let Δ = the coefficient matrix. Stability requires that $tr\Delta < 0$ and $det\Delta > 0$ However, we have:

$$tr\Delta = 0 \qquad (3.9)$$

$$det\Delta = -\zeta\{[\alpha(1 + \varepsilon \eta) + \varepsilon \gamma \theta]/(1 + \varepsilon \eta + \gamma)\}, (<0). \qquad (3.10)$$

Therefore, the system has a saddle-point, meaning that there is just one stable path to equilibrium (the "stable arm") and all other trajectories are unstable. As previously explained by Kam and Smithin (2004), however, in the modern mainstream economics literature this finding in itself is usually regarded as sufficient justification to proceed to a comparative static analysis around the equilibrium. This is on the grounds that it is always possible to invoke the existence of a "jump variable" within the system, based on the likely behavior of the various players in the economy, and able to shift the system on to the single stable arm.

Although this is by now standard practice in mainstream economic theory, as a general proposition it is not, in fact, as convincing an argument as the graduate-level textbooks make it seem. In the mathematical jargon, it requires specifying a plausible "transversality condition", grounded in the actual behavior of the actors in the system, to achieve the desired goal. In reality (as opposed to working through a purely mathematical exercise), there may exist several types of economic scenario in which it is not possible to do this. We make this observation as a general caveat. In the present case, however, as it specifically involves asset markets in foreign exchange, it nonetheless seems plausible to appeal to the likely behavior of the participants in these markets to provide the solution. These players will be constantly involved in valuing, revaluing and rearranging their portfolios, and hence it becomes possible to suggest that the asset values can be either inflated or deflated sufficiently, as the case may be, such that the system eventually arrives on the stable arm.[2] Therefore, in the next section we proceed to a comparative static analysis.

4   COMPARATIVE STATICS IN THE FLEXIBLE EXCHANGE RATE CASE

The equilibrium solution in the flexible exchange rate case is:

$$y = 1/(1 + \varepsilon\eta + \gamma)d - [(1 + \varepsilon)/(1 + \varepsilon\eta + \gamma)]t$$

$$-[(\alpha - \varepsilon\theta)/(1 + \varepsilon\eta + \gamma)]q + [\varepsilon/(1 + \varepsilon\eta + \gamma)][a - w_0 - r] \quad (3.11)$$

$$p = p_0 + t + w_0 - a - \theta q + \eta y \quad (3.12)$$

$$0 = \alpha q + \gamma y + rb \quad (3.13)$$

$$0 = r^* - r + \zeta b. \quad (3.14)$$

Next, work out the comparative static derivatives. These are:

$$\delta y/\delta d = [1/(1 + \varepsilon\eta + \gamma)], \qquad \delta y/\delta r = -[\varepsilon/(1 + \eta + \gamma)],$$
$$\delta y/\delta t = -[(1 + \varepsilon)/(1 + \varepsilon\eta + \gamma)], \quad \delta y/\delta a = [\varepsilon/(1 + \eta + \gamma)]$$
$$\delta p/\delta d = [\eta/(1 + \varepsilon\eta + \gamma)], \qquad \delta p/\delta r = -\eta[\varepsilon(1 - \theta) + \alpha]/(1 + \varepsilon\eta + \gamma),$$
$$\delta p/\delta t = [\eta(1 + \varepsilon)/(1 + \varepsilon\eta + \gamma)], \quad \delta p/\delta a = -[(1 + \gamma)/(1 + \varepsilon\eta + \gamma)],$$
$$\delta q/\delta d = 0, \qquad\qquad\qquad \delta q/\delta r = -[\zeta b + r)/\alpha\zeta],$$
$$\delta q/\delta t = 0, \qquad\qquad\qquad \delta q/\delta a = 0, \qquad\qquad (3.15)$$
$$\delta b/\delta d = 0, \qquad\qquad\qquad \delta b/\delta r = 1/\zeta,$$
$$\delta b/\delta t = 0, \qquad\qquad\qquad \delta b/\delta a = 0.$$

The signs of the comparative static derivatives may then be conveniently summarized as in Table 3.1. Therefore, the results show that low real interest rates on money (that is, an expansionary monetary policy, or "cheap money" – in the true sense of the term) will tend to increase the

Table 3.1 *Signs of the comparative static derivatives in the floating exchange rate case*

	δd	δt	δr	δa
$\delta y \mid$	+	−	−	+
$\delta p \mid$	+	+	−	−
$\delta q \mid$	0	0	+	0
$\delta b \mid$	0	0	+	0

growth rate, just as old-time mercantilists would have suggested. It will also increase the inflation rate, but note that inflation will not accelerate (that is, get out of control) after the initial increase. We are back in a realm in which there is a trade-off between inflation and growth, at least as far monetary policy is concerned. Meanwhile the real exchange rate will depreciate, and the foreign debt position will be reduced (or the credit position increased), in what seems like the classic monetary mercantilist scenario alluded to above.

An expansionary fiscal policy by means of an increase in government spending as a percentage of GDP (illustrated here by an increase in the demand variable *d*), will also increase the growth rate, much as a Keynesian advocate of "stimulus" would argue. Again there will be a somewhat higher inflation rate, but not an ever-accelerating rate. Interestingly enough, a change in the demand variable ultimately has no effect on either the real exchange rate or the foreign debt position. This occurs because by construction the, for example, expansionary fiscal policy is carried out against the background of a stable monetary policy, that is, stable real interest rates (Smithin, 2007). This reinforces the point that the real exchange rate, like the real interest rate, is above all a monetary variable.

A fiscal stimulus brought about by a reduction in the average tax rate rather than an increase in spending – either way entailing an increase in the budget deficit – is another means of increasing the growth rate, via a combination of demand side and incentive (supply-side) effects. In this case, however, it is important to note that the inflation rate *falls* rather than rises, because of the impact of lower taxes on production costs. As with increases in spending, tax cuts ultimately seem to have little or no effect on the real exchange rate or the foreign debt position.

The final change to be considered is the impact of an increase in productivity, as might occur, for example, in the Schumpeterian model of growth due to technological innovation. In the present model this may be represented by an increase in the exogenous variable, *a*. In a similar manner to the effect of tax cuts this will lead to an increase in the growth rate, together with a fall in the inflation rate. This recalls, for example, the discussion of the so-called "new economy" scenario of the 1990s (Atesoglu and Smithin, 2007; Smithin, 2009). Once again, however, we should point out that this situation is "allowed" to occur because of the backdrop of a stable monetary policy, with no interruption in the provision of financing. The opposite case, a fall in the productivity variable, a, would alternatively lead to 1970s-style "stagflation", with growth falling and the inflation rate rising.

5 A MACROECONOMIC MODEL OF A SMALL OPEN ECONOMY WITH A "HARD PEG" (AN IRREVOCABLE FIXED EXCHANGE RATE REGIME)

If, instead of floating the exchange rate, we institute a fixed exchange rate system which is confidently expected to be a "hard peg", an "irrevocable" fixed exchange rate, or a "credible" fixed exchange rate regime (which are some of the expressions commonly used), the macroeconomic model set out in equations (3.1) to (3.4) above must be changed to:

$$y = [1/(1 + \varepsilon\eta + \gamma)]d - [(1 + \varepsilon)/(1 + \varepsilon\eta + \gamma)]t$$

$$- [(\alpha - \varepsilon\theta)/(1 + \varepsilon\eta + \gamma)]q + [\varepsilon/(1 + \varepsilon\eta + \gamma)](a - w_0 - r) \quad (3.16)$$

$$p = p_0 + t + w_0 - a - \theta q + \eta y \quad (3.17)$$

$$\delta f/\delta \tau = \alpha q + \gamma y + r(1 + \upsilon)f \quad (3.18)$$

$$\delta q/\delta \tau = p. \quad (3.19)$$

In the case of a hard peg, evidently the nominal exchange rate will not be expected to change, nor will there be any risk premium charged in forward foreign exchange market, so that $\zeta = 0$. The implication is that nominal interest rates must always be equal systemwide, $i = i^*$, where i is the domestic nominal rate of interest, and i^* is the foreign nominal rate. However, with endogenous money, and therefore the potential for various "cost-push" sources of inflation, this does not guarantee that *real* interest rates would be the same everywhere. For real interest parity (RIP) to hold there would have to be a combination of covered interest parity (CIP) and uncovered interest parity (UIP), both of which hold in the dynamic system of equations (3.14) through (3.18), *plus* purchasing power parity (PPP), which does not necessarily hold outside of the equilibrium state.[3] As exchange rates are now fixed, changes in foreign exchange reserves will be occurring, and therefore a new variable must be introduced, namely:

f = real foreign debt net of real foreign exchange reserves (both denominated in domestic currency) as a percentage of base-year GDP.

Also, a new parameter (treated as such mainly for mathematical convenience):

υ = the ratio of net real foreign debt to real foreign exchange reserves.

In the next section, we discuss the stability properties of the irrevocable fixed rate case.

6   STABILITY IN THE IRREVOCABLE FIXED EXCHANGE RATE CASE

Once again setting all exogenous variables equal to zero, the dynamic system will reduce to:

$$\delta f/\delta \tau = r(1 + \upsilon)f + \alpha q + \gamma y \tag{3.20}$$

$$\delta q/\delta \tau = -\theta q + \eta y. \tag{3.21}$$

Totally differentiating, and noting also that the real interest rate r is now no longer in principle an exogenous variable, we obtain:

$$[\delta(\delta f/\delta \tau)] = [r(1 + \upsilon)]\delta f + \alpha \delta q + \gamma \delta y + [(1 + \upsilon)f]\delta r \tag{3.22}$$

$$[\delta(\delta q/\delta \tau)] = -\theta \delta q + \eta \delta y. \tag{3.23}$$

From the definition of the real interest rate and using equation (3.16), we also have:

$$\delta r = \{[\theta(1 + \gamma) + \alpha \eta]/(1 + \gamma)\}\delta q \tag{3.24}$$

$$\delta y = -[\alpha/(1 + \gamma)]\delta q. \tag{3.25}$$

Therefore, the dynamic system can be rewritten in matrix form as:

$$\left|\frac{[\delta(\delta f/\delta\tau)]}{[\delta(\delta q/\delta\tau)]}\right| =$$

$$\begin{vmatrix} r(1 + \upsilon) & \{1 + f(1 + \upsilon)[\theta(1 + \gamma) + \alpha\eta]\}/(1 + \gamma) \\ 0 & - [\theta(1 + \gamma) + \alpha\eta]/(1 + \gamma) \end{vmatrix} \begin{vmatrix} \delta f \\ \delta q \end{vmatrix} \quad (3.26)$$

Let Δ = the coefficient matrix. Stability requires that $tr\Delta < 0$ and $det\Delta > 0$. However, we have:

$$tr\Delta = r(1 + \upsilon) - [\theta(1 + \gamma) + \alpha\eta]/(1 + \gamma), \qquad (?) \qquad (3.27)$$

$$det\Delta = -[r(1 + \upsilon)][\theta(1 + \gamma) + \alpha\eta]/(1 + \gamma), \qquad (< 0). \ (3.28)$$

Therefore, this system also has a saddle-point, but now the equilibrium solution has certain essential features that make the argument about how equilibrium might be achieved much more precarious than in the floating exchange rate case. The equilibrium solution is, in fact:

$$y = (1/\eta)(a - p_0 - t - w_0) \qquad (3.29)$$

$$d = [(1 + \gamma)/\eta](a - p_0 - w_0) - (1/\eta)(1 + \gamma - \eta)t + \varepsilon r^* \qquad (3.30)$$

$$p = 0 \qquad (3.31)$$

$$q = 0 \qquad (3.32)$$

$$f = -[\gamma/\eta(1 + \upsilon)](a - p_0 - t - w_0)(1/r^*). \qquad (3.33)$$

Therefore, if there is to be equilibrium the system *must* involve zero inflation, that is, the same inflation rate as in the rest of the world, and also PPP here exemplified by $q = 0$. Something similar to a neoclassical "natural rate" of growth emerges in equation (3.29), though the term is a clear misnomer in this case. There is nothing "natural" about the equilibrium growth rate, as it is basically imposed by the nature of the exchange rate regime. The only policy variable that can now affect the GDP growth rate is a change in the average tax rate t. A cut in taxes will increase the GDP growth rate, essentially because of incentives, as in the usual supply-side argument. There is a problem with this artificially imposed version of supply-side economics, however, because equation (3.30) is overdetermined and as it stands is inconsistent. There are only exogenous variables on both sides of the expression. To make it work it seems that the demand variable, d, must become endogenous rather than exogenous, if the unique saddle-point equilibrium is ever to be reached. In short, it would have to be achieved deliberately by the management of government spending.

For example, any tax cut would have to be balanced by some change in government spending, and moreover (against the usual instincts of policy makers), this may have to be *either* a cut *or* an increase, depending on the value of the parameters. Similarly, an exogenous increase in the real wage, for example (say, through an increase in the $w0$ term, without any concomitant increase in productivity), would have to be offset by government spending cuts. On the other hand, an increase in foreign real interest rates would need to be countered by spending increases! These may seem like familiar propositions about the need to carefully manage the public finances, but note that there are some anomalies here that differ from the conventional wisdom about what the concept of "fiscal responsibility" usually means. Also these rules are *not* imposed by market forces or anything of the kind, in fact, just the opposite. They are necessary only because of the commitment by the governmental authorities to the exchange rate regime. In effect, the willingness to adjust/manage the government budget, in this way, becomes the necessary transversality condition if the single stable arm of the system is ever to be reached.

It is evident, therefore, that there is a difficult balancing act to perform, both politically and financially, if equilibrium is ever to be attained. Failing this, the practical analogy to the mathematical problem may be that the system is likely to break down in a foreign exchange crisis as (it can surely be argued) frequently does occur in reality. It may be objected to this that "rational agents" will not initially "believe" in the system if it can ultimately end in crisis. The point is, though, that "rational expectations" in themselves are not enough. The policy makers and market participants would also have to be working with the *correct* model of the economy. It seems evident that many in the real world are not doing so, simply by noting that there are, and have been, many expert advocates over the years of such things as currency unions, currency boards, "dollarization", the gold standard, other commodity standards, a single world currency, and so forth.

7 A MACROECONOMIC MODEL OF A SMALL OPEN ECONOMY WITH FIXED EXCHANGE RATES, BUT RESIDUAL FRICTION AND REMAINING PERCEIVED CURRENCY RISK

Perhaps ironically, a fixed exchange rate regime that is initially perceived as less secure than a hard peg may in reality have a greater chance of longevity, and precisely because a currency risk premium will re-emerge in such circumstances, it also allows the domestic monetary authorities a greater degree of control over both interest rate and fiscal policy. A related argument to be made in this context is that the introduction of various frictional elements into the system (some form of capital controls being the obvious example) will also allow more room to maneuver on the part of the domestic policy makers. The old Bretton Woods system of 1944–71, for example, was called a "fixed but adjustable" regime, and also had various capital control provisions, so there clearly would have been a substantial element of currency risk in that case.

The following set of equations may be used to represent this type of situation:

$$y = [1/(1 + \varepsilon\eta + \gamma)]d - [(1 + \varepsilon)(1 + \varepsilon\eta + \gamma)]t$$

$$- (\alpha - \varepsilon\theta)(1 + \varepsilon\eta + \gamma)q + [\varepsilon/(1 + \varepsilon\eta + \gamma)](a - w_0 - r) \quad (3.34)$$

$$p = p_0 + t + w_0 - a - \theta q + \eta y \quad (3.35)$$

$$\delta f/\delta\tau = \alpha q + \gamma y + r(1 + \upsilon)f \quad (3.36)$$

$$\delta q/\delta\tau = r - r^* + \zeta f. \quad (3.37)$$

This system is almost the same as that outlined in (3.16) through (3.19) above, but with one main difference. The nominal exchange remains fixed and is not *expected* to change. However, there is now nonetheless a currency risk premium on debt obligations denominated in domestic currency, as there is some perceived risk that these expectations will not be fulfilled. Therefore, the parameter ζ is reintroduced, and now stands for the sensitivity of the currency risk premium to real foreign debt *net of* real foreign exchange reserves, as a percentage of base-year GDP ($\zeta > 0$). The implication is also that nominal interest rates need not now be equal systemwide, that is, $i \neq i^*$.

8   STABILITY IN THE CASE OF FIXED EXCHANGE RATES WITH RESIDUAL FRICTIONS AND REMAINING PERCEIVED CURRENCY RISK

Once more setting all exogenous variables equal to zero, the dynamic system becomes:

$$\delta f/\delta \tau = \alpha q + \gamma y \tag{3.38}$$

$$\delta q/\delta \tau = \zeta f, \tag{3.39}$$

where the domestic real interest is once again under the control of the domestic monetary authorities, and for the purposes of the stability exercise can be set at zero. In matrix form, the system becomes:

$$\begin{vmatrix} \delta f/\delta \tau \\ \delta q/\delta \tau \end{vmatrix} = \begin{vmatrix} 0 & [\alpha(1 + \varepsilon\eta) + \varepsilon\gamma\theta]/(1 + \varepsilon\eta + \gamma) \\ \zeta & 0 \end{vmatrix} \begin{vmatrix} f \\ q \end{vmatrix} \tag{3.40}$$

Let Δ = the coefficient matrix. Stability requires that $tr\Delta < 0$ and $det\Delta > 0$ However, we have:

$$tr\Delta = 0, \tag{3.41}$$

$$det\Delta = -\zeta\{[\alpha(1 + \varepsilon\eta) + \varepsilon\gamma\theta]/(1 + \varepsilon\eta + \gamma)\}, \qquad (<0) \tag{3.42}$$

Therefore, this system again has a saddle-point, as in the original case of floating exchange rates.

9 COMPARATIVE STATICS IN THE CASE OF FIXED EXCHANGE RATES WITH RESIDUAL FRICTION AND REMAINING PERCEIVED CURRENCY RISK

In this case of "fixed" exchange rates, but with remaining perceived currency risk, the equilibrium solution will be:

$$y = [1/(1 + \varepsilon\eta + \gamma)]d - [(1 + \varepsilon)/(1 + \varepsilon\eta + \gamma)]t$$

$$- [(\alpha - \varepsilon\theta)/(1 + \varepsilon\eta + \gamma)]q + [\varepsilon/(1 + \varepsilon\eta + \gamma)][a - w_0 - r] \tag{3.43}$$

$$p = p_0 + t + w_0 - a - \theta q + \eta y \tag{3.44}$$

$$0 = \alpha q + \gamma y + r(1 + \upsilon)f \tag{3.45}$$

$$0 = r^* - r - \zeta f. \tag{3.46}$$

Next, again work out the comparative static derivatives:

Table 3.2   Signs of the comparative static derivatives in the "virtual" floating exchange rate case

	δd	δt	δr	δa
$\delta y \mid$	+	−	−	+
$\delta p \mid$	+	+	−	−
$\delta q \mid$	0	0	+	0
$\delta b \mid$	0	0	+	0

$$\delta y/\delta d = [1/(1 + \varepsilon\eta + \gamma)], \qquad \delta y/\delta r = -[\varepsilon/(1 + \eta + \gamma)],$$
$$\delta y/\delta t = -[(1 + \varepsilon)/(1 + \varepsilon\eta + \gamma)], \quad \delta y/\delta a = [\varepsilon/(1 + \eta + \gamma)]$$
$$\delta p/\delta d = [\eta/(1 + \varepsilon\eta + \gamma)], \qquad \delta p/\delta r = -\eta[\varepsilon(1 - \theta) + \alpha]/(1 + \varepsilon\eta + \gamma),$$
$$\delta p/\delta t = [\eta(1 + \varepsilon)/(1 + \varepsilon\eta + \gamma)], \quad \delta p/\delta a = -[(1 + \gamma)/(1 + \varepsilon\eta + \gamma)],$$
$$\delta q/\delta d = 0, \qquad\qquad \delta q/\delta r = -[\zeta f + r)/\alpha\zeta],$$
$$\delta q/\delta t = 0, \qquad\qquad \delta q/\delta a = 0, \tag{3.47}$$
$$\delta f/\delta d = 0, \qquad\qquad \delta f/\delta r = 1/\zeta,$$
$$\delta f/\delta t = 0, \qquad\qquad \delta f/\delta a = 0.$$

The signs of the comparative static derivatives are then summarized as in Table 3.2. The most obvious point about the results in the table is that they simply replicate those of the flexible exchange rate case discussed earlier. This shows that the reintroduction of the currency risk premium, the possibility of exchange rate adjustments, and/or the introduction of other frictional elements can recreate the conditions of a "virtual" floating exchange rate regime (as stated in the caption to Table 3.2), and thus may still provide the necessary degrees of freedom for domestic policy makers.

10   CONCLUSION

In effect, the framework set out in this chapter has been able to illustrate several of the "growth scenarios" that have been suggested by a number of different schools of economic thought, including the original mercantilists, as well as to predict the impact of these on the real exchange rate and the foreign debt position. The main conclusion is that the key to "capitalism in one country" (to return to our original expression) is the existence of a separate monetary and financial system, with either a floating exchange rate regime, or at least one in which adjustments can be made as frequently as required, without excessive political or other difficulties. By the same token, it may explain the problems that have often been experienced by jurisdictions that are not in a comparable situation.

NOTES

*   An earlier version of this chapter was published in Spanish (Kam and Smithin, 2011). The authors would like to thank Robert Guttmann, Noemi Levy, Warren Mosler, Tom Palley, Mario Seccareccia and Mark Setterfield for helpful comments and suggestions that have improved this chapter; and Louis-Phillipe Rochon for organizing the "Political Economy of Central Banking" conference sponsored by Laurentian University, and the Social Sciences and Humanities Research Council (SSHRC), at which the first draft was presented in May 2009.
1. See also Smithin (2003), Kam and Smithin (2008) and Barrows and Smithin (2009).
2. This is not the same argument as that stating that "stabilizing speculation" will tend to reduce nominal exchange rate volatility, as in Friedman (1953). In the present model, nominal exchange rates will need to change to whatever extent is necessary to achieve the eventual real exchange rate equilibrium. The real exchange rate itself is considered to be a monetary variable. See also Iwai (2009).
3. It must hold in equilibrium, however, if that equilibrium is ever to be reached, as shown below.

REFERENCES

Atesoglu, H.S. and J. Smithin (2007), "Un modelo macroeconomico simple", *Economia Informa*, **346**: 105–19.

Barrows, D. and J. Smithin (2009), *Fundamentals of Economics for Business*, 2nd edn, Toronto and Singapore: Captus Press and World Scientific.

Bougrine, H. and M. Seccarecccia (2008), "Financing development: removing the external constraint", paper presented at the "Financing Development: Where Do We Find the Money?", international conference, Laurentian University, Sudbury, ON, Canada, October 17–18.

Friedman, M. (1953), "The case for flexible exchange rates", in *Essays in Positive Economics*, Chicago, IL: University of Chicago Press, pp. 157–203.

Humphrey, T. (1998), "Mercantilists and classicals: insights from doctrinal history", in *Federal Reserve Bank of Richmond Annual Report*, pp. 2–27.

Ingham, G. (2004), *The Nature of Money*, Cambridge: Polity Press.

Iwai, K. (2009), "The second end of laisser-faire", paper presented the "Money – Interdisciplinary Perspectives", international workshop, Free University of Berlin, June.

Kam, E. (2005), "A note on time preference and the Tobin effect", *Economics Letters*, **89**: 127–32.

Kam, E. and J. Smithin (2004), "Monetary policy and demand management for the small open economy in contemporary conditions with (perfectly) mobile capital", *Journal of Post Keynesian Economics*, **26**: 679–94.

Kam, E. and J. Smithin (2008), "Unequal partners: the role of international financial flows and the exchange rate regime", *Journal of Economic Asymmetries*, **5**: 125–37.

Kam, E. and J. Smithin (2011), "Capitalismo en un sólo país?: Una revaloración de los sistemas mercantilistas desde el punto de vista financiero", in N.O. Levy Orlik and T.S. López González (eds), *Las Instituciones Financieras y el Crecimiento Económico en el Contexto de la Dominación del Capital Financiero*, Mexico City: Juan Pablo, pp. 37–58.

Keynes, J.M. (1964), *The General Theory of Employment Interest and Money*, London: Harcourt Brace, 1st edn London: Macmillan, 1936.

Kim, J.-C. (2009), "Identity, money and trust: the origin and ontology of modern money in England, 17th–early 19th centuries", PhD thesis proposal in political science, York University, Toronto.

Palley, T.I. (2004), "The effectiveness of monetary policy in open-economy macro-economics: Dornbusch versus Tobin", in M. Lavoie and M. Seccareccia (eds), *Central Banking in the Modern World: Alternative Perspectives*, Cheltenham, UK and Northampton, MA, USA: Edward Elgar, pp. 211–25.

Seccarecccia, M. (2003/04), "Is dollarization a desirable alternative to the monetary *status quo*? A critical evaluation of competing currency arrangements for Canada", *Studies in Political Economy*, **71/72**: 91–109.

Smithin, J. (2003), *Controversies in Monetary Economics: Revised Edition*, Cheltenham, UK and Northampton, MA, USA: Edward Elgar.

Smithin, J. (2006), "The theory of interest rates", in P. Arestis and M. Sawyer (eds), *A Handbook of Alternative Monetary Economics*, Cheltenham, UK and Northampton, MA, USA: Edward Elgar, pp. 273–90.

Smithin, J. (2007), "A real interest rate rule for monetary policy?", *Journal of Post Keynesian Economics*, **30**: 101–18.

Smithin, J. (2009), *Money, Enterprise and Income Distribution: Towards a Macroeconomic Theory of Capitalism*, London: Routledge.

Smithin, J. (2010), "The importance of money and debt/credit relationships in the enterprise economy", in H. Bougrine and M. Seccareccia (eds), *Introducing Macroeconomic Analysis: Ideas, Questions, and Competing Views*, Toronto: Esmond Montgomery, pp. 49–60.

4. Proposals for the banking system, the FDIC, the Fed, and the Treasury

Warren Mosler

1 INTRODUCTION

The purpose of this chapter is to present proposals for the banking system, the Federal Deposit Insurance Corporation (FDIC), the Federal Reserve (Fed), and the Treasury. Government begins with an assumption that it exists for public purpose, and I use that as the guiding assumption of my proposals. I begin with my proposals for the banking system, as banking operations influence both Fed and Treasury operations.

2 PROPOSALS FOR THE BANKING SYSTEM

US banks are public/private partnerships, established for the public purpose of providing loans based on credit analysis. Supporting this type of lending on an ongoing, stable basis demands a source of funding that is not market dependent. Hence most of the world's banking systems include some form of government deposit insurance, as well as a central bank standing by to loan to its member banks.

Under a gold standard or other fixed exchange rate regime, bank funding cannot be credibly guaranteed. In fact, fixed exchange rate regimes by design operate with an ongoing constraint on the supply side of the convertible currency. Banks are required to hold reserves of convertible currency, to be able to meet depositors' demands for withdrawals. Confidence is critical for banks working under a gold standard. No bank can operate with 100 percent reserves. They depend on depositors not panicking and trying to cash in their deposits for convertible currency. The US experienced a series of severe depressions in the late 1800s, with the "panic" of 1907 disturbing enough to result in the creation of the Federal Reserve in 1913. The Fed was to be the lender of last resort to ensure that the nation would never again go through another 1907. Unfortunately, that strategy failed. The depression of 1930 was even worse than the panic of 1907. The gold standard regime kept the Fed from being able to lend its banks the convertible currency they needed to meet withdrawal demands.

After thousands of catastrophic bank failures, a "bank holiday" was declared and the remaining banks were closed by the government while the banking system was reorganized. When the banking system reopened in 1934, convertibility of the currency into gold was permanently suspended (domestically), and bank deposits were covered by federal deposit insurance. The Fed was unable to stop depressions. It was going off the gold standard that did the trick.

It has been 80 years since the Great Depression. It would now take exceptionally poor policy responses for even the current severe recession to deteriorate into a depression, though misguided and overly tight fiscal policies have unfortunately prolonged the restoration of output and employment.

The hard lesson of banking history is that the liability side of banking is not the place for market discipline. Therefore, with banks funded without limit by government-insured deposits and loans from the central bank, discipline is entirely on the asset side. This includes being limited to assets deemed "legal" by the regulators and minimum capital requirements also set by the regulators.

Given that the public purpose of banking is to provide for a payments system and to fund loans based on credit analysis, additional proposals and restrictions are in order:

1. Banks should only be allowed to lend directly to borrowers, and then service and keep those loans on their own balance sheets. There is no further public purpose served by selling loans or other financial assets to third parties, but there are substantial real costs to government regarding the regulation and supervision of those activities. And there are severe consequences for failure to adequately regulate and supervise those secondary market activities as well. For that reason (no public purpose and geometrically growing regulatory burdens with severe social costs in the case of regulatory and supervisory lapses), banks should be prohibited from engaging in any secondary market activity. The argument that these areas might be profitable for the banks is not a reason to extend government-sponsored enterprises into those areas.
2. US banks should not be allowed to contract in LIBOR (London Inter-Bank Offered Rate). LIBOR is an interest rate set in a foreign country (the UK) with a large, subjective component that is out of the hands

of the US government. Part of the current crisis was the Fed's inability to bring down the LIBOR settings to its target interest rate, as it tried to assist millions of US homeowners and other borrowers who had contracted with US banks to pay interest based on LIBOR settings. Desperate to bring US dollar interest rates down for domestic borrowers, the Fed resorted to a very high-risk policy of advancing unlimited, functionally unsecured, US dollar lines of credit called "swap lines" to several foreign central banks. These loans were advanced at the Fed's low target rate, with the hope that the foreign central banks would lend these funds to their member banks at the low rates, and thereby bring down the LIBOR settings and the cost of borrowing US dollars for US households and businesses. The loans to the foreign central banks peaked at about US$600 billion and did eventually work to bring down the LIBOR settings. But the risks were substantial. There is no way for the Fed to collect a loan from a foreign central bank that elects not to pay it back. If, instead of contracting based on LIBOR settings, US banks had been linking their loan rates and lines of credit to the US Fed Funds rate, this problem would have been avoided. The rates paid by US borrowers, including homeowners and businesses, would have come down as the Fed intended when it cut the Fed Funds rate.

3. Banks should not be allowed to have subsidiaries of any kind. No public purpose is served by allowing bank to hold any assets "off balance sheet".

4. Banks should not be allowed to accept financial assets as collateral for loans. No public purpose is served by financial leverage.

5. US banks should not be allowed to lend offshore. No public purpose is served by allowing US banks to lend for foreign purposes.

6. Banks should not be allowed to buy (or sell) credit default insurance. The public purpose of banking as a public/private partnership is to allow the private sector to price risk, rather than have the public sector pricing risk through publicly owned banks. If a bank instead relies on credit default insurance it is transferring that pricing of risk to a third party, which is counter to the public purpose of the current public/private banking system.

7. Banks should not be allowed to engage in proprietary trading or any profit-making ventures beyond basic lending. If the public sector wants to venture out of banking for some presumed public purpose, it can be done through other outlets.

8. My last proposal for the banks in this draft is to utilize FDIC-approved credit models for evaluation of bank assets. I would not allow mark to market of bank assets. In fact, if there is a valid

argument to marking a particular bank asset to market prices, that likely means that asset should not be a permissible bank asset in the first place. The public purpose of banking is to facilitate loans based on credit analysis, rather than market valuation. And the accompanying provision of government-insured funding allows those loans to be held to maturity without liquidity issues, in support of that same public purpose. Therefore, marking to market rather than evaluation by credit analysis both serves no further public purpose and subverts the existing public purpose of providing a stable platform for lending.

3   PROPOSALS FOR THE FDIC

I have three proposals for the FDIC. The first is to remove the US$250,000 cap on deposit insurance. The public purpose behind the cap is to help small banks attract deposits, under the theory that if there were no cap, large depositors would gravitate toward the larger banks. However, once the Fed is directed to trade in the Fed Funds markets with all member banks, in unlimited size, the issue of available funding is moot.

The second is to not tax banks in order to recover funds lost on bank failures. The FDIC should be entirely funded by the US Treasury. Taxes on solvent banks should not be on the basis of the funding needs of the FDIC. Taxes on banks have ramifications that can either serve or conflict with the larger public purposes presumably served by government participation in the banking system. These include sustaining the payments system and lending based on credit analysis. Any tax on banks should be judged entirely by how that tax serves or does not serve public purpose.

My third proposal for the FDIC is to do its job without any assistance by Treasury (apart from funding any FDIC expenditures). The FDIC is charged with taking over any bank it deems insolvent, and then selling that bank, selling the bank's assets, reorganizing the bank, or any other similar action that serves the public purpose government participation in the banking system. The TARP (Troubled Asset Relief Program) was at least partially established to allow the US Treasury to buy equity in specific banks to keep them from being declared insolvent by the FDIC, and to allow them to continue to have sufficient capital to continue to lend. What the TARP did, however, was reveal the total failure of both the Bush and Obama administrations to comprehend the essence of the workings of the banking system. Once a bank incurs losses in excess of its private capital, further losses are covered by the FDIC, an arm of the US government. If the Treasury "injects capital" into a bank, all that happens is that once losses exceed the same amount of private capital, the US Treasury, also an arm of the US government, is next in line for any losses to the extent of its capital contribution, with the FDIC covering any losses beyond that. So what is changed by Treasury purchases of bank equity?

After the private capital is lost, the losses are taken by the US Treasury instead of the FDIC, which also gets its funding from the US Treasury. It makes no difference for the US government and the "taxpayers" whether the Treasury covers the loss indirectly when funding the FDIC, or directly after "injecting capital" into a bank. All that was needed to accomplish the same end as the TARP program – to allow banks to continue to function and acquire FDIC-insured deposits – was for the FDIC to directly reduce the private capital requirements. Instead, and as direct evidence of a costly ignorance of the dynamics of the banking model, both the Bush and Obama administrations burned through substantial quantities of political capital to get the legislative authority to allow the Treasury to buy equity positions in dozens of private banks. And, to make matters worse, it was all accounted for as additional federal deficit spending.

While this would not matter if Congress and the administrations understood the monetary system, the fact is that they do not, and so the TARP has therefore restricted their inclination to make further fiscal adjustments to restore employment and output. Ironically, the overly tight fiscal policy continues to contribute to the rising delinquency and default rate for bank loans, which continues to impede the desired growth of bank capital.

4   PROPOSALS FOR THE FED

First, the Fed should lend unsecured to member banks, and in unlimited quantities at its target Fed Funds rate, by simply trading in the Fed Funds market. There is no reason to do otherwise. Currently the Fed will only loan to its banks on a fully collateralized basis. However, this is both redundant and disruptive. The Fed demanding collateral when it lends is redundant because all bank assets are already fully regulated by federal regulators. It is the job of the regulators to make sure that all FDIC-insured deposits are "safe" and "taxpayer money" is not at risk from losses that exceed the available private capital. Therefore, the FDIC has already determined that funds loaned by the Fed to a bank can only be invested in "legal" assets and that the bank is adequately capitalized as required by law. There is no room for funding from the Fed to be "misused" as banks already can obtain virtually unlimited funding by FDIC-insured deposits. The only difference between banks funding with FDIC-insured deposits and funding directly from the Fed might be the interest rate the bank may have to pay, however it is the further purpose of the Fed's monetary policy to target the Fed Funds rate.

The Fed also tends to set quantity limits when it lends to its member banks, when there is every reason to instead lend in unlimited quantities. Bank lending is not reserve constrained, so constraining lending to the banks by quantity does not alter lending. What constraining reserves does is alter the Fed Funds rate, which is the rate banks pay for reserves as well as the Fed's target rate. So the only way the Fed can fully stabilize the Fed Funds rate at its target rate is to simply offer to provide unlimited funds at that rate as well as offer to accept Fed Funds deposits at that same target rate. And with no monetary risk or adverse economic consequences for lending unlimited quantities at its target rate, there is no reason not to do this. Another benefit of this policy would be to entirely eliminate the interbank Fed Funds market. There is no public purpose served by banks trading Fed Funds with each other when they can do it with the Fed, and transactions costs are reduced as well. And to eliminate the interbank markets entirely, the Fed has the further option to provide funding with an entire term structure of rates to its banks to both target those rates and also eliminate the need for any interbank trading.

Second, I would limit the Fed to using banks as agents for monetary policy. I would not pursue the policy of attempting to establish additional public/private partnerships for the purpose of buying various financial assets. Instead, if I agreed with the need to purchase those assets, I would enable the banking system to do this along the same lines proposed for the new public/private partnerships. That might take the form of allowing banks to put these "qualifying assets" in a segregated account, where losses to bank capital would be limited to, for example, 10 percent of the investment in those accounts. This would have the same result as the recently proposed public/private partnerships but within the existing highly regulated and supervised banking system. Banks are the appropriate instrument of monetary policy for targeting the risk-adjusted term structure of interest rates. Why go to the expense and risk of creating new public/private partnerships when there are already approximately 8,000 member banks already set up for that purpose?

Third, I would make the current zero interest rate policy permanent. This minimizes cost pressures on output, including investment, and thereby helps to stabilize prices. It also minimizes rentier incomes, thereby encouraging higher labor force participation and increased real output. Additionally, because the non-government sectors are net savers of financial assets, this policy hurts savers more than it aids borrowers, so a fiscal adjustment such as a tax cut or spending increase would be appropriate to sustain output and employment.

Fourth, I would instruct the Fed to offer credit default insurance on all Treasury securities through its banking system to any buyer. There is no default risk in US Treasury securities, but, if market participants do want to buy such credit default insurance, I would make it available through the Fed. This would keep the premiums and the perception of risk down to a level determined by the Fed. I would suggest that they offer it freely at 5 basis points for any maturity.

5 PROPOSALS FOR THE TREASURY

First, I would cease all issuance of Treasury securities. Instead, any deficit spending would accumulate as excess reserve balances at the Fed. No public purpose is served by the issuance of Treasury securities with a non-convertible currency and floating exchange rate policy. Issuing Treasury securities only serves to support the term structure of interest rates at higher levels than would be the case. And, as longer-term rates are the realm of investment, higher-term rates only serve to adversely distort the price structure of all goods and services.

Second, I would not allow the Treasury to purchase financial assets. This should be done only by the Fed as has traditionally been the case. When the Treasury buys financial assets instead of the Fed, all that changes is the reaction of the President, the Congress, the economists, and the media, as they misread the Treasury purchases of financial assets as federal "deficit spending" that limits other fiscal options.

6 CONCLUSION

I conclude with my proposals to support aggregate demand and restore output and employment:

1. A full payroll tax holiday where the Treasury makes all the contributions for employees and employers. This immediately restores the purchasing power of those still working and enables them to make their mortgage payments which also stabilizes the banking system.
2. I would distribute US$150 billion of revenue sharing to the state governments on a per capita basis. This would stabilize state governments currently cutting back on public services due to revenue shortfalls caused by the recession. Distribution on a per capita basis makes it "fair" and does not "reward bad behavior".
3. I would have the federal government fund US$8/hr full-time jobs for anyone willing and able to work, that includes healthcare benefits. This provides an employed labor buffer stock that is a superior price

anchor to our current unemployed buffer stock. This helps support an expansion in private sector employment as the economy improves. It has been demonstrated that the private sector prefers to hire those already working rather than those who are unemployed.

These three proposals, along with the above proposals for the banking system, the FDIC, the Fed, and the Treasury, will quickly restore the US economy to positive growth, full employment, and establish a banking system that will promote the intended public purpose and require less regulation while substantially reducing the systemic risk inherent in our current institutional arrangements.

5. Financial market organizations, central banks and credits: the experience of developing economies

Noemi Levy-Orlik*

1 INTRODUCTION

There are important and vital discussions over the limit of finance and its effect on economic growth. The first disagreement is over the need to build institutions to direct finance to production. One of the main differences is about how finance is generated: through bank credit issuance (money advances) or financial intermediation. Keynesian and heterodox economists stress the importance of banks, and their main argument is that money is a social relation, the interest rate is a monetary variable not limited by natural interest rates (profits), money is endogenous and, more importantly, it affects production (it is not neutral). Therefore one of the principal deterrents of economic growth is credit constraints. In this context, the central bank's main function is to stabilize the financial system through accommodating banks' demand reserves and formulating monetary policies to support productive activity rather than financial gains.

In contrast, mainstream economists assume that savings finance investment, consequently financial intermediation guarantees finance for production. Money is a commodity that reduces the cost of barter, turning the exchange of commodity into an indirect process, whereby money (as another commodity) enhances the process of intermediation (Graziani, 2003: ch. 2), the rate of interest is a real variable, and money is neutral (that is, it does not modify the level of economic activity). The principal restriction of economic growth lies in the economic structure, specifically in imperfect movements of production factors (mainly capital), which impede the capital market from collecting enough savings. As long as prices (interest rates) are "correct" (in equilibrium), financial intermediation guarantees that economic activity will operate at full-employment levels; the central bank's main concern is to keep inflation under control.

The discussion of how finance is produced and what are the core financial institutions is crucial in developing economies, since the industrialization process requires the mobilization of large amounts of financial resources and it faces uneven competition. Hence, central banks and public financial institutions, along with government economic intervention, play a vital role in guaranteeing financial resources for economic growth and neutralizing credit constraints. Therefore we adopt the heterodox view, arguing that credit issuance (and not savings) is a prerequisite of economic growth, and it depends on the credit demand of solvent borrowers and the central bank's willingness to stabilize the financial system. Also it is vital that the central bank determines its discount rate, which should favor productive activities rather than financial returns. In developing economies the financial structure that best performs these functions is the bank-based system along with government intervention in the economy. The capital-based system has not been efficient in providing financial resources to the productive sectors since its objective is to maximize financial rather than productive returns.

This chapter is organized as follows. Section 2 discusses credit issuance, highlighting the way finance is created and how central banks intervene in providing credit and improving borrowers' solvency. Section 3 examines how the bank-based structure has evolved in developing economies and Section 4 analyzes the transition from the bank- to the market-based system. Section 5 discusses the Mexican financial structure in terms of credit mobility and central bank functions under new financial settings. Section 6 concludes.

2 CREDIT ISSUANCE AND CENTRAL BANKS' BEHAVIOR IN DEVELOPING ECONOMIES

There are two contradicting positions in terms of providing financial resources for production and regarding central banks' functions. The neoclassical view is based in the prior savings argument, which assumes that finance is provided by savings that are intermediated to investment, where the rate of interest is a real variable whose flexibility guarantees equality between savings and investment. Capital markets are the more important institutions in this theoretical framework.

Savings are supplied by household intertemporal preferences and investment is determined by the marginal productivity of capital; thrift and productivity are the main forces behind the natural (equilibrium) rate of interest. The process of intermediation takes place in capital markets under the assumption of the perfect market paradigm "which assumes an ideal world of complete and perfect capital market, with full and symmetric information amongst all market participants" (Lewis, 1992: 204). Under this view, banks are seen as traders or equity-financed mutual funds, and the main objective of government policy is to guarantee perfect market competition and perfect distribution of information.

Central banks control the money supply (money is exogenous) in their capacity as government banker, bank of banks and the guardian of international reserves. Thus, central banks establish the monetary base that, given a monetary multiplier, determines the money supply, with a causation movement from money supply to money demand, inflation being caused by demand factors. Government spending is the only source of money expansion (Graziani, 2003: ch. 2).

Different historical events modified the dominant view of central banks' behavior. Blinder (1998) is one of the first modern economists to acknowledge that capital mobility induces money demand instability, preventing central banks from controlling the money supply. Thus these institutions are left with no other choice than to determine short-term monetary interest rates which, however, need not affect the interest rate structure. Money remains neutral as it is unable to modify production. This view has been validated by the new consensus theory (see Blanchard, 2000 [2003]), based on Knut Wicksell's argument which differentiates central bank (monetary) interest rates from the real (natural) interest rate, the latter guaranteeing production at full employment levels (see Lavoie, 2004 for a critical discussion). The central bank reaction function (known as the Taylor rule, see Taylor, 1993) sets a monetary interest rate taking into account the gaps of inflation (observed and expected), of income (observed and potential), and of the interest rate (natural and monetary rate, deducted inflation).

John Maynard Keynes (and earlier, Thorstein Veblen and Ralph Hawtrey, see Toporowski, 2005) and Post Keynesians assume that money is not a commodity,[1] and that it is structurally non-neutral since it impacts on production. Banks can create debts independently of real resources, and debts which are structurally linked to wages and production. Keynes's (1937) arguments on banks' liquidity preference in the transition to a superior stage of production is of central importance in this discussion.

Moore (1988) and the circuitist theory argue that debts precede money (Innes, 1913, quoted in Parguez and Seccareccia, 2000) and they are not related to any commodity (money is a social relation), from where it follows that real resources do not intervene in the process of debt creation, but debts do need to be cancelled out. Hence financial stability depends on the process of debt destruction and borrowers' creditworthiness becomes a central issue of financial stability.

Central banks need to perform the lender-of-last-resort function and, more importantly, supply all commercial bank reserves if the monetary circle does not close in the production period. Their main role is to ensure that short-term imbalances do not induce massive financial institution bankruptcies. Another important central bank task is to determine its discount rate, independently of the amount of credit demanded and supplied. Thus, the rate of interest is a distributive variable that can affect credit availability.

Some important points should be clarified in terms of central and commercial bank performances. First, central banks need not increase liquidity to back commercial bank credit so long as debts are wiped out in each monetary circuit. However, when the Le Bourva law of large numbers does not operate (see Lavoie, 1992) and one bank issues more credit than the rest within one period of time, the central bank is required to intervene in order to fill the gap between the deficit and surplus banks, through issuing debt money creation.

Central bank money supply does not induce inflation since it is demand determined and amplifies the supply of goods and services (considered constant in the neoliberal theoretical framework) and does not induce inflation. A reverse causation takes place: higher prices or unpaid debts expand money demand and supply. Hence, instability is induced not by central bank money issuance but by changes of the market conditions and wrong decisions in terms of credit issuance.

Second, the economic system confronts credit constraints rather than bank credit rationing, which means that the main challenge of the financial system is the reduced number of creditworthy borrowers rather than banks not accommodating credit demand from solvent borrowers (Rochon, 2006). The main argument behind this assertion is that banks lend to all solvent borrowers since their returns come from financial margins (the lending and borrowing interest rate gap), commissions and, more importantly, credit issuance does not compete with other bank activities (such as buying and selling bonds, repos, derivatives, securitization, and so on). In other words, the banks' main function is to issue credit, which if granted to solvent borrowers is paid back in the same circuit period, or in the future, without affecting the equilibrium of the bank balance sheet. In other words, commercial banks first deal with the asset side, and look for funds to put the balance sheet into equilibrium.

The central bank interest rate has an important role in determining who has access to bank lending and the conditions for future repayments; thereby it can modify borrowers' creditworthiness. If the central bank raises its interest rate, the commercial bank lending rate goes up, limiting credit access to some enterprises. Additionally, changes in the central bank's discount rate could increase interest payments above the firms' return, leaving them unable to fulfill previous debt commitments. Central bank interest rate movements (and the future level of effective rates) are considered to be an "interest rate risk" (Moore, 1998: 48) or "macro-economic uncertainty" (Rochon, 2006: 180), which affects all firms in the economy. More importantly, changes in the central bank interest rate can modify the distribution of profit between financial and non-financial corporations. Consequently, higher interest rates may turn solvent borrowers into non-creditworthy agents and modify solvent borrowers' permanency criteria.

Banks can also affect the credit issuance criteria on the basis of "credit risks" or "micro-uncertainty" (ibid.) by determining the borrower's payment ability, which is based on three elements: the cash receipts or the expected borrower's income; the credit history of the borrower; and his/her financial wealth (shares and bonds); and the particular enterprises that are affected. This is independent of macroeconomic conditions and expectations.

The first component (expected income) is related to the project's production performance and the borrower's managerial ability, particularly whether the production or investment projects will yield the expected returns to repay credit advances (including interest). The moral hazard problem deals with the borrower's credit history, which throws light on his/her behavior (in terms of debt repayment). It can exclude an important number of solvent borrowers who do not have a previous credit record (new entrepreneurs with no financial assets, which are micro and small enterprises with no credit record). Finally, a borrower's wealth (financial assets and productive capital) is crucial in determining borrowers' solvency, since it can be used as collateral[2] in cases of unpaid debts or due to changing conditions or wrong predictions in terms of profit creation; therefore, the main problem is asset price volatility.

Under this framework, uncertainty switches from financial markets (Keynes's liquidity preference or Hyman Minsky's corporation leverage rate) to creditors' payment capacity; the central bank discount rate is a fundamental variable. Moore (1988: 266) argues that interest rates are made dependent on

> the techniques of monetary policy, the sensitivity of economic behavior to interest rates changes, the size of openness of the economy, the degree of capital mobility, the extent to which the central bank is willing foreign exchange reserves and exchange rates to fluctuate, the expected domestic and foreign inflation rate, the willingness of the government to regulate and impose controls on the economy, and the extent to which policy is coordinated across countries.

Summing up, debts only turn into money when they are not repaid. A borrower's solvency is a central concern in credit issuance and is subject to speculative decisions. Commercial banks need to ensure that enough profits will be accrued to cancel credit issuance, while central banks should guarantee the smooth functioning of the economy in terms of credit solvency and accommodating commercial bank reserves. It is crucial that the central rate of interest supports productive returns rather than rentiers' financial gains.

Debt creation and repayment are subject to particular conditions in developing countries. The first element to highlight is that investment finance becomes a major factor in developing countries since these economies need to "catch up" with developed countries, mobilizing huge quantities of financial resources to acquire capital goods, which usually are not produced by developing countries. Technology advances take place through imitation processes in relatively short time periods, requiring high amounts of liquidity that are redeemed in long periods; therefore, industrialization processes are subject to high "micro and macro uncertainties". Historical experience has shown that successful industrialization processes require government intervention through public investment and financial public institutions that secure credit provisions for economic development and, more importantly, reduce the credit and interest (and exchange) risks.[3]

Latin American developing countries also face reduced internal markets (due to technological dependency); since their high-tech productive sectors are relatively small, relative wages remain low, therefore firms producing for internal markets face difficulties in selling their production realization (they cannot use their full productive capacity). The differences between high-tech corporations producing for external markets, and small firms with indigenous technology producing for internal markets, prevent an even economic development (Fajnzylber, 1990). Hence, important productive sectors are dominated by micro, small and medium-sized enterprises not eligible for bank credit. Consequently, domestic and farming goods are credit constrained, unless the state channels financial resources to these sectors.

A final consideration is that the banking sector in Latin America (especially in Mexico) has accrued political power, imposing a large gap between the lending rate and the funding interest rate (or deposit rate), as well as high bank commission and other bank income, unwilling to undertake any credit risk. Historically their lending capacity has been relatively low in relation to other countries' experiences. The next two sections will analyze how developing countries dealt with the macro and micro credit constraints in the bank- and capital-based financial structures.

3 BANK-BASED FINANCIAL STRUCTURE: CREDIT ISSUANCE AND THE CENTRAL BANK FUNCTION IN DEVELOPING COUNTRIES

The bank-based system was the dominant financial structure before the demise of the Bretton Woods international monetary order, with the exception of Great Britain and the United States, and was aimed at overcoming credit constraints.

In developing countries, the main characteristics of the bank-based financial arrangement were high state intervention, industrial policies that determined "priority" sectors and institutions such as the central bank, development (public) banks and development trusts, which channeled financial resources into production and assumed most economic growth credit risks. This institutional arrangement took place within an environment of limited international capital mobility, thus interest rate movements were limited. Its characteristics were as follows.

First, banks were considered to be the core institutions in the financial structure and finance for economic growth became one of the most important government policies (money is not neutral). Second, the objective of government intervention in the financial and productive sectors aimed to reduce the credit risks of new productive sectors. Specifically, in the Latin American bank-based system, central banks were extremely active in overcoming credit restraints, through selective credit policies directed at strategic productive and social sectors, central bank financial development trusts and public (or development) banks, which channeled finance to specific sectors. Third, central banks determined interest rates and banks' operation norms, within a context of weak capital markets since external capital mobility was hindered: speculation was limited and the risk of interest rate changes was low.

In Mexico, the central bank's most important tools for carrying out monetary and selective credit policies were: the legal reserve requirement; trust funds; direct controls on strategic financial variables; and rediscount facilities. Development (public) banks also played an important role in financing economic development.

The legal reserve requirement was based on a complex set of regulations to determine commercial bank credit volume and, more importantly, allocated credits in the strategic productive sector. Sánchez Lugo (1976) argues that the legal reserve requirement policy was used in an unorthodox manner in the Mexican bank-based system, since its main purpose was to provide financial resources to productive sectors, rather than limit the volume of bank credit.

It operated through two distinct mechanisms. First, private financial intermediaries had to deposit in the central bank a proportion of their liability demand deposits (although they were free of risk, and were paid interest), which were used to finance public spending, especially productive investment spending, and also financed public deficit,[4] operating as a means of wiping out debts. Second, financial intermediaries channeled financial resources into "priority" sectors indicated by the government's industrial policy. Government priority sectors had a lower reserve requirement than activities considered unimportant. Additionally, these regulations shaped the time structure of bank deposits and the geographical location of commercial banks, according to regional development objectives (Baqueiro and Ghigliazza, 1983).

Furthermore, the legal reserve requirement was used to fine tune interventions in order to neutralize domestic and external shocks by means of a marginal reserve requirement that temporarily affected the shape of bank liabilities, and was able to establish sterilization practices or penalize rapidly growing liabilities in foreign currencies.

The legal reserve requirement regulation policy was the core instrument in selective credit policies since it determined the share of specific types of credit, leaving little room for commercial bank decisions (in 1975, banks could allocate only 25 percent of the total credit issued, see ibid.).

The other important central bank instruments were the establishment of direct controls on the leverage degree of financial intermediaries, as well as on the rate of growth of their liabilities, and the rates of interest they should pay for different types of deposits. Lending interest rates were not controlled, although the central bank set upper limits in a few types of loans to the lowest-income groups and imposed a cap on deposit interest rates.

Central banks also set up development trust funds that played a decisive role in providing finance to "strategic" projects as well as technical assistance such as appropriate technology, trading and guidance to credit users (Fernández-Hurtado 1976). These funds operated as second-level banking institutions and offered guarantees and rediscount facilities to other intermediaries. Their main funding sources were government contributions, international credits and placement of their own securities, which were mainly held by the Banco de México (Mexico's central bank).

The rediscount facilities served two main purposes. First, selective credit policy was supported through channeling financial resources to priority sectors, via the public development trusts. Second, it was used as a device to assist banks in fulfilling legal reserve obligations, when their deposits grew slowly or they faced unexpected withdrawals.

Finally, public banks were delegated to assist particular sectors and were directly financed by their own securities issues, deposits from the

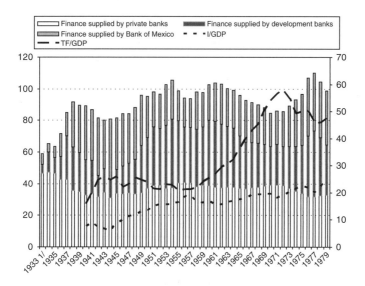

Note: TF: total finance; GDP: Gross Domestic Product; I: investment.

Sources: Own calculations based on indicatores Económicos and Economia Mexicana en Cifras, 1986.

Figure 5.1   Investment coefficient, total finance in terms of GDP and main financial sources, 1933–1979

public and, most importantly, government contributions and foreign loans (Orci, 1983); these institutions were not subject to legal reserves requirements (untill 1974). An important weakness of public banks was the structural imbalance between the liability demand deposits and the credit issuance, in contrast to commercial bank credit which, in the 1970s, operated against the legal reserve requirement policy, advising people to buy external reserves rather than make deposits in domestic currency (see Quijano, 1981: 159–70).

The bank-based system was particularly successful in promoting economic growth and increasing the investment coefficient, which rose from 7.6 percent in 1940 to 22.2 percent in 1979, one of the highest coefficients of the Mexican economy. Bank credits in terms of GDP trebled between the 1940s and the final years of the 1970s, reaching 60 percent of GDP (Figure 5.1). The main providers of these credits were public financial institutions – development banks and public trusts (Figure 5.1) – while private banks supplied less than 40 percent of total finance. The Mexican central bank's main asset was the tenancy of bonds from the non-financial public sector, reflecting the financial links between the central bank and public trusts (Table 5.1).

Table 5.1   Central bank asset balance sheet structure (% of total assets)

Central bank asset composition	1980	1990	2000	2005	2008
International reserves	11.6	35.16	52.06	71.13	74.4
Investment assets (securities)	71.66	47.31	NA	NA	9.2
Public Trust*	70.97	NA	NA	NA	NA
Non-financial public sector**	NA	46.45	NA	NA	NA
IPAB bond holding	NA	NA	NA	NA	9.2
Credits	9.18	8.69	31.95	13.64	4.4
Credit institutions	4.95	NA	NA	NA	3.6
Financial intermediaries	NA	7.4	NA	NA	NA
Official Trust (inc. IPAB)	NA	NA	16.59	NA	0.8
Debtors for securities repos	NA	NA	NA	6.38	7.1
Other	7.56	8.83	15.48	8.51	4.80

Notes:
NA: Not available or the data are insignificant.
*   Institutions that received central bank finance for productive investment.
**   Financial resources provided by the central bank to pay previous credit commitments.

Source: Based on Bank of Mexico data.

4   THE CAPITAL-BASED SYSTEM: THE TRANSITION TO CREDIT RESTRAINTS IN DEVELOPING ECONOMIES

This system became dominant after the 1970s, with non-bank financial entities as the core institutions of the capital-based system. The main assumption of this financial structure is that financial intermediation is the most efficient way to finance economic growth, since private or public financial instruments are the chief means of accruing savings that can be turned into liquid assets (see Zysman, 1983; Allen, 1990). Institutional investors, such as insurance companies, pension funds and investment banks, played a key function in enhancing the supply and demand of the secondary and primary markets (they broadened and deepened the financial market) since financial instruments could easily be converted into cash with no fall in price. Conversely, financial inflation was considered positive since it made financial intermediation more attractive (Toporowski, 2000; this point will be discussed further below). It was thought that financial deepness was a key factor in development (Demirgüc-Kunt and Levine, 2001).

Another important feature of this financial system has been the privatization of economic activity; consequently government public spending was restrained, and public investment in particular was limited. Government intervention was confined to guaranteeing free market conditions and promoting private economic activity, since it was believed that public spending has a crowding-out effect on private spending, inducing inflation, and reinforcing the idea of money neutrality.

This financial structure modified the workings of central banks. Its main objective shifted from economic growth to keeping inflation under control. Therefore, central banks concentrated on imposing a monetary rate of interest that would match the natural interest rate, following the Taylor rule, which untill the 2008 crisis was pro-cyclical. Financial disequilibria (especially the current account deficit) were confronted with high interest rates to reduce economic activity; there were steep interest rates hikes, which induced credit constraints and, more importantly, credit defaults.

In order to guarantee that central banks would concentrate on inflation stabilization policies, they were converted into autonomous entities that operated independently from government authorities. Central bank policies related to financing public economic activity or channeling financial resources into specific economic sectors and/or agents ceased. In this context, credit risk was shifted to private borrowers, which would be partially neutralized by government guarantees or even backed by international institutions (Winpenny, 2005). Furthermore, interest rates became unstable due to increased movement of external capital, and borrowers were faced with interest rate risks or macro uncertainty.

The banks' structure and their financial operations also changed, resulting in a diversification of their assets. Governments financed their spending through bonds, which increased bank bondholding, while large enterprises became corporations, increasing their finance department, and causing banks to lose the most secure borrowers (government and large enterprises). Another result, following international trends, was the dismantling of financial segmentation. Derivate operations also took place as a result of the huge exchange rate devaluations of the 1980s and the interest rate movements.

The combination of deposit and investment banks modified the assessment of borrowers' creditworthiness (solvent borrowers). Credit issuance was accompanied by new bank funding sources, whereby credits turned into securities, packed in special investment vehicles that carried investment grade ratings, determined by a statistical rating company, which were sold to other financial institutions. Kregel (2008: 3) referred to this bank behavior as "originate and distribute" in which banks seek to maximize their fees and commissions from originating assets (credits), managing these assets in off-balance sheet affiliate structures, underwriting the primary distributions of securities collateralized with those assets and serving them. Under this system, he adds, banks have reduced their efforts to evaluate micro uncertainties since credits do not remain on their balance sheet until they are paid, leading to securitization activities.

The typical bank–borrower relationship dominant in the Bretton Woods financial era, where bank officials and committees valued enterprises' risks in producing profits, was substituted by rating agencies that determined credit issuance in terms of probability models, giving collateral asset prices a central role.

Although these new procedures temporarily stabilized commodities prices, rates of interest and exchange rates, they encouraged speculative activities and induced financial gains (and losses), increasing financial instability. Speculation took place in the financial market, unrelated to financing production and, more importantly, had negative effects on investment spending, since productive returns were below short-term financial gains. The functioning of this financial structure increased financial inflation which meant a higher money influx into the financial system in relation to money reflux (see Toporowski, 2000), thus redistributing returns in favor of asset wealth holders and against producers.

5   MEXICO'S TRANSITION TO THE CAPITAL-BASED SYSTEM

Mexico initiated the dismantling process of the bank-based financial structure in the 1970s. In particular, the legal reserve requirement policy was simplified in 1976 to promote universal banks, which became highly concentrated, increasing their political power *vis-à-vis* the domestic government (Tello, 1983). After the 1982 economic crisis, the public primary account balance turned into surplus, public development trusts disappeared, and development banks were converted into second-level institutions, reducing the number of banks and credit issuance (see Levy and Girón, 2005). Treasury bonds were first issued in 1978 and became negotiable in 1981, raising the money market activity; furthermore, the legal reserve requirements along with selective credit policies and rediscount facilities, with other compensatory mechanisms, disappeared in 1988. Central banks were banned from directly financing government activity. The capital market was globalized in the 1990s, increasing stock market activity. Through the North American Free Trade Agreement (NAFTA), foreign direct investment could operate in almost all economic sectors, and the Mexican financial structure was modified to resemble the American financial system, imposing non-bank banks, and increasing the number of insurance companies, investment banks and other institutional investors, such as pension funds, whose main task was to deepen the financial market, and thereby increase financial intermediation.

Weakening bank operations (credit issuances) and limiting the central bank's function to control inflation had various effects on the Mexican financial system. First, the risks of credit and interest rates were switched to private borrowers, turning domestic entrepreneurs (micro, small and medium-sized enterprises) into non-solvent borrowers, with no government program to reverse this situation (for example, government credit guarantees).

Second, the central bank asset balance sheet was drastically modified. Central bank bondholdings of non-financial public trusts disappeared, reducing the importance of this entry (bondholding), and almost all credits issued by the central bank were channeled into private banks and financial intermediaries, with international reserves becoming the most important entry of central banks' assets (see Table 5.1). The monetary authorities assumed that higher international reserves would stabilize the exchange rate and thereby control inflation. By 2000, international reserves represented half of total central bank assets, increasing to 71 and 74 percent by 2005 and 2008, respectively.

Third, interest rates became more volatile and, more importantly, commercial banks' financial margin increased once the banking system was deregulated (Figure 5.2), increasing macro uncertainties. Specifically, the financial margin between Treasury bills and bank deposit rates remained relatively stable from the late 1970s to the 1994 financial crisis, increasing afterwards to levels above 200 and 300 percent. This means that Treasury bills became an important income source after credit issuance was stopped (central bank monetary policy after the 1994 crisis aimed to restore banks' profits). Furthermore, banks' lending[5] and deposit margins soared, increasing above 50 percent in the 1980s, and doubling and trebling in the following decades (Figure 5.2). Extremely high interest rates and commission were imposed to limit the number of creditworthy borrowers, with government Treasury bonds being an important funding source. Hence, the banking system decided not to lend to micro, small and medium-sized enterprises, turning these agents into non-creditworthy borrowers.

The interest rates of credit cards (simple average interest rates) oscillated around 35 and 40 percent between 2003 and 2009 (not including commission), while the Treasury bond rate fluctuated between 7 and 8 percent. In the same period, the average housing total credit cost was much lower, around 14 to 17 percent. This is explained by the presence of development (public) banks that backed mortgage loans (Sociedad

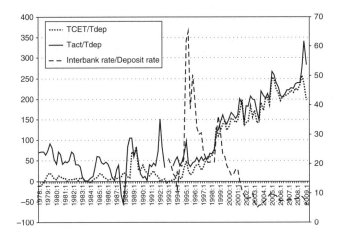

Notes:
TCET: Treasury bills; Tdep: deposit rate of interest in net terms;
Tact: active interest rate. 1978–92: the lending rate source is IMF sources; 1993–2009: short-term interest rate of private bonds. Since 1992, active interest rate was central bank lending rate.

Source: Own calculation based on Bank of Mexico data.

Figure 5.2   Financial margins

Hipotecaria Federal: SHF);[6] and, more importantly due to the reforms to the Mexican housing trust (INFONAVIT).

The banking system underwent a process of dis-intermediation, quite drastic from 1987 onwards, mainly as a result of the reduction in bank credits, increasing during 1991–94, when the last credit boom took place. During these years, credits represented around 40 percent of total bank assets, later falling due to credit default, which soared in the post-1994 crisis (1995–99) (Figure 5.3). The reason for the higher share of unpaid debts and credit reduction is quite simple: interest rates rose to levels near 100 percent and effective demand fell. The interesting point is that during the first decade of the twenty-first century, the relation of credit to bank assets and in terms of GDP remained low.

The ratio of banks' credit to GDP remained relatively constant between 1982 and 1988, following an upward tendency (1989–94), in which banks were free to fulfill borrowers' demand,[7] reaching 41.5 percent of GDP in 1994 (in 1989 it had barely achieved 14.5 percent); then following a downward tendency, recuperating slightly in 2005 (Figure 5.3). It is important to highlight that the post-1994 economic growth period (2000 and 2007) did not herald higher credits, since banks became highly reluctant to issue

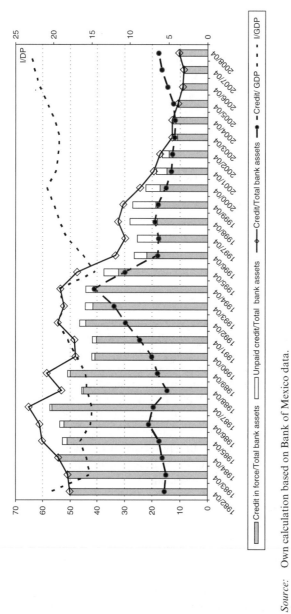

Source: Own calculation based on Bank of Mexico data.

Figure 5.3   Credit in terms of GDP, total bank assets, and investment coefficient

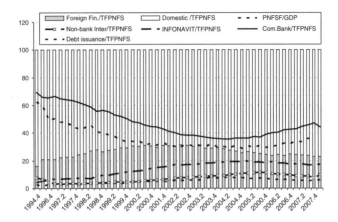

Notes: TFPNFS: total finance to private non-financial sector; Non-bank Inter: non-bank intermediaries; Com.Bank: commercial banks; Foreign finan: foreign finance.

Source: Own calculation based on Bank of Mexico data.

Figure 5.4   Main financial intermediaries

credit and there were fewer solvent borrowers since the production model moved to a *maquila* structure and wages remained relatively low. Bank credits were low since capital goods were imported by multinationals and finance by external capital flows.

Another important element is that the private financial non-bank institutions were unable to increase alternative sources of finance that would neutralize the fall in bank credits; the government-supported financial intermediary INFONAVIT was one of the more dynamic providers of finance. The ratio of total finance to the private non-financial sector in terms of GDP halved between 1994 to 2008, with bank credits being the component that reduced most, falling 30 percent in relation to the domestic finance of the private non-financial sector (Figure 5.4). Most astonishingly, financial non-bank intermediaries (including non-bank institutions, concentrating in one or multiple activities – Sofoles and Sofomes, factoring and leasing institutions and savings and lending societies) did not exceed 11 percent of all private non-financial sectors. Regarding stock and debt issuance, although its participation in all private non-financial sectors nearly doubled, it represented only 7 percent of GDP. INFONAVIT finance soared throughout the period. In 1994, INFONAVIT finance represented around 4.2 percent, averaging around 20 percent in 2000, shrinking slightly afterwards. Note that external finance did not increase the total finance of the private non-financial sectors. In 1994, it represented around 16 percent, increasing to 30 percent in 2000, and decreasing to around 20 percent in 2008.

Thus, it can be concluded that a social trust (backed by government) along with a development bank (SHF), neutralized banks' commercial credit shrinkage, with INFONAVIT becoming the most dynamic source of finance. Hence, the financial restructured system continued to depend on a social trust, backed by the Mexican government and a development bank.

6 CONCLUSIONS

Financing economic growth (and development) is subject to micro and macro uncertainties, and credit constraints can halt economic activity. There is no technical difficulty in producing credit advances, since money is a social relation that does not require real resources to be produced. The main deterrent to issuing finance is the availability of solvent borrowers, which depends on many factors: banks' assessment of future returns (a borrower's capacity to produce profits) and central bank interest determination which has the capacity to ease (or make more difficult) borrowers' eligibility and payment conditions. It should be stressed that lower interest rates do not induce mechanically lower lending rates or more eligible creditworthy borrowers, or ease credit payment conditions. Solvent borrower demand is necessary.

The problem becomes more difficult in developing countries, which require higher volumes of debt to "catch up" developed countries, which increases credit and interest risks, since expected returns are not known. Therefore several circuit periods are required to cancel out debts and there is no certainty of producing sufficient returns to cover previous debt commitment. Even institutions such as the World Bank acknowledge this situation, arguing for government guarantees for highly risky projects to avoid government direct interference in the economy (in public investment or imposing public financial institutions).

Historical records show that countries undergoing industrialization processes did not have a financial system dominated by market rules, guided by perfect market paradigms, which favor financial gains. Nearly all successful industrialization processes require government intervention, public financial institutions or government spending (and public deficit) to overcome credit risks and secure sufficient financial resources to overcome credit restraints. Looking at the Mexican experience, it can be shown that the periods of highest economic growth of the Mexican economy took place during the bank-based system, were domestic and, more importantly, public institutions (development banks and trusts) played an important role in providing finance for economic development. Government economic intervention through industrialization policies (setting up "priority" sectors), selective credit policies and direct public investment are the most important features of the industrialization process.

The capital-based system modified the financial structure. The more important feature is that credit and interest rate risks were passed on to private borrowers, increasing micro and macro uncertainties, with no serious government guarantees to neutralize these risks. In this context, central bank objectives changed, concentrating on the control of inflation,[8] leaving aside the commitment of stable economic growth. This was reflected in the increased share of international reserves in central bank assets, over 70 percent from 2000 onwards. Commercial banks also modified their balance sheet components, reducing the ratio of credit issuance in terms of total bank assets and, in terms of GDP, without other financial (non-bank) entities being able to neutralize the bank credit shrinkage due to a squeeze on creditworthy borrowers. The most significant characteristic of the capital-based system is that a social trust, backed by public institutions, was able to increase housing financing and induce economic growth. Therefore, the capital-based system failed to overcome credit constraints and, more importantly, central banks concentrating on the control of inflation have not been able to induce economic growth.

NOTES

*　 This chapter is part of the research project "The Impact of 'Financialization' on Developing Countries", sponsored by the Research Council of UNAM (PAPIIT).
1.　 Keynes argues the money is a special commodity because it has a production elasticity equal to zero, a substitution elasticity near to zero and its transference cost (present to the future or past to the present) is also near zero. Therefore, increasing money production would not induce higher employment and no other commodity can perform the function of money; for a discussion, see Levy (2001: ch. 1).
2.　 Kalecki put forward the idea that capitalists ought to have capital before becoming capitalists. He writes: "The access of firms to stock markets, that is, the amount of rentist capital that can be acquired is determined by the amount of the capital enterprises has . . . [thereby the] most important requisite to turn into an entrepreneur is to be a proprietor of capital" (Kalecki, 1971: 105).
3.　 Latin American economies faced a distorted industrialization process since the more dynamic productive sectors (related to external markets) were controlled by foreign multinationals, which transferred second-hand technology from their centers, with small spillover effects on domestic economies. Prebisch (1949 [1998]) frequently referred to the lack of creative industrialization. Additionally, these multinationals were supported by government industrialization policies (Amsden, 2001 [2004])
4.　 From 1958 onwards, Banco de México has been banned from creating money through increasing the number of notes in circulation.
5.　 It should be highlighted that the active bank interest rate does not reflect the income banks accrue from lending, since commission and other income are not considered. Moreover, bank lending rate data are only available between 1970 and 1992 (IMF CD ROM). Since then the IMF has published the central bank lending interest rates.
6.　 The SHP was conceived as a public and provisional institution (until a robust mortgage

financial market had been established) and should have been replaced in 2009 by a private market former. The SHF confers two types of insurance: (a) it guarantees payment default that covers up to 35 percent of each mortgage credit; and (b) it offers partial guarantees insurance for issuance that covers certain requirements. Furthermore, the SHF increases Sofoles bond liquidity (Borhis) through secondary market participation and induces market formers.

7. In 1989, bank deregulation was completed and banks could issue credit to borrowers they considered solvent, so long as they complied with the BIS-I reserve preventive ratio (8 percent of capital in relation to total bank assets).
8. Note that central banks continued to fight inflation by stabilizing the exchange rate risks through overvaluing their exchange rate. This strategy has been dominant since Latin American countries initiated their industrialization process.

REFERENCES

Allen, C.S. (1990), "Democratic Politics and Private Investment: Financial regulation in the Federal Republic of Germany and the United States", Research Report No. 2, November, American Institute for Contemporary German Studies, Johns Hopkins University, Baltimore, MD.

Amsden, A. (2001 [2004]), *The Rise of "The Rest." Challenges to the West from Late-Industrializing Economies*", Oxford: Oxford University Press (paperback).

Baqueiro, A. and S. Ghigliazza (1983), "Política Monetaria en México: El Marco Institucional", in H.E. González (ed.), *El Sistema Económico Mexicano. Un análisis sobre su situación*, México: Premia Editora, pp. 83–131.

Blanchard, O. (2000 [2003]), *Macroeconomia*, 2nd edn, Upper Saddle River, NJ: Prentice Hall.

Blinder, A. (1998), *Central Banking in Theory and Practice*, Cambridge, MA: MIT Press.

Demirgüç-Kunt, A. and R. Levine (2001), *Financial Structure and Economic Growth*, Cambridge, MA: MIT Press.

Fajnzylber, F. (1990), "Industrialización en América Latina: de la caja negra al casillero vacío", reprinted in *Cincuenta años de Pensamiento en la CEPAL*, Vol. II, CEPAL-FCE, pp. 817–52.

Fernández Hurtado, E. (1976), "Reflexiones sobre aspectos fundamentales de la Banca Central en México", in *Cincuenta años de la Banca Central*, México: Ed. Trimestre Económico, FCE, pp. 15–26.

Gnos, C. and L.-P. Rochon (2007), "The new consensus and Post-Keynesian interest rate policy", *Review of Political Economy*, **19** (3), July, 369–86.

Graziani, A. (2003), "Neoclassical monetary theory", in Graziani, *The Monetary Theory Production*, Cambridge: Cambridge University Press, pp. 33–58.

Kalecki, M. (1971), "Entrepreneurial capital and investment", ch. 9. in *Selected Essays on the Dynamics of the Capitalist Economy 1933–1970*, Cambridge: Cambridge University Press.

Keynes, J.M. (1937), "Alternative theories of the rate of interest", reprinted in *Collected Writings of John Maynard Keynes*, Vol. XIV, ed. D. Moggridge, London: Macmillan, 1973, pp. 201–14.

Kregel, J. (2008), "Minsky's cushions of safety systemic risk and the crisis in the U.S. subprime mortgage market", Public Policy Brief No. 93, Levy Economics Institute of Bard College, Annandale-on-Hudson, NY (www.levy.org).

Lavoie, M. (1992), "Money creation and credit multipliers", *Review of Political Economy*, **4** (4), 447–66.
Lavoie, M. (2004), "The new consensus on monetary policy seen from a Post-Keynesian perspective", in Lavoie and M. Seccareccia (eds), *Central Banking in the Modern World: Alternative Perspectives*, Cheltenham, UK and Northampton, MA, USA: Edward Elgar, pp. 15–34.
Levy, N. (2001), *Cambios institucionales del sector financiero y su efecto sobre el fondeo de la inversión México, 1960–1994*, Mexico: Impresores Fernández, ch. 1, pp. 27–43.
Levy, N. and A. Girón (2005), *México: los bancos que perdimos. De la desregulación a la extranjerización del sistema financiero*, Mexico: Grupo Edición, Instituto de Investigaciones Económicas y Facultad de Economía.
Lewis, M.K. (1992), "Modern banking in theory and practice", *Revue Économique*, **43** (2), 203–28.
Moore, B. (1988), *Horizontalists and Verticalists: The Macroeconomics of Credit Money*, Cambridge: Cambridge University Press.
Orci, L.M. (1983), 'Política crediticia en México: generación y uso de recursos", in H.E. González (ed.), *El Sistema Económico Mexicano: Un Análisis sobre su Situación*, Mexico: Premia Editora.
Parguez, A. and M. Seccareccia (2000), "The credit theory of money: the monetary circuit approach", in J. Smithin (ed.), *What Is Money?*, New York: Routledge, pp. 101–23.
Prebisch, R. (1949 [1998]), "El Desarrollo económico de la América Latina y algunos de sus principales problemas", reprinted in *Cincuenta años de pensamiento en la CEPAL*, Vol. I, CEPAL-FCE, pp. 65–129.
Quijano, J.M. (1981), *México: Estado y Banca Privada*, México: CIDE.
Rochon, L.P. (2006), "Endogenous money, central banks, and the banking system: Basil Moore and the supply of credit", in M. Setterfield (ed.), *Complexity, Endogenous Money and Macroeconomic Theory*, Cheltenham, UK and Northampton, MA, USA: Edward Elgar, pp. 170–201.
Sánchez Lugo, L. (1976), "Instrumentos de política monetaria y crediticia", in E. Fernández-Hurtado (ed.), *Cincuenta Años de Banca Central: Ensayos Commemorativos 1925–1975*, México: Fondo de Cultura Económica, pp. 369–87.
Taylor, J. (1993), "Discretion vs policy rules in practice", *Carnegie-Rochester Conference Series on Public Policy*, **39**, December, 195–214.
Tello, C. (1983), *Nacionalización de la banca en México*, México: Siglo XXI.
Toporowski, J. (2000), *The End of Finance, Capital Market Inflation, Financial Derivatives and Pension Fund Capitalism*, Frontiers of Political Economy, London: Routledge.
Toporowski, J. (2005), "Critical theories of finance in the twentieth century: unstable money and finance", in Toporowski (ed.), *Theories of Financial Disturbance: An Examination of Critical Theories of Finance from Adam Smith to the Present Day*, Cheltenham, UK and Northampton, MA, USA: Edward Elgar, pp. 45–74.
Winpenny, J. (2005), "Guaranteeing development? The impact of financial guarantees", Working Paper 107, Development Centre, OECD, Paris.
Zysman, J. (1983), *Governments, Markets and Growth: Finance and the Politics of Industrial Change*, Ithaca, NY: Cornell University Press.

PART II

Central bank policy in times of crisis

6. Financial crisis, state of confidence, and economic policies in a Post Keynesian stock-flow consistent model

Edwin Le Heron*

1 INTRODUCTION

While in 2007 it was only a financial crisis and, particularly, a banking crisis, now economic growth and employment are deteriorating sharply. The aim of this chapter is to understand how the financial crisis was transformed into a global real economic crisis and how it passed through banking behavior. We are particularly interested in psychological variables such as the state of confidence, because these variables play a key role in the Post Keynesian tradition through expectations. We develop a model of a "financialized" economy suffering a strong fall in the state of confidence of banks, firms and households. In order to do so, we analyzed two policy mixes. We contrast a rule on public expenditures with a rule on public deficits, and a usual Taylor rule with a truncated Taylor rule. In the first case, the government implements a fiscal policy with automatic stabilizers and the central bank has a dual mandate: inflation and growth. There is a coordination between fiscal and monetary policies. The second policy mix implements an orthodox fiscal policy (balanced budget) and the independent central bank implements inflation targeting.

In Section 2, we present the most important equations of a Post Keynesian stock-flow consistent (SFC) model (Dos Santos and Zezza, 2004; Godley and Lavoie, 2007; Le Heron and Mouakil, 2008; Le Heron, 2009) with a private bank sector introducing more realistic features. We introduce the borrower's and the lender's risks from the Minskian approach. In Section 3, we simulate a model to study the effects of a financial crisis on the banking behavior within our two-policy mix. The aim is to deal with the consequences of a fall in the state of confidence of banks, firms and households. We make a comparison for the two assumptions on the policy mix and we analyze the channel of transmission on the economic activity. Section 4 concludes.

2 A POST KEYNESIAN STOCK-FLOW CONSISTENT GROWTH MODEL OF A "FINANCIALIZED" ECONOMY

We resumé only the most specific features of our model[1] with five sectors: government, firms, households, private banks and the central bank. SFC modeling is based on two tables (Appendix 6A2). For the transactions matrix (flows), see Appendix Table 6A2.1 and for the balance sheet matrix (stocks), see Appendix Table 6A2.2. The complete model (Appendix 6A3) contains 61 equations.

All production must be financed. However, current production is financed by the working capital of entrepreneurs (retained earnings) and by contracted revolving funds granted by banks at the current rate of interest. These two factors constitute a shock absorber to possible monetary rationing by banks. We are essentially limiting our study to the effects that a fall in the state of confidence of banks, firms and households might have on new financing for investment and growth of production. Let us proceed to examine the gross supply (φ) and the net supply (ΔF) of finance by banks – that is to say, the new flow of money, as opposed to the existing stock of money (Δ). Also, there is a stock of money demand equal to transaction, precaution, finance and speculative motives, whereas the desired gross finance demand (φ^d) represents the new flow of financing required by firms (I_D) plus the redemption of the debt (amortization = amort) minus the undistributed profits (P^u). Thus the internal funds of firms (IF) represent the undistributed profits (P^u) minus the redemption of the debt (amort). Assuming a closed economy, demand for money can be satisfied by banks, either by the stock markets or by credit. At the end of the period, net financing demand (ΔF_D) can be constrained by net money supply from banks (ΔF). ΔF determines monetary creation in the period.

The national income (Y) adds the household consumption (C), investment of the firms (I) and the public expenditure (G). The rate of growth of the national income is gr_y.

Two Fiscal Policies for the Government

Government expenditures are only final sales of consumption goods. The government collects only taxes from households on wages. The government finances any deficit issuing bills, so that the supply of Treasury bills (B) in the economy is identical to the stock of government debt. In other words, it is given by the pre-existing stock of debt plus its current deficit (GD). The current deficit of the government includes the redemption of the national debt. We assume that private banks give limitless credit to government at the long-term rate of interest (i_l). To analyze the consequences of the crisis, we make two different assumptions for the fiscal policy. We contrast a rule on public expenditures (F1) with a rule on public deficits (F2).

Assumption 1 (F1): a rule on public expenditures
First, we assume that public expenditure (G) is always growing at the growth rate (gr_{y-1}) of the national income with a lag of one year. The final effect of the fiscal policy is measured by the government deficit (GD). Tax revenue is proportional to income and hence varies in line with the public expenditure. The financial cost of the national debt varies with interest rate. The global impact is linked to the key interest rate and, then, to the monetary policy, thus there is a coordination between the monetary and the fiscal policies. With F1, the economy has a weak self-stabilizing tendency due to the fiscal policy, though the fiscal policy effect comes through the effects of the interest rate on the budget deficit:

$$G = G_{-1} \cdot (1 + gr_{y-1}) \qquad (6.1\text{-F1})$$

$$GD \equiv G + (i_{b-1} \cdot B_{-1}) - T - P_{cb}. \qquad (6.2\text{-F1})$$

Assumption 2 (F2): a rule on public deficits
Second, we assume that a "neutral" fiscal policy corresponds to a constant ratio (r_{GD}) of government deficit to the last national income: GD/Y_{-1}. This is more or less the case of the Maastricht Treaty of the European Union. Then we use the first accounting identity to calculate the adequate public expenditure. We shall take the ratio (r_{GD}) equal to zero as is required by the Maastricht treaty. Contrary to the previous assumption, the public debt is zero, since the budget is always balanced. As the interest rate does not act on fiscal policy, there is no coordination between the fiscal and monetary policies:

$$GD = r_{GD} \cdot Y_{-1}, \quad \text{with } r_{GD}: \text{constant} \qquad (6.1\text{-F2})$$

$$G \equiv GD - (i_{b-1} \cdot B_{-1}) + T + P_{cb}. \qquad (6.2\text{-F2})$$

Firms

The investment function is the most important one in a growth model. The stock of capital (K) increases with the flow of net investment (I) that is financed by the total of external funds from commercial banks (gross finance = φ) and by the internal funds of firms. The self-financing of firms corresponds to the retained earnings (P^u) minus the redemption of the debts of firms (amort). Firms issue equities (E), bonds with fixed rates of interest (OF) and commercial papers (CP), and borrow money from banks (variable rate) (L) to finance investments. Amortization concerns only the debt: loans, bonds and commercial papers:

$$I \equiv \varphi + IF \tag{6.3}$$

$$IF = p^u - \text{amort} \tag{6.4}$$

$$\text{amort} = (a_1 \cdot L_{-1}) + (a_{of} \cdot of_{-1}) + (a_{cp} \cdot CP_{-1}). \tag{6.5}$$

In our model, we focus on the difference between actual investment (I) and the desired investment of firms (I_D). The banks agree to finance totally or in part the second one according their lender's risk (LR) (see equations (6.14), (6.15), (6.17)). A rationing in investment financing can exist ($\varphi < \varphi^d$ or $I < I_D$). The desired rate of accumulation (gr_{kD}) is a function of an exogenous state of confidence (γ_0), the capacity utilization rate (u) and of the borrower's risk (BR), which is measured by the rate of cash flow (r_{cf}) and by the financial condition index (FCI). The rate of cash flow is the ratio of retained earnings to capital and the financial condition index captures the sensitivity of investment to the level of endebtedness, to the long-term interest rate, to the short-term interest rate and to the financial capitalization ratio. The lender's risk and the borrower's risk come from Minsky's (1975) analysis:

$$I_D = gr_{kD} \cdot K_{-1} \tag{6.6}$$

$$\varphi^d = I_D - IF \tag{6.7}$$

$$gr_{kD} = \gamma_0 + (\gamma_1 \cdot r_{cf-1}) + (\gamma_2 \cdot u_{-1}) - (\gamma_3 \cdot FCI_{-1}), \quad \text{with } \gamma_i: \text{constant} \tag{6.8}$$

where the rate of capacity utilization is defined as the ratio of output to full capacity output (Y_{fc}):

$$r_{cf} = P^u/K_{-1} \tag{6.9}$$

$$u = Y/Y_{fc}. \tag{6.10}$$

The capital to full capacity ratio (σ) is defined as a constant:

$$Y_{fc} = K_{-1} \cdot \sigma, \text{ with } \sigma: \text{constant} \tag{6.11}$$

$$FCI = (\mu_1 \cdot i_1 \cdot L/K) + (\mu_2 \cdot i_{cb} \cdot CP/K) - (\mu_3 \cdot E/Y), \quad \text{with } \mu_i: \text{constant.} \tag{6.12}$$

We measure the output gap in ratio, with Y_{fc} the output of full capacity and not of the capacity that corresponds to the potential output. Distributed dividends (P^d) are a fraction (25 percent) of profits realized in the previous period. This part can be higher in a "financialized" economy:

$$P^d = (1 - s_f) \cdot P_{-1}, \text{ with } s_f: \text{constant.} \tag{6.13}$$

Households

We assume that households determine their consumption expenditure on the basis of their expected disposable income and their wealth of the previous period which consists entirely of bank deposits. Following the Kaleckian tradition, wages are mostly consumed while financial income is largely devoted to saving. The consumption decision depends on the state of confidence of households and determines the amount that they will save out of their disposable income. The financial behavior of households is simplified: they hold only a banking deposit account.

Private Banks

Banks do not make loans to households, but firms' financing is fundamental in a monetary economy of production. Firms begin by being self-financed then turn to external finance (ΔF_D). Banks only finance projects they consider profitable, but confidence in their judgment is variable and can justify various strategies. Banks examine firms' productive and financial expectations and also their financial structure. This investigation is made according to their confidence in the state of long-term expectations of yields on capital assets, influencing what Keynes (1936 [1973]) referred to as "animal spirits". The state of confidence of banks is notably taking into account by an exogenous variable (γ_4). After the study of expected production and of demand of financing that integrates the firm's borrowing risk, bankers can refuse to finance. The state of confidence of banks summarizes these factors.

Banks know a lender's risk (LR) when underwriting finance and creating money. Lender's risk is the sum of three fundamental risks: risk of default, risk of liquidity and market risk. Market risk can be split into other risks. Fluctuations in capital asset prices modify their value and explain capital risk – which is very high for equities and fixed-yield bonds. For the fixed-yield bonds, capital risk is inversely proportional to interest rates. The risk of income mainly concerns the highly uncertain dividends of equities and the variable yield of loans. Finaly, monetary policy involves a money market risk when fluctuations in the money interest rates occur.

In equations (6.14), (6.17), (6.20) and (6.21), the risks of default and of liquidity are accounted for by the gap between the leverage ratio and a conventional leverage ratio. We also introduce the value of the securities lodged as collateral and the cost of indebtedness for the risk of default. The market risk is taken into account by the expected capital gains on equities (CG_e^a) and on fixed-yield bonds (CG_{of}^a), but also by the central bank interest rate.

When the lender's risk is at a maximum ($LR = 1$), commercial banks refuse to finance the net investment of firms: $\Delta F = 0$. Desired investment (I_D) faces a serious finance rationing. The flow of net investment is only financed by self-funding, that is the retained earnings (P^u), minus the amortization of the debt, minus the capital losses of firms (CG). Thus the money supply (in stock) can be reduced with the redemption of the debt. If the lender's risk is null ($LR = 0$), desired investment is fully financed: $\Delta F = \Delta F_D$ or $\varphi = \varphi^d$. This is the horizontalist case. The capital losses of firms are also the capital gains of banks, measured by the capital losses on equities (CG_e) and on fixed rate bonds (CG_{of}):

$$\varphi = \varphi^d \cdot (1 - LR), \quad \text{with } 0 \leq LR \leq 1 \tag{6.14}$$

$$\Delta F = \varphi - \text{amort} + CG \tag{6.15}$$

$$CG = CG_e + CG_{of}. \tag{6.16}$$

In the model, the lender's risk (LR) is measured by the difference between the current leverage ratio and the conventional leverage ratio (quantity of indebtedness), by the variation in the value of the securities lodged as collateral (V_C) and by the cost of indebtedness (i_{cb}). The higher current indebtedness of firms (($CP + OF + L)/K$) is over the accepted indebtedness, the more the lender's risk is. The accepted indebtedness is conventional, but this conventional indebtedness can increase during a boom and decrease during a crisis. The variation in the value of the securities lodged as collateral (V_C) is measured by the value of equities (E) on the value of equities of the last period. The financial value is the value of the equities on the market:

$$LR = -\gamma_4 + a_1 \cdot (lev_{-1} - lev_c) - (b_1 \cdot V_C) + (c_1 \cdot i_{cb}),$$

with γ_4, a_1, b_1, c_1 and lev_c: constant   (6.17)

$$lev = (CP + OF + L)/K \tag{6.18}$$

$$V_C = E/E_{-1}. \tag{6.19}$$

We follow the methodology developed by Godley and Lavoie (2007) and inspired by Tobin (1958, 1969) and Kalecki (1937) to define the portfolio behavior of banks. Banks can hold four different assets: bonds (with fixed rate of interest) $OF = of \cdot p_{of}$, equities $E = e \cdot p_e$, loans at variable long-term interest rate (L) and commercial paper (CP) at short-term interest rate.

Monetary authorities determine endogenously the key rate on the money market (i_{cb}) following a Taylor rule. While central banks fix the short-term rates, private banks' liquidity preference determines banking rates (short-, medium- and long-term interest rates). Significant rates for growth and financing (loan) are the long-term interest rates (i_l). The link between short- and long-term interest rates is complex. Macroeconomic banking interest rates (i_l) are the production costs of money plus a risk premium. The first element corresponds to functioning costs (wages, investment, immobilization); payment costs for monetary liabilities (subject to the firm's competition for households savings) and the cost of high-powered money determined by the central bank; and to a rate of margin (χ) corresponding to standard profits of banks. The production costs of money are equal to (i_{cb}) plus a relatively constant mark-up (χ).

Risk premiums are not constant because they are the fruits of the banks' liquidity preference. Risk premiums cover lender's risk (lr). Five expectations strongly influence risk premiums: anticipations about the productivity, economic evolution and budget; expected inflation; the level of future short-term rates of interest; financial markets' evolution and capital assets' prices; and foreign long-term rates. In the model, we use the same lender's risk as the one seen previously (equation (6.17)), that is a mix of state of confidence, leverage ratio and variation in the value of the securities lodged as collateral. But with the different coefficients (γ_5), (a_2) and (b_2), (lr) can be negative and reduces the mark-up. Therefore the long-term interest rate becomes endogenous and the spread between (i_{cb}) and (i_l) is not constant. Contrary to the horizontalist view, we introduce an endogenous curve of the interest rates. To explain the short-term interest rates (i_b or i_{cp}), i_{cb} and χ are sufficient. On the contrary, (lr) is the primary variable in order to explain long-term interest rates (i_1, i_{of}). Banks apply a spread (χ_3) between the key rate and the rate on deposits in order to realize profits:

$$i_1 = i_{cb} + lr + \chi_1, \quad \text{with } \chi_1: \text{constant } \chi_1 > \chi_2 \qquad (6.20)$$

$$lr = -\gamma_5 + a_2 \cdot (lev_{-1} - lev_c) - (b_2 \cdot V_C), \qquad (6.21)$$

with $\gamma_5, a_2, b_2, lev_c$ constant and c = convention on the "normal" debt ratio

$$i_{cp} = i_{cb} + \chi_2, \quad \text{with } \chi_2: \text{constant } \chi_1 > \chi_2 \qquad (6.22)$$

$$i_d = i_{cb} - \chi_3. \qquad (6.23)$$

The initial structure of interest rates is as follows: $i_1 > i_{of} > i_{cp} > i_b = i_{cb} > i_d$.

Economic activity also depends on the animal spirits of banks. Finance scarcity can only be the consequence of a deliberate choice. "Desired scarcity" of financing is the sign of banks' liquidity preference. From an optimal structure of their balance sheet, we can measure the profits of commercial banks (P_b) obtained by monetary financing:

$$P_b \equiv i_{b-1} \cdot B_{-1} + i_{l-1} \cdot L_{-1} + i_{cp-1} \cdot CP_{-1} + i_{of} \cdot of_{-1}$$

$$+ P^d - i_{d-1} \cdot D_{-1} - i_{cb-1} \cdot REF_{-1}. \qquad (6.24)$$

Central Banking

The central bank has neither operating costs nor net worth and pays all its profits to the government. Following the theory of endogenous money, we assume that the central bank is fully accommodating. We use a Taylor rule for the modeling of its behavior. First, the central bank fixes the key rate of interest (i_{cb}) using a Taylor rule and second, it provides whatever advances (*REF*) are demanded by banks at this rate. Taylor propounded his first rule in 1993, modeling the dual mandate of the Fed (Taylor, 1993). It was founded on the output gap and on the inflation gap. But today, independent central banks prefer inflation targeting. A truncated rule (without the output gap) appeared as a theoretical answer (Batini and Haldane, 1999). From the Taylor rule, we can summarize monetary policy according to three dimensions: strategy, flexibility and intensity. Strategy represents the mandate and therefore the long-term policy. Flexibility measures the deviation in the short term of the policy from the strategy. Intensity is the weight put, respectively, on output gap and inflation gap. With the "Taylor principle", coefficients must be superior to one to avoid that inflation expectations produce inflation.

The first hypothesis (M1) is that the central bank uses a standard Taylor rule, modeling the dual mandate of the Fed. The key interest rate (i_{cb}) is a negative function of the output gap and a positive function of the inflation gap. The output gap is the difference between the full capacity output (Y_{fc}) and the current output (Y). Full capacity output is a Post Keynesian approach. We refused the New Keynesian potential output that is founded on a NAIRU (non-accelerating inflation rate of unemployment). The inflation gap is the difference between current inflation and the target of inflation (Π^*). As in the standard Taylor rule, we add a neutral interest rate, exogenously fixed at 2 percent as Keynes did in the *General Theory*. The inflation target is 1 percent. At the steady state, the key interest rate is equal to 3 percent, so the real key interest rate is equal to the neutral interest rate $(i_{cb} - \Pi^* = i^* = 2\%)$. The monetary rule M1 is:

$$i_{cb} = i^* + \Pi + \alpha_4 \cdot OG_R + \alpha_6(\Pi - \Pi^*). \qquad \text{(6.25-M1)}$$

The second hypothesis (M2) is a truncated Taylor rule similar to inflation targeting, which contains only the inflation gap. With inflation targeting, the fear of inflation is higher. We should have: $\alpha_5 > \alpha_6$. We put $\alpha_6 = 0.5$ and $\alpha_5 > 1$. The monetary rule (M2) is:

$$i_{cb} = i^* + \alpha_5(\Pi - \Pi^*). \qquad \text{(6.25-M2)}$$

A special kind of Phillips curve models inflation. When inflation is low and close to its target, we consider that the anticipations of inflation are anchored on the target. In this case, inflation does not react to the variations of the output gap (OG_R). Inflation depends only on the anticipated inflation (Π^a) that is anchored on the target: $\Pi^a = \Pi^*$. This leads to a horizontal curve. But if the variations in output are too important (for instance, close to full capacity output), inflation reacts. Inflation reappears over OG_{Rmini} and disinflation or deflation under OG_{Rmaxi}. The idea that for small disturbances the inflation rate is stable while for large disturbances it is unstable was coined by Leijonhufvud (1973[1981]) in the notion of a "corridor". The economy has stability inside the corridor, while it will lose stability outside. Such a "corridor of stability" can provide another way of looking at Keynes's insight that the economy is not violently unstable.

To write the equation of inflation, we use the output gap and the inflation gap:

$$\Pi = \Pi^* + d_1 \cdot (OG_{Rmini} + OG_R) + d_2 \cdot (OG_{Rmaxi} + OG_R). \quad (6.26)$$

3 AN EXPERIMENT ABOUT THE FINANCIAL CRISIS AND CONFIDENCE WITH TWO POLICY MIXES

We make simulations[2] by imposing exogenous shocks arising from the financial crisis over four years (5, 6, 7 and 8). Shocks are stronger in 6 and 7 than in 5 and 8. Numerous features in our standard model correspond to a financialized economy: an important financial market, four different financial assets, the lender's risk, the borrower's risk, a time structure of interest rate, and so on. We assume that financial crisis involves essentially a drop in the state of confidence of the economic agents and, in our model, especially that of banks. The aim is to deal with the channels of transmission of these psychological variables on the real sector. We want to show that psychological reactions (lower confidence) are sufficient to explain the spread of financial crisis to the real sector. We also try to understand the effects of the policy mix on it. Model and shocks are the same for both economies, even if the steady states are a little bit different because the policy mix is different. We develop four processes for the crisis.

A Drop in the State of Confidence of Commercial Banks: B

First, the state of confidence of banks decreases sharply and then the lender's risk increases. We change exogenously (γ_4) and (γ_5) in equations (6.17) and (6.21) of lender's risk. Furthermore, the level of the conventional leverage ratio (quantity of firms' indebtedness considered as normal (lev_c)) falls strongly in these equations. Finally, the variation in the value of the securities lodged as collateral (V_C) is certainly negative at the beginning of the financial crisis. But this change is endogenous. Accordingly lender's risk and rationing of finance increase.

A Drop in the State of Confidence of Firms: F

Second, the state of confidence of firms (γ_0) falls with the development of the financial crisis. We change exogenously (γ_0) in equation (6.8) of the desired rate of accumulation. Pessimistic expectations of firms depress effective demand. We could also increase the weight of the financial condition index in this equation (γ_3) to take into account the higher borrower's risk.

A Drop in the State of Confidence of Households: H

Third, the state of confidence of households is going down and their propensity to consume is falling, involving a negative demand shock.

Generalized Crisis in the State of Confidence (Banks, Firms, Households): B + F + H

Fourth, we put the three processes together for a generalized fall of the state of confidence. In the experiments, the respective importance of the crisis in the different economic sectors is not relevant. To respect the stylized facts of the last crisis, we assume that the drop in the state of confidence of banks is higher than those of other sectors (firms and then households). Polls on expectations and confidence of various kinds of agents can be used. The liquidity preference increases for all the economic agents.

The consequences of the financial crisis are examined for two kinds of policy mix:

- For country (1), monetary policy is determined by a standard Taylor rule (M1) that corresponds to a dual mandate: output gap and inflation gap. The fiscal policy rule (F1) has a stabilizing effect. But this effect is insufficient to restore the economy to the previous steady state. There is a coordination between the monetary and the fiscal policies.
- For country (2), monetary policy is determined by a "truncated" Taylor rule (M2) that corresponds to a unique mandate of the independent central bank: inflation gap only. Fiscal policy (F2) is neutralized, because we assume the fiscal rule that the ratio of the current deficit of the government on the GDP is constant and equal to zero, as imposed by the Maastricht Treaty for the European Union.

The drop in the state of confidence of banks and firms involves a supply shock. In contrast the drop in the state of confidence of household involves a shock of demand. As risk is deflation, the equations of complete or truncated Taylor react similarly. In fact the output gap as the anticipation of lower prices requires lower interest rates.

In our economy, the steady state is not the full-employment equilibrium. The output gap is positive, with a significant rate of unemployment. Potential output corresponds to the full capacity output. To simplify, we

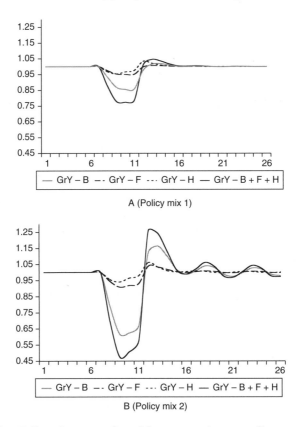

Figure 6.1   Fall in the state of confidence over 4 years: effects on the growth rate of the economy

introduced inflation only in our special Phillips curve and we do not take into account the difference between real and monetary variables in the rest of the model. Inflation could be integrated into the determinants of lender's risk and borrower's risk and into the portfolio matrix, in order to better integrate the wealth effects. Monetary policy tries to neutralize expectations of inflation.

In the short term, the growth rate in the national income decreases strongly. Depressed effective demand that is the cause of higher unemployment can be explained by the loss of confidence of firms but also of banks. In our approach, private banks are no longer neutral. Following the approaches of Minsky and Keynes, financial features and confidence explain the crisis. Figures 6.1A and B show that country (1) resists much better than country (2) a fall in the state of confidence.[3]

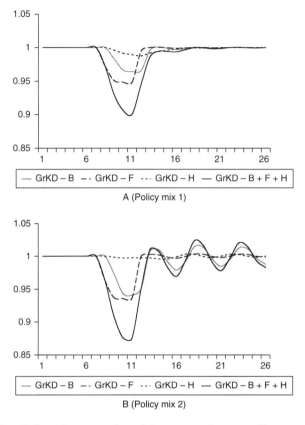

A (Policy mix 1)

B (Policy mix 2)

*Figure 6.2   Fall in the state of confidence over 4 years: effects on the
desired growth rate of accumulation of capital of firms*

The fall in the growth rate is much lower. In addition, the emergence of economic cycles is obvious in country (2). With the removal of the fiscal tool, the economic situation deteriorates sharply and becomes more strongly cyclical.

The drop in state of confidence of firms is the first explanation to the depressed effective demand, that is, the desired growth rate of accumulation of capital (Figures 6.2A and B). But, particularly with the policy mix (2), banks also have an important responsibility, because financing conditions deteriorate. The rate of utilization of productive capacity falls more in the second country than in the first. The financial behavior of firms largely explains these developments. With the depressed financial condition index and the lower cash flow ratio, the borrower's risk increases seriously.

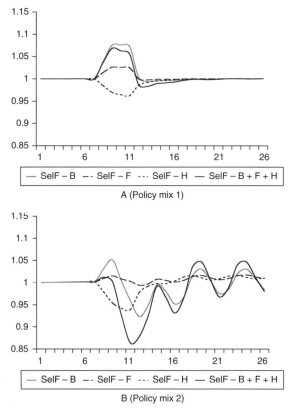

Figure 6.3   Fall in the state of confidence over 4 years: effects on the ratio of self-financing of firms

The effects on the self-financing of firms are very interesting (Figures 6.3A and B). With the higher borrower's and lender's risks, firms and banks reduce external financing: self-financing of firms increases. This corresponds to a supply shock and a credit crunch. On the contrary, the lost confidence of households involves a shock of demand and self-financing of firms decreases. With the policy mix (1), the higher government deficit allows an increase of the cash flow of firms. Their self-financing increases. Government indebtedness substitutes one of firms. With the policy mix (2), the weight of bank and household behaviors is stronger and durably lowers self-financing of firms. We understand why the reading of the ratio of self-financing is difficult and why it does not show the good state of economy.

One key element of the experiments is the increase of the lender's risk

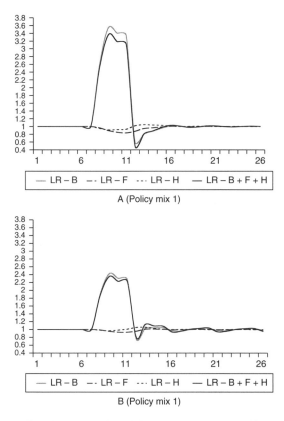

Figure 6.4   Fall in the state of confidence over 4 years: effects on the lender's risk of commercial banks

(Figures 6.4A and B). The fall of collateral value, the supposed lowest solvency of firms and the new strict convention of firm endebtedness explain the rise of the lender's risk.

The consequence is a financing rationing of the investment of firms by private banks: $\varphi < \varphi^d$ (Figures 6.5A and B). We can understand the credit crunch. The financing rationing of firms explains in part an increasing rate of unemployment. There is a sharp volatility in the financial markets (stocks and bonds) and a significant fall in the profit of banks. During the crisis, private banks try reaching a new equilibrium in their asset allocation. The structure of their balance sheet changes clearly. These elements could explain the transfer of the financial crisies to the real world.

We see the beginning of the deflation (Figures 6.6A and B). With the

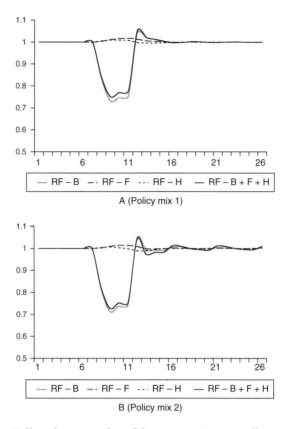

Figure 6.5   Fall in the state of confidence over 4 years: effects on the rationing of finance from banks

deep crisis, monetary policy tries to avoid deflation, then the two kinds of Taylor rule work similarly: the key interest rate goes down quickly to stop the fall in prices. The influence of the output gap on the key interest rate is the same but is lower than that of inflation, even with the standard Taylor rule. With the disinflation, the truncated Taylor rule reacts more. If the fear is inflation, the opposite occurs because the output gap pushes the other way.

Contrary to IS–LM, to New Keynesians or to usual PK–SFC models, the curve of interest rates is not exogenous. The spread between the short- and long-term interest rates is not constant. Figures (6.7A and B) show the same evolution as the stylized facts of the last crisis: a quick rise of this spread (almost 3 percent), which corresponds to higher lender's risk, when the central bank decreases the key rate.

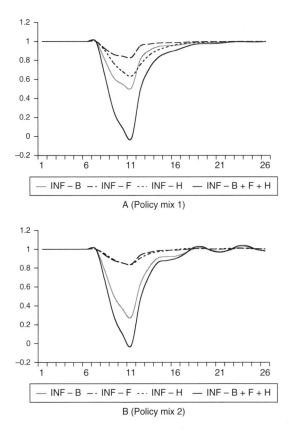

*Figure 6.6   Fall in the state of confidence over 4 years: effects on the rate
of inflation*

A fall of the state of confidence in the private sector involves
the government "becoming" optimistic and supports the effective
demand with an increasing fiscal deficit. This is the case of country
(1) (Figure 6.8). But, by hypothesis, there is a balanced budget in
country (2).

4   CONCLUSION

In this chapter, to better understand the last financial crisis and its
generalization to the real world, we have tried to take into account
the behavior of private banks, the financial risks of firms and banks,
and the psychological variables (state of confidence). In order to do

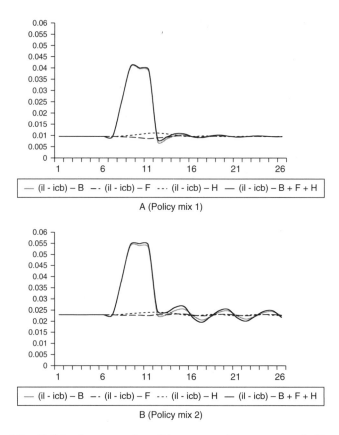

Figure 6.7   Fall in the state of confidence over 4 years: spread effects (long-term interest rate (i_l) – short-term interest rate (i_{cb}))

so, Keynes and Minsky provide an adequate framework. We have analyzed more deeply the problems of coordination between fiscal and monetary policy. We can argue that it is better to include a stabilizing fiscal policy. Indeed, simulations showed a high volatility in production with policy mix (2) and financial instability may also be an unforeseen consequence. This stock-flow consistent model is a first step into this research agenda.

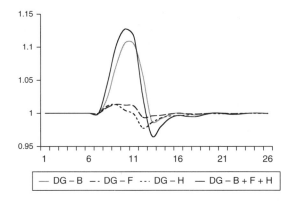

Figure 6.8   Fall in the state of confidence over 4 years: effects on the fiscal deficit with policy mix 1

NOTES

*   Our grateful thanks to J. Creel, W. Godley, M. Lavoie, J. Mazier, T. Mouakil, D. Plihon, M. Sawyer, E. Tymoigne and G. Zezza for their helpful comments on previous drafts.
1.   For more detail, see Le Heron and Mouakil (2008) and Le Heron (2009) for the Post Keynesian model, and Le Heron (2008) for the Keynesian stock-flow consistent model. See Appendix 6A1 for the glossary of variables.
2.   We use the E-views 5.5 software. In Le Heron (2011), in order to simulate the shocks in the state of confidence, we use the different monthly indicators elaborated by the French National Institute of Statistics and Economic Studies (INSEE). The indexes are calculated from monthly polls on a representative population.
3.   In all the figures (except Figures 6.6 and 6.7), all values on the vertical axis are homogenized to one for the steady state. The drops in the state of confidence are, respectively: B for Banks, F for Firms, H for Households and B+F+H for all the private sectors.

REFERENCES

Batini, N. and A. Haldane (1999), 'Forward-looking rules for monetary policy", in J. Taylor (ed.), *Monetary Policy Rules*, Chicago, IL: University of Chicago Press, pp. 157–92.

Dos Santos, C. and G. Zezza (2004), "A Post-Keynesian Stock-Flow Consistent Macroeconomic Growth Model: preliminary results", Working Paper 402, The Levy Economics Institute, Board College, Annandale-on-Hudson, New York, February.

Godley, W. and M. Lavoie (2007), *Monetary Economics: An Integrated Approach to Credit, Money, Income, Production and Wealth*, London: Palgrave Macmillan.

Kalecki, M. (1937), "The principle of increasing risk", *Economica*, **4** (13), 440–47.

Keynes, J.M. (1936 [1973]), *The General Theory*, The Collected Writings of J.M. Keynes, vol. VII, London: Macmillan.

Le Heron, E. (2008), "Fiscal and monetary policies in a Keynesian stock-flow consistent model", ch. 8 in J. Creel and M. Sawyer (eds) *Current Thinking on Fiscal Policy*, London: Palgrave Macmillan, pp. 145–75.

Le Heron, E. (2009), "Monetary and fiscal policies in a Post Keynesian stock-flow consistent model", ch. 18 in R. Wray and M. Forstater (eds), *Keynes and Macroeconomics after 70 years: Critical Assessments of the General Theory*, Cheltenham, UK and Northampton, MA, USA: Edward Elgar, pp. 468–506.

Le Heron, E. and T. Mouakil (2008), "A Post Keynesian stock-flow consistent model for the dynamic analysis of monetary policy shock on banking behavior", *Metroeconomica*, **59** (3), 405–40.

Leijonhufvud, A. (1973 [1981]), "Effective demand failures", *Swedish Journal of Economics*, **75** (1), 27–48. Reprinted in Leijonhufvud (1981), *Information and Coordination. Essays in Macroeconomic Theory*, New York: Oxford University Press.

Minsky, H. (1975), *John Maynard Keynes*, New York: Columbia University Press

Taylor J. (1993), "Discretion versus policy rules in practice", *Carnegie-Rochester Conference Series on Public Policy*, **39**, 195–214.

Tobin, J. (1958), "Liquidity preference as behavior toward risk", *Review of Economic Studies*, **67**, 65–86.

Tobin, J. (1969), "A general equilibrium approach to monetary theory", *Journal of Money, Credit, and Banking*, **1**, 15–29.

APPENDIX 6A1   GLOSSARY OF VARIABLES

Y — National income
Y_{fc} — Output of full capacity
gr_y — Growth rate in the national income
Π — Inflation
Π^* — Inflation target
N — Employment
N_{fe} — Full employment
OG — Output gap
OG_R — Ratio of output gap
Un — Unemployment
r_{un} — Rate of unemployment
L — Loans (variable long-term rate)
CP — Commercial paper
B — Treasury bills
E — Equities
e — Number of equities
P_e — Price of equities
OF — Bonds (fixed rate)
of — Number of bonds
P_{of} — Price of fixed rate bonds
LF — Loss function of the society

Central Bank

P_{cb} — Central bank profits
REF — Reserve requirements (CB refunds)
H — High-powered money
i_{cb} — Central bank key interest rate
i^* — Neutral interest rate

Commercial Banks

P_b — Bank's profits
V_b — Net wealth of banks
CG — Capital gains of banks (capital losses of firms)
CG_e — Capital gains on equities
CG_e^a — Expected capital gains on equities
CG_{of} — Capital gains on bonds
CG_{of}^a — Expected capital gains on bonds
i_{cp} — Interest rate on commercial paper
i_d — Interest rate on deposits
i_l — Interest rate on loans
i_b — Interest rate on Treasury bills
FCI — Financial Condition Index
LR — Lender's risk

APPENDIX 6A1   (continued)

lr — Lender's risk for long-term interest rate
γ_4, γ_5 — State of confidence of banks
r^a_{of} — Expected yield of bonds
r^a_e — Expected return on equities
p_d — Expected distributed profits
lev — Leverage ratio
V_C — Variation of the value of collateral

P — Firm's profits
p_d — Distributed profits
p_u — Undistributed profits
r_{cf} — Borrower's risk (ratio of cash flow)
γ_0 — State of confidence of firms

Firms

I — Net investment
I_D — Investment demand
W — Wages
K — Stock of capital
V_f — Net wealth of firms
u — Capacity utilization rate
gr_k — Growth rate in the stock of capital
gr_{kD} — Desired growth rate in the stock of capital
ΔF — Net finance
φ — Gross finance
φ^d — Desired gross investment
IF — Internal Funds
$amort$ — Amortization (debt redemption)

Government

G — Government expenditure
GD — Government deficit
i_{GD} — Constant ratio of government deficit
P_{cb} — Central bank profits
T — Taxes

Households

C — Consumption
D — Bank deposits
Y^a_w — Expected disposable income of workers
Y^a_v — Expected disposable financial income
Y_w — Disposable income of workers
Y_v — Disposable financial income
Y_h — Disposable income of household

APPENDIX 6A2   MATRIX TABLES

Table 6A2.1   Transactions matrix

Operation \ Sector	Govt	Firms Current	Firms Capital	House-holds	Private banks Current	Private banks Capital	Central Bank (CB) Current	Central Bank (CB) Capital	Σ
Consumption		$+C$		$-C$					0
Government expenditures	$-G$	$+G$							0
Net investment		$+I$	$-I$						0
Wages		$-W$		$+W$					0
Taxes	$+T$			$-T$					0
Interest on Treasury bills	$-i_{b-1} \cdot B_{-1}$				$+i_{b-1} \cdot B_{-1}$				0
Interest on loans		$-i_{l-1} \cdot L_{-1}$			$+i_{l-1} \cdot L_{-1}$				0
Interest on comm. paper		$-i_{cp-1} \cdot CP_{-1}$			$+i_{cp-1} \cdot CP_{-1}$				0
Interest on bonds		$-i_{of} \cdot of_{-1}$			$+i_{of} \cdot of_{-1}$				0
Interest on bank deposits				$+i_{d-1} \cdot D_{-1}$	$-i_{d-1} \cdot D_{-1}$				0
Interest on CB advances					$-i_{cb-1} \cdot REF_{-1}$		$+i_{cb-1} \cdot REF_{-1}$		0
Profits of firms		$-P$	$+P^u$	$+P^d$					0
Profits of banks					$-P_b$	$+P_b$			0
Profits of CB	$+P_{cb}$						$-P_{cb}$		0

Table 6A2.1 (continued)

Sector / Operation	Govt	Firms Current	Firms Capital	House-holds	Private banks Current	Private banks Capital	Central Bank (CB) Current	Central Bank (CB) Capital	Σ
Δ HPM						$-\Delta H$		$+\Delta H$	0
Δ T bills	$+\Delta B$					$-\Delta B$			0
Δ equities			$+\Delta e \cdot p_e$			$-\Delta e \cdot p_e$			0
Δ loans			$+\Delta L$			$-\Delta L$			0
Δ commercial paper			$+\Delta CP$			$-\Delta CP$			0
Δ bonds			$+\Delta of \cdot p_{of}$			$-\Delta of \cdot p_{of}$			0
Δ bank deposits				$-\Delta D$		$+\Delta D$			0
Δ CB advances						$+\Delta REF$		$-\Delta REF$	0
Σ	0	0	0	0	0	0	0	0	0

Table 6A2.2 Balance sheet matrix

Sector / Assets	Government	Firms	Households	Private banks	Central bank	Σ
Capital		$+K$				$+K$
HPM high-powered money				$+H$	$-H$	0
Treasury bills	$-B$			$+B$		0
Equities		$-e \cdot p_e$		$+e \cdot p_e$		0
Loans		$-L$		$+L$		0
Commercial paper		$-CP$		$+CP$		0
Bonds (fixed yield)		$-of \cdot p_{of}$		$+of \cdot p_{of}$		0
Bank deposits			$+D$	$-D$		0
CB advances				$-REF$	$+REF$	0
Net wealth	$-B$	$+V_f$	$+D$	$+V_b$	0	$+K$

APPENDIX 6A3   THE COMPLETE MODEL, 2 VERSIONS WITHIN 4 HYPOTHESES

Policy mix (1) = F1–M1

Policy mix (2) = F2–M2

(1)	$Y = C + I + G$	National income
(2)	$gr_y = \Delta Y / Y_{-1}$	Growth rate of national income
(3)	$T = \tau \cdot W_{-1}$	Taxes
(4)	$B = B_{-1} + GD$	Treasury bills
(5)	$i_b = i_l$	Interest rate on Treasury bills

With τ: constant

F 1: Model 1 with a countercyclical fiscal policy

(F1-6)	$G = G_{-1} \cdot (1 + gr_{y-1})$	Government expenditure
(F1-7-i)	$GD = G + i_{b-1} \cdot B_{-1} - T - P_{cb}$	Government deficit

F 2: Model 2 with a neutral fiscal policy: GD/Y_{-1} constant

(F2-6-i)	$G = GD - i_{b-1} \cdot B_{-1} + T + P_{cb}$	Government expenditure
(F2-7)	$GD = \gamma_{GD} \cdot Y$	Government deficit

With r_{GD}: constant ratio

(8)	$K = K_{-1} + I$	Stock of capital
(9-iii)	$I \equiv \varphi + IF$	Net investment
(10)	$IF = P^u - \text{amort}$	Internal funds
(11)	$\text{amort} = a_1 \cdot L_{-1} + a_{of} \cdot of_{-1} + a_{CP} \cdot CP_{-1}$	Amortization
(12)	$I_D = gr_{kD} \cdot K_{-1}$	Investment demand
(13)	$\varphi^d = I_D - IF$	Desired gross investment
(14)	$gr_{kD} = \gamma_0 + \gamma_1 \cdot r_{cf-1} + \gamma_2 \cdot u_{-1} - \gamma_3 \cdot FCI_{-1}$	Desired growth in stock of capital
(15)	$r_{cf} = P^u/K_{-1}$	Ratio of cash flow
(16)	$u = Y/Y_{fc}$	Capacity utilization rate

With γ_i: constant

(17)	$Y_{fc} = K_{-1} \cdot \sigma$	With σ : constant	Output of full capacity
(18)	$FCI = \mu_1 \cdot i_1 \cdot L/K + \mu_2 \cdot i_{cb} \cdot CP/K - \mu_3 \cdot E/Y$	With μ_i : constant	Financial Condition Index
(19)	$OG_R = Y_{fc} - Y / Y_{fc}$		Output gap ratio
(20)	$W = Y / (1 + \rho)$	With ρ : constant	Wages
(21-ii)	$P \equiv Y - W - i_{l-1} \cdot L_{-1} - i_{CP-1} \cdot CP_{-1} - i_{of} \cdot of_{-1}$		Firm's profits
(22)	$P^d = (1 - s_f) \cdot P_{-1}$	With s_f : constant	Distributed profits
(23-ix)	$Pu = P - Pd$		Undistributed profits
(24)	$e = e_{-1} \cdot (1 + gr_{y-1})$	With gr_e : constant	Number of equities
(25)	$C = \alpha_1 \cdot Y_w^a + \alpha_2 \cdot Y_v^a + \alpha_3 \cdot D_{-1}$	With α_i : constant	Consumption
(26)	$Y_w^a = Y_{w-1} + \theta_h \cdot (Y_{v-1} - Y_{v-1}^a)$	With θ_h : constant	Expected disposable income of workers
(27)	$Y_v^a = Y_{v-1} + \theta_h \cdot (Y_{v-1} - Y_{v-1}^a)$	With θ_h : constant	Expected disposable financial income
(28)	$Y_w = W - T$		Disposable income of workers
(29)	$Y_v = i_{d-1} \cdot D_{-1}$		Disposable financial income
(30)	$Y_h = Y_w + Y_v$		Disposable income of households
(31-iv)	$D \equiv D_{-1} + Y_h - C$		Bank deposits
(32)	$\varphi = \varphi^d \cdot (1 - LR)$		Gross finance
(33)	$\Delta F \stackrel{?}{=} \varphi - amort + CG$		Net finance
(34)	$CG = CG_e + CG_{of}$		Capital gains of banks
(35)	$LR = \gamma_4 + a_1 \cdot (lev_{-1} - lev_c) - b_1 \cdot V_C + c_1 \cdot i_{cb}$	With $\gamma_4, a_1, b_1, lev_c$ and c_1: constant	Lender's risk
(36)	$lev = (CP + OF + L) / K$		Leverage ratio
(37)	$V_C = E / E_{-1}$		Value of the collateral
(38)	$OF = (\lambda_{10} + \lambda_{11} \cdot r_{of}^a - \lambda_{12} \cdot r_e^a - \lambda_{13} \cdot i_1 - \lambda_{14} \cdot i_{CP}) \cdot F$		Bonds (fixed rate)
(39)	$E = (\lambda_{20} - \lambda_{21} \cdot r_{of}^a + \lambda_{22} \cdot r_e^a - \lambda_{23} \cdot i_1 - \lambda_{24} \cdot i_{CP}) \cdot F$		Equities
(40)	$L = (\lambda_{30} - \lambda_{31} \cdot r_{of}^a - \lambda_{32} \cdot r_e^a + \lambda_{33} \cdot i_1 - \lambda_{34} \cdot i_{CP}) \cdot F$		Loans (variable long-term rate)

APPENDIX 6A3   (continued)

Policy mix (1) = F1–M1 | Policy mix (2) = F2–M2

(41) $CP = F - OF - E - L$ Commercial paper

With i_{of}: constant

(42) $r^a_{of} = i_{of} + CG^a_{of}/OG_{-1}$ Expected yield of bonds
(43) $CG^a_{of} = CG_{of-1} + \theta_b \cdot (CG_{of-1} - CG^a_{of-1})$ Expected capital gains on bonds
(44) $CG_{of} = \Delta p_{of} \cdot of_{-1}$ Capital gains on bonds
(45) $of = OF/p_{of}$ Number of bonds
(46) $p_{of} = p_{of-1}(1 + i_{of})/(1 + i_l)$ Price of bonds

(47) $r^a_e = (P^{da} + CG^a_e)/E_{-1}$ Expected return on equities
(48) $P^{da} = P^d_{-1} + \theta_b \cdot (P^d_{-1} - p^{da}_{-1})$ Expected distributed profits
(49) $CG^a_e = CG_{e-1} + \theta_b \cdot (CG_{e-1} - CG^a_{e-1})$ Expected capital gains on equities
(50) $CG_e = \Delta p_e \cdot e_{-1}$ Capital gains on equities
(51) $p_e = E/e$ Price of equities

(52) $i_l = i_{cb} + lr + \chi_1$ Interest rate on loans
With χ_1: constant
(53) $lr = \gamma_5 + a_2 \cdot (lev_{-1} - lev_c) - b_2 \cdot V_C$ Lender's risk for long-term interest rate
With γ_5, a_2 and b_2, Lev_c constant
= convention on leverage ratio

(54)	$i_{CP} = i_{cb} + \chi_2$	Interest rate on commercial paper
(55)	$i_d = i_{cb} - \chi_3$	Interest rate on deposits
(56-v)	$P_b \equiv i_{b-1} \cdot B_{-1} + i_{l-1} \cdot L_{-1} + i_{CP-1} \cdot CP_{-1} + i_{of} \cdot of_{-1} + P^d - i_{d-1} \cdot D_{-1} - i_{cb-1} \cdot REF_{-1}$	Bank's profits
(57)	$H = \eta \cdot D$	High-powered money (bank reserves)
(58-vii)	$P_{cb} \equiv i_{cb-1} \cdot REF_{-1}$	Central bank profits

With χ_2: constant $\chi_1 > \chi_2$

M1: Policy mix 1 with a Taylor rule (inflation gap and output gap) RM1

(M1-59)	$i_{cb} = i^* + \Pi - \alpha_4 \cdot OG + \alpha_5 (\Pi - \Pi^*)$	Central bank key interest rate

M2: Policy mix 2 with a truncated Taylor rule (only inflation gap) RM2

(M2-59)	$i_{cb} = i^* + \alpha_5 (\Pi - \Pi^*)$	Central bank key interest rate
(60-vi)	$REF \equiv REF_{-1} + \Delta H + \Delta B + \Delta F - CG - P_b - \Delta D$	Reserve requirements (CB refunds)
(61)	$\Pi = \Pi^* + d_1 \cdot (OG_{Rmini} - OG_R) + d_2 \cdot (OG_{Rmaxi} - OG_R)$	Inflation (NKPC)

Missing equation: (62-viii) $REF = H$

7. Central bank responses to financial crises: lenders of last resort in interesting times

Robert Dimand and Robert Koehn

The present signs indicate that the bankers of the world are bent on suicide. At every stage they have been unwilling to adopt a sufficiently drastic remedy. And by now matters have been allowed to go so far that it has become extraordinarily difficult to find any way out. It is necessarily part of the business of a banker to maintain appearances and to confess a conventional respectability which is more than human. Lifelong practices of this kind make them the most romantic and the least realistic of men. (John Maynard Keynes, 1931b, p. 178)

"The central bankers have all learned the lesson of the 1930s," said Robert Barbera, the chief economist of ITG, a Wall Street firm. That lesson was that if the choice is between allowing the system to collapse and writing a lot of checks, you write the checks and forget about ideology. Unfortunately, none of them learned the lesson of the 1920s, which is that when asset prices soar, it is not a good idea to sit around doing nothing, as the Fed did for most of the housing boom. Cheerleading, which it sometimes did, is even worse. (Norris, 2008, p. B8)

1 INTRODUCTION: THE DIVERSITY OF CENTRAL BANK RESPONSES TO CRISIS

The daunting challenges facing central bankers in the financial crisis that began in August 2007 are reflected in the shocked tone of the minutes of the Federal Open Market Committee (FOMC) meeting of December 15 and 16, 2008 (Andrews, 2009). Normally, such minutes are staid and circumspect – and normally FOMC meetings require only one day. At the December 2008 meeting (the Federal Reserve Board of Governors plus presidents of Federal Reserve banks), some participants wished to abandon any explicit target for overnight interbank interest rates (the Federal Funds rate) while others feared such an admission that the Fed had lost control of financial markets. The target for the Federal Funds rate was lowered yet again, from 1 percent to a range from zero to 1 quarter of 1 percent; yet the Fed's own "Taylor rule" formula, weighting inflation and the output gap, would have indicated a target interest rate of –5 percent, were such a negative rate feasible.[1] Dismayed by their inability to go further with their accustomed methods, the FOMC members looked to supplement the reduction of the target overnight rate by buying mortgage-backed securities and perhaps long-term Treasury bonds and seeking ways to induce banks to borrow more from the Fed to lend to the public. The distress of the FOMC, although more transparently documented, was undoubtedly shared by central bankers throughout the world, yet the Federal Reserve System, the Bank of England, the European Central Bank (ECB), and the Bank of Canada have reacted very differently to the crisis and taken different views of their responsibility. These differing reactions reflect the differing structures and mandates of these central banks, but also the central banking traumas of the past: the German hyperinflation of the early 1920s, the collapse of the US banking system during the debt-deflation of the early 1930s, the aftermath of "the Norman conquest of $4.86", and, in Canada, the "Coyne affair" upheaval over central bank independence. Ben Bernanke, Mervyn King, Mark Carney, and Jean-Claude Trichet are painfully conscious of the misfortunes of Eugene Meyer, Montagu Norman, James Coyne, and Rudolf Havenstein. The Federal Reserve remembers the failure of 9,000 banks and the 1933 "bank holiday" that shut down the entire US banking system. The Bank of England remembers Winston Churchill reflecting that the return to the gold standard at the prewar parity was "the biggest blunder" in his life, into which he was "misled by the Governor of the Bank of England" (quoted by Ahamed 2009, p. 239). The Bank of Canada has not forgotten the days when Scott Gordon entitled a book *The Economists versus the Bank of Canada* (1961) and the Government of Canada introduced a bill in Parliament to declare the governorship vacant, only to have the bill rejected by the Senate. The ECB, like the Bundesbank, obsessively recalls the German price level rising to one trillion times its previous level while the Reichsbank president promised that, with 38 new high-speed printing presses, the central bank would print enough currency to catch up with the soaring prices. Each of these central banks has been shaped by a particular historical trauma, which is reflected in how each central bank has responded to the present crisis.

This consciousness is more than just a matter of oral tradition or a general cultural inheritance within central banks: Bernanke (1981, 1983, 1995, 2000) built his academic career on analysis of the debt-deflation of the early 1930s, which King (1994) also examined (with very different emphasis) in his European Economic Association presidential address (see Dimand and Koehn, 2008) – but it happens that neither of them gave comparable attention to the preceding US financial boom of the middle and late 1920s, fueled by expansionary monetary policy in a weak regulatory environment. In the case of the ECB, although its first two presidents (dividing a single term) have been Dutch and French, the relevant historical trauma is the Bundesbank view of Germany in the early 1920s, as held by Otmar Issing, the first chief economist of the ECB and previously chief economist of the Bundesbank. For Canada, lectures by the recently retired governor David Dodge (2008a, 2008b) provide insight into the prevailing viewpoint at the top of the Bank of Canada.

Even when central bankers or other persons draw lessons from history or otherwise gain insight into the role of greed, self-delusion, limited knowledge, and fundamental uncertainty in financial markets, it is still difficult to avoid pitfalls. The University of Colorado at Boulder psychology professor Stephen Greenspan analyzed in *The Annals of Gullibility* (2008) how people fall for Ponzi schemes, yet lost more than half his retirement savings to Bernard Madoff's Ponzi scheme (Shermer, 2009). Robert Rubin, reflecting on his experience at Goldman Sachs and as Treasury Secretary, warned that "Entranced by the model, a trader could easily forget that assumptions are involved and treat it as definitive" (with specific reference to the Black–Scholes assumption that "future volatility in stock prices will resemble past volatility"), and remarked on "a seeming tendency in human nature not to give appropriate weight to what might occur in remote, but potentially very damaging conditions" (Rubin and Weisberg, 2003, pp. 81, 99) – the "black swans" of Taleb (2007). Unfortunately, while he was expressing these insights, Rubin was chairman of the executive committee of Citigroup, which subsequently wrote off $88.3 billion of toxic assets, having relied on quantitative models that assumed that past observations predicted future risk and that ignored the low-frequency, high-impact possibility of a systemic financial crisis.

2   THE PERFECT STORM: THE SITUATION FACING THE CENTRAL BANKS

Several striking features of the current financial crisis are unprecedented only if "unprecedented" is redefined (as indeed often seems to be the case in the financial sector) to mean "it hasn't happened since last time, and that was *several* years ago, and anyway the CFO has personally assumed that nothing so inconvenient will happen so that we can scoop up the higher expected return without there really being any risk". As Eduardo Porter (2008) points out, the Ponzi schemes of Bernard Madoff and Allan Stanford are in a long tradition of such scams (including of course the eponymous Charles Ponzi). During the present crisis, the difficulty of valuing mortgage-based securities made them illiquid once confidence was shaken. Large markets, seemingly with deep reserves of liquidity, suddenly dried up entirely for $330 billion of auction-rate notes in the US (see Morgenson, 2008) and C$33 billion of asset-based commercial paper (ABCP) in Canada, in both cases securities that were sold to investors (Quebec's Caisse de Depots, investing for the Quebec Pension Plan, held more than C$12 billion of ABCP when the market froze) as being as safe and liquid as Treasury bills but offering a higher interest rate (which apparently did not cause purchasers to question the supposed safety and liquidity). But such mishaps have occurred before. Many remembered that in 1994 Kidder Peabody, then the investment banking arm of General Electric, had revealed that a rogue trader, Joe Jett, had created $350 million of fictitious profits to earn himself a bonus of $9 million. But that contretemps provided cover for a more serious problem: Kidder Peabody owned $16 billion of illiquid mortgage-backed bonds.[2]

> The mortgage-bond market was in paralysis, and Kidder, as the biggest owner of inventory on Wall Street, found it couldn't even get a fix on the value of its holdings because there were no buyers . . . Even though the number was lower than it had been, Kidder was dangerously leveraged: every $1 of its equity was supporting $93 of assets, compared with average leverage for the industry of $1 to $27. (O'Boyle, 1998, pp. 353, 348)

With such leverage, even a slightly bad year brings disaster.

Nonetheless, 10 years after Kidder Peabody's débâcle, the investment bankers succeeded in 2004 in lobbying the Securities and Exchange Commission to eliminate the leverage limits on the five biggest US investment banks (Merrill Lynch, Morgan Stanley, Goldman Sachs, Lehman Brothers, and Bear Stearns), so that they could invest aggressively in mortgage-backed collateralized debt obligations (CDOs) and other sophisticated financial instruments (Labaton, 2008).[3] Of the five, only Goldman Sachs chose to keep its leverage ratio below $1 of capital to $30 of equity, and so it is the only remaining free-standing institution among the five (with the partial exception of Morgan Stanley, now an affiliate of Mitsubishi UFJ but not a subsidiary). The current Union Bank of Switzerland (UBS) was created a few years ago when UBS lost a billion dollars on derivatives and was taken over by the Swiss Bank Corporation, as Switzerland's Big Three became Big Two. Apparently learning nothing from that experience, or from the experience of Kidder Peabody, which, incorporated into Paine Webber, is now part of UBS's American investment banking arm, UBS has now written off $50.6 billion on mortgage-backed securities and other derivatives. Swiss attitudes to banks have been so changed by these events that when one of us visited Switzerland in February 2009, mainstream pro-business newspapers in Geneva and Lausanne were calmly reporting, without comment or dissent, that the CEO of SWATCH was moving all the company's accounts to the postal savings bank and the cantonal bank of Aargau because the Big Two Swiss banks were run by cretins and bandits.

The Savings and Loans (S&Ls) crisis of the 1980s, which required $500 billion of public money in bailouts (for a final cost of $150 billion after selling off troubled assets), might have served as a warning against partially deregulating a financial sector while leaving explicit or implicit public guarantees in place. Investment banking and mortgage lending became steadily less regulated from the late 1990s onward, just as the borrowing and investing of S&Ls had been deregulated. The language became enriched by such terms as exploding ARMs (adjustable rate mortgages, on which payments would rise sharply after an initial period, unless the mortgage was refinanced), no-docs loans, liar loans, and NINJA loans (no income, no job or assets), designed to be swiftly repackaged by the original lenders and sold off as CDOs to other financial institutions that knew little about the debtors, but cared only about the rating given the CDO by a rating agency. Because the deregulation was only partial, the role of the handful of rating agencies is enshrined in law, with the agencies competing for clients by cultivating reputations for giving more generous ratings (Lowenstein, 2008; *The Economist*, 2009b; Rosenkranz, 2009). In many US states, unlike Canada, mortgages are non-recourse loans, so that if a borrower takes a mortgage for 125 percent of the market value of a house and then walks away, the owner of the mortgage (presumably no longer the original issuer) cannot pursue the debtor, beyond seizing the house itself (Fitzgerald, 2008; Schwartz, 2009). There was heavy reliance on fancy mathematical models that were suited to independent risks with stable probability distributions rather than systemic risk and non-ergodic uncertainty (Davidson, 1991; Overbye, 2009), although it is also the case that large, supposedly sophisticated financial institutions not only fell prey to fundamental uncertainty but also failed to use mathematical models properly to handle even calculable risks (Nocera, 2009). In retrospect, the combination of partial deregulation, a belief that finally how to outsmart the market had been figured, and an asset price boom fueled by accommodative monetary policy (whether the boom was in "New Economy" stocks in the 1920s, dot-com stocks in the late 1990s, or house prices in the 2000s) was a recipe for disaster comparable to giving a bunch of insolvent S&Ls deposit guarantees and turning them loose to try to win enough in high-risk real estate speculation to have a positive net worth. Such behavior fits Robert Shiller's concept of "irrational exuberance" (Shiller,

2000, 2009) better than it matches the neoclassical conception of forward-looking rational investors and policy makers. Even Judge Richard Posner (2009), founder of Chicago "law and economics", acknowledges the failure of unregulated financial capitalism. But as David Dodge (2008a, 2008b) points out, once an asset bubble has started, it is very tempting for a central bank to put off intervening to halt the bubble, since such intervention precipitates the credit crunch that the central bank hopes to avoid. Central bankers such as Bernanke have drawn lessons from the 1930s about how to respond to debt-deflation, but not lessons from the 1920s about avoiding the preceding asset price bubble (see, for example, Ferguson, 2009). Much of mainstream economic theory is unhelpful in learning such lessons, because many formal models of supposedly monetary economies impose the "transversality condition" that all debts are paid, in which case, as Charles Goodhart (2008) acidly observes, all private liabilities are as safe and liquid as money, so there is no role for money.

3 THE SHADOW OF THE BANK HOLIDAY: BERNANKE AND THE FED

Ben Bernanke (1981, 1983) began his academic career with a dissertation on how the debt-deflation of the early 1930s led not just to a contraction of the money supply, as the public withdrew cash from uninsured bank deposits and banks scrambled to shift from loans to reserves, but to a breakdown of the US payments system, a failure of bank money as a medium exchange in the bank holiday of 1933. US bank failures increased from 659 in 1929 to 1,352 in 1930 and 2,294 in 1931, although dipping to 1,456 in 1932, but these bank closings were only the prelude to collapse. According to Hughes and Cain (2007, pp. 504–5):

> By 4 March 1933, all banks in 38 states had suspended business. Two days later, Roosevelt finished the job by declaring a nationwide bank holiday. When the banks reopened under federal supervision, some 4,000 more were found to be insolvent and were liquidated. Ben Bernanke concluded that the effects of the banking crisis in the early 1930s (especially in 1931) were so severe that the banking system was simply unable to resume as a competent mechanism of intermediation for the rest of the 1930s.

After the bank holiday, the surviving banks held exceptionally high levels of excess reserves until the United States entered the Second World War, instead of expanding lending, and other financial institutions displayed comparable risk aversion.

In 2002, soon after joining the Board of Governors of the Federal Reserve System, Bernanke spoke at Milton Friedman's 90th birthday party. Referring to Friedman and Schwartz's *Monetary History of the United States* (1963), Bernanke delighted the assembled monetarists by concluding, "Let me end my talk by abusing slightly my status as an official representative of the Federal Reserve System. I would like to say to Milton and Anna: Regarding the Great Depression. You're right, we did it. We're very sorry. But thanks to you, we won't do it again" (quoted by Bragues, 2009, p. FP19). At the time, this was just a jaunty witticism. In 2002, depressions, financial crises, and banking meltdowns were things that might happen in less favored parts of the world, from Mexico in 1994 (and in 1992 the Swedish banking crisis and the unraveling of Europe's Exchange Rate Mechanism) through Brazil, Russia, Thailand, South Korea, and Indonesia in 1997–98 to Argentina and Mexico in 2002 (see Spotton Visano, 2006 for an overview of crises and their causes and consequences), but seemed inconceivable in the United States.[4] After all, the United States had vast financial markets with deep liquidity and highly sophisticated, recently deregulated investment bankers, and where only a year before monetary economists had learnedly debated how to conduct monetary policy once the national debt had been reduced to zero (a problem that has since ceased to cause worry). Bernanke's remarks did not seem quite as amusing after he returned to the Board of Governors as chairman in 2006, and was responsible for seeing that the Fed did not "do it again".

Beyond being constrained by the gold exchange standard, the leadership of the Fed in the early 1930s was clueless about what was going on. In a letter to Clark Warburton in 1946 (published by Cargill, 1992, pp. 1275–6), Irving Fisher recalled:

> In the summer of 1931 I called on Eugene Meyer, the chairman of the Federal Reserve Board. I said: "I am getting alarmed to see demand deposits diminish. It seems to me this may cause great trouble." He said: "What do you call the figure?" Amazed, I said: "The full name is individual deposits subject to check without notice." He rang a bell and asked his assistant to bring in the last controller's report open to the page where the figures were given for individual deposits subject to check without notice. In a few minutes the report came in and I pointed and said: "You see that during the last several call dates there has been a continuous reduction." He said, "Yes, I see it." Of course his main object should have been to see it all along and long before his attention was called to it.

Meyer's failure to grasp what was happening to the financial system and that he had a responsibility as head of the Fed to do something about it can be seen in David Halberstam's *The Powers That Be* (1979, pp. 252–61), in which Meyer figured because of his later career as publisher of the *Washington Post* (eventually inherited from him by his daughter Katharine Graham). Halberstam (p. 254) noted that Meyer had held various government positions ("All his jobs were important. Many of them had to do with the financing of World War I and the reconstruction of Europe after the war") and reported that Meyer "had been bothered by the inaction of Hoover. His old friend had seemed to draw in, and had been unwilling to face the reality of the national crisis". Faithfully recording Meyer–Graham family tradition about the founding father, Halberstam did not realize, or did not think it worth mentioning, that Meyer had headed the Federal Reserve in the Depression or that perhaps Meyer, not just Herberk Hoover, might have done more to face up to the crisis. Bernanke, who has studied the monetary turmoil of the early 1930s, does not wish to share Meyer's well-earned reputation for befuddled inertia in the midst of a financial meltdown.

From August 2007, when two hedge funds run by BNP Paribas suspended withdrawals (the funds specialized in US mortgage-backed securities), the Federal Reserve repeatedly reduced its target Federal Funds rate and injected liquidity into credit markets, faltering only when it allowed Lehman Brothers to fail (after which the confidence shocks to Lehman's counterparties forced the Fed to prevent any further liquidations). In contrast, the Bank of England resisted pressure to provide comparable support to the British financial system until its policy stance was overwhelmed by the collapse of Northern Rock in September 2007, a policy reversal that damaged Governor Mervyn King's reputation (*The Economist*, 2007). While the Fed and then the Bank of England reduced short-term interest rates (Shaikh and Jones, 2009), the ECB held its interest rate target unchanged after onset of the crisis, basing its interest rate decisions solely on fear of inflation. From August 2007 to June 2008, while the Fed reduced its overnight interest rate target by 325 basis points from 5.25 to 2.0 percent, the ECB kept its comparable rate unchanged at 4.0 percent – and then in July 2008, the ECB raised its rate by 25 basis points, keeping to the "Bagehot principle" of lending freely at penalty rates to illiquid but supposedly solvent banks (the ECB later cut rates). This was not because Europe's banking system was unscathed by the US subprime and Alt-A mortgage crisis. Spanish, Irish, and British housing price bubbles burst. Five of Germany's seven Landesbanken (the banks of the state governments) had their credit ratings reduced and German banks were estimated to hold over a trillion dollars of troubled assets, so that the German government intervened to guarantee all bank deposits. Other European countries had similar problems (although the worst hit, Iceland, whose government took over foreign currency debts of Icelandic banks equal to seven times GDP, is outside the eurozone). But the ECB based its monetary policy primarily on targeting inflation rather than on its role as lender of last resort, leaving national fiscal policies to stabilize the banking system by guaranteeing deposits (Carmichael, 2008; Carmichael and Scofield, 2008).

Much of Bernanke's academic research in the late 1990s concerned the benefits of setting an explicit target for inflation (Bernanke et al., 1999). The Bank of England, the Bank of Canada, and other central banks have such inflation targets – in New Zealand, the central bank governor's salary is pegged to success in meeting the inflation target. The ECB does not quite have inflation-only targeting, but is so inflation obsessed that it might as well have. In contrast, the Federal Reserve sets no explicit target for inflation, and implicitly sets interest rates by a Taylor rule, according to a formula that weights both inflation and the output gap. Given his research on inflation targets, Bernanke might have been expected to push the Fed toward adopting an explicit inflation target, but he has not done so. Instead, he has emphasized the lender-of-last-resort function of the Fed, and has been quicker than Mervyn King at the Bank of England to accept the moral hazard problem of keeping large institutions from failure. Why? Bernanke's academic writings suggest an answer. Bernanke (1981, 1983, 1995, 2000) repeatedly stressed the devastating effect on economic activity of the collapse of the US system of financial intermediation brought about by debt-deflation in the 1930s. Beyond these historical studies, several of his contributions to macroeconomic theory, such as Bernanke and Blinder (1988) and Bernanke and Gertler (1989), concern the ways in which a decline in the capital of lenders or the collateral of borrowers can reduce lending and real economic activity. In addition to Fisher (1933), Bernanke cited Hyman Minsky (1975, 1982) and the MIT economic historian Charles Kindleberger (1978), one of Bernanke's teachers at MIT, but he distanced himself from their willingness to acknowledge deviations from rational behavior: "I do not deny the possible importance of irrationality in economic life; however it seems that the best research strategy is to push the rationality principle as far as it will go" (Bernanke, 2000, p. 43) – after all, he was submitting his work on the Depression as an MIT dissertation. The lesson that Bernanke drew from these studies is that, faced by such a debt-deflation crisis, the paramount concern of a central banker must be to sustain the functioning of the system of financial intermediation, leaving to some later, quieter time worries about exchange rates, future inflation, or the moral hazard of rescuing improvident institutions (see, for example, Norris, 2008).

4 ANOTHER VIEW OF DEBT-DEFLATION: KING OF THREADNEEDLE STREET

Mervyn King, the "King of Threadneedle Street", has also studied the debt-deflation of the early 1930s (King, 1994), citing Keynes (1931b), Fisher (1933), Minsky (1975, 1982), and Tobin (1980) as sources of the debt-deflation analysis (in addition to sources cited by Bernanke or King, see also Keynes, 1931a, 1936, pp. 264, 268, 271; Fisher, 1932). But, although he examined the same historical episode of debt-deflation and read much of the same literature as Bernanke, King drew a different lesson, and, especially in August and September 2007, he responded differently to the crisis, resisting as long as possible aggressive expansionary policies. His 1994 presidential address to the European Economic Association, on the subject of debt-deflation, indicates why. Both Bernanke and King recognize two channels through which an unanticipated fall in the price level, raising the real value of inside debts fixed in nominal terms, and a collapse of asset prices, can reduce the level of economic activity. First, the scramble for liquidity disrupts the system of financial intermediation, causes bankruptcies, raises risk premiums, and reduces the availability of credit. Second, the rise in the real value of inside debts transfers wealth from borrowers to lenders. Since borrowers presumably became borrowers because they have higher propensities to spend than lenders do, such a transfer reduces aggregate expenditure (and, because there is so much more inside debt than outside money, this destabilizing effect of a price decline can overwhelm the stabilizing Pigou real balance effect of a lower price level). Bernanke emphasized the first channel, and argued that the disruption of financial intermediation caused much of the harm of the Great Depression in the US. King's focus was on the second channel, and he concluded that the plausible differences in spending propensities between borrowers and lenders were not large enough for this channel of debt-deflation to be of critical importance. A possible reason why King's attention was not more drawn to the disruption of financial intermediation is a difference in the historical experiences of the countries in which Bernanke and King were writing. Britain, unlike Austria, Germany, Italy, or the United States, did not experience a banking crisis in the early 1930s. The historical sin of the Fed, for which Bernanke apologized at Milton Friedman's 90th birthday party, was permitting the disintegration of the banking system, with more than 9,000 banks failing and the whole system temporarily closed in the bank holiday. The historical sin of Montagu Norman and the Bank of England was the return to the gold standard in 1925 at the pre-war parity, necessitating deflation of wages and prices and prolonged unemployment, the "Norman conquest of $4.86" (Keynes, 1925; Moggridge, 1972).

Letting the exchange rate of the pound sterling float (or, rather, sink) in August 1931 provided escape from that mistake, without forcing attention on the fragility of the banking system. The lesson Ben Bernanke drew from the Great Depression was the paramount importance of maintaining the liquidity of the financial system, while the lesson Mervyn King drew (at least until the collapse of Northern Rock, followed by the near-failures of HBOS and the Royal Bank of Scotland) was the need to pursue a stable aggregate demand policy, unconstrained by the fixed exchange rates of 1925–31 (or of the Exchange Rate Mechanism of 1992).

5   REMEMBERING HAVENSTEIN IN FRANKFURT

While Bernanke is haunted by the Fed's failure to prevent the collapse of the US system of financial intermediation and the bankruptcy of 9,000 uninsured banks from 1929 to 1933, Otmar Issing and his successors at the ECB, like the Bundesbank, are haunted by a different specter (Carmichael, 2008; Carmichael and Scofield, 2008). In 1914, one US dollar exchanged for 4.2 Reichsmarks. In 1923, one US dollar exchanged for 4.2 trillion Reichsmarks, and the German price level was one trillion times (a one followed by 12 zeros) as high as it had been in 1914, as the post-war German government, its fiscal base devastated, printed money to pay its expenses (see Bresciani-Turroni, 1937). Trust funds, pension funds, and the assets of insurance companies, all of which by law had to be invested entirely in bonds and other claims to fixed amounts of money, were worthless. John Maynard Keynes (1923), then a young, orthodox Marshallian quantity theorist, calculated that the real quantity of money in Germany, M/P, had fallen by 92 percent, as the opportunity cost of holding real money balances soared. However, Rudolf Havenstein, Reichsbank president since the turn of the century, held that since the price level P had risen so much faster than the quantity of currency, the rise in prices could not have been caused by the increased quantity of money. Accordingly, he promised the German people that, with 38 new high-speed printing presses, the Reichsbank would be able to print enough money for the quantity of money to catch up with the price level. As a headline in *The Economist* (2008a) puts it, "The lessons of German history haunt the single currency".

The mindset of the Bundesbank and the ECB is illustrated by a machine in the Bundesbank's Money Museum, where

> [M]useum-goers are . . . invited to grab a lever, and choose how much money to supply to a slowing economy . . . The machine shows prices running out of control, warning lights come on and the game ends. "Sorry, but you've failed,"

reads an illuminated rebuke. "Go back and review the basics of money again." The real-life costs are spelled out, a few metres away, by sombre displays and newsreels describing the miseries of currency instability. They show Germany's hyperinflation in 1923, when it became cheaper to burn banknotes than to buy fuel. Then came deflation and mass unemployment in the early 1930s, triggering despair that – the museum commentary suggests – helped the Nazis to power. Other sections explain how post-war Germany was saved by the strict policies of the Bundesbank. A display marked "conflicts" describes how politicians from Konrad Adenauer to Helmut Schmidt all failed to browbeat the bank into bending the rules on inflation. Each time, visitors are told, the bank was ultimately proved right. (*The Economist*, 2008a, p. 62)

6 THE BANK OF CANADA'S GOOD LUCK

On May 16, 2009, *The Economist* (2009c) offered a salute in its special report on international banking, entitled "Don't blame Canada: a country that got things right". The following day, in the *Sunday New York Times Magazine*, financial historian Niall Ferguson (2009, p. 20; original italics) notes that, while Citigroup's ratio of on- and off-balance-sheet assets to common equity reached 56 to 1 in 2008, "The good health of Canada's banks is due to *better* regulation. Simply by capping leverage at 20 to 1, the Office of the Superintendent of Financial Institutions spared Canada the need for bank bailouts". The Bank of Canada has lowered its overnight rate to 0.25 percent and made a conditional "near-guarantee" of keeping the rate there for a year, barring new major developments, in the hope that the boost to confidence from such a commitment (or near-commitment) would make it unnecessary for the Bank of Canada to engage in anti-depression credit expansion as vigorously as the Fed (Scofield, 2009). The Canadian economy is in a nasty recession, especially the oil and automobile sectors, the ABCP market collapsed, and, although less severe than the US (in part because of different laws on non-recourse mortgage loans, no income tax deductions for mortgage interest), Canada has its own problems in subprime lending (MacArthur and McNish, 2009), but the banking system did not collapse, or even totter very much, attracting praise from outside Canada. In particular, *The Economist* (2009c) offers a graph showing how much slower the assets of the Royal Bank of Canada (RBC) have grown since 1997 than the now-troubled Royal Bank of Scotland. While praise is always welcome, it is worth remembering that the Canadian banks very much wanted to grow more rapidly and to imitate their American counterparts. In 1998, they begged the government to let them merge and to roll back restrictions on their activities, so that they could compete in the global marketplace like Citigroup or UBS.

Paul Martin, then Minister of Finance, turned the banks down, for which he is now hailed as "Man of the Year" (Marche, 2008) – but at the time, political opposition to bank mergers centered as much or more on losses of banking jobs, closing of duplicate bank branches, and increased oligopoly power to raise service charges than on systemic fragility. Some academic critics, notably at a Laurentian University conference organized by Brian MacLean, worried about systemic fragility, but it was not their concern that overcame the political power of the big banks. Canada's bankers were bitterly unhappy at the time, but in retrospect that they were fortunate that Canada's politicians could not face branch closures and higher ATM fees and so blocked the lemming-like urge of Canada's big banks to merge and to move aggressively into the US market, including the mortgage and derivatives markets. Mind you, in the absence of wisdom, sheer dumb luck has its uses.

The Bank of Canada did not always bask in such praise. In 1960 and 1961, most of Canada's leading economists signed a petition calling for the ousting of Bank Governor James Coyne (see Gordon, 1961) for his tight-money policy, and his outspoken, idiosyncratic views about high interest rates to encourage Canadians to save more and so own more of the Canadian economy instead of leaving it so open to foreign investment (he did not give sufficient consideration to the effect of high Canadian interest rates on the capital inflow). The Governor's isolation enabled the government of the day to use him as a scapegoat for an unpopular mix of fiscal and monetary policy (Babad and Mulroney, 1995). It introduced a bill in Parliament to declare his office vacant, a bill that passed the House of Commons but was defeated in the Senate (whereupon Coyne resigned, claiming vindication from the government's aspersions on his personal integrity). Since then, the Bank of Canada has avoided such vulnerability and isolation by keeping to the conventional orthodoxies of the mainstream of the economic profession and the business community, adopting monetary aggregate targets when those became mainstream, and then inflation targets when that became the standard for conventional central bankers.

7 CONCLUSION: LEARNING FROM THE PAST

The past affects different central bankers in different ways. Ben Bernanke does not wish to be the next Eugene Meyer: the lesson Bernanke took from the debt-deflation of the 1930s is that the entire system of credit and financial intermediation can freeze unless the Federal Reserve (supported by the Treasury) intervenes strongly in a crisis to maintain liquidity and confidence, even if such action as lender of last resort (with the Treasury as capital supplier of last resort) conflicts with inflation targeting and involves a moral hazard risk for financial institutions that consider themselves too big to fail. Mervyn King does not wish to be the next Montagu Norman: the lesson that King took from studying the Great Depression is that the fixed exchange rates of the gold standard obstructed a monetary policy geared to stabilization of domestic aggregate demand. Duisenberg, Trichet, Issing, and their ECB colleagues have nightmares of being the next Rudolf Havenstein: they take their lesson from the early 1920s rather than the early 1930s, and fear that any inflation may become uncontrollable (see Carmichael, 2008; Carmichael and Scofield, 2008; *The Economist*, 2008a, 2008c, 2009a). Dodge, Carney, and their colleagues at the Bank of Canada do not wish to be the next James Coyne, vulnerable as a lightning rod for dissatisfaction with the performance of the economy, because out of step with the mainstream of the most conventional economic orthodoxy (see Gordon, 1961; Babad and Mulroney, 1995). The historical traumas that haunt central bankers are those that ruined the reputations of past central bankers.

But other lessons from the past have not been taken to heart by these central bankers to the same extent. Bernanke and King focused their studies on the debt-deflation of the early 1930s, rather than on the preceding boom in a weakly regulated economy. In the middle and late 1920s, as in the dot-com bubble of the late 1990s or the subprime mortgage–CDO–CDS housing price bubble leading to the present crisis, speculators easily persuaded themselves that "this time is different" in the "New Economy". Central bankers, financial regulators, and policy makers forget (and were encouraged by lobbyists to forget) that stabilizing the US economy and financial system in the 1930s was not just a matter of monetary expansion, budget deficits, and a floating exchange rate, but of structural reforms such as the Securities and Exchange Commission, the Glass–Steagall Act separating commercial and investment banking, Social Security, and the Federal Deposit Insurance Corporation. They forgot that the Savings and Loans fiasco of the 1980s resulted from easing regulation of borrowing and investment by thrift institutions while continuing to guarantee their liabilities, a parallel to the more recent consequences of easing regulation of mortgage lending and removing limits on the leverage of the five largest investment banks. Investors, regulators, and central bankers all forgot that the experience of Kidder Peabody showed that mortgage-backed securities could abruptly become illiquid, or that the misfortunes of the Lloyd's insurance exchange (Raphael, 1994), where four years of losses wiped out 20 years of profits, demonstrated yet again that risks need not be independent or normally distributed or subject to be being tamed by mathematical models – in short, that markets are subject to fundamental uncertainty in the sense of Keynes and Knight (Davidson, 1991; Taleb, 2007). It is not the case that nothing is learned from experience. Indeed, *The Economist* (2008b, p. 86), perhaps a bit prematurely, headlined one story, "Fuld of experience: by learning from past mistakes, Dick Fuld has brought Lehman Brothers back from the brink". But learning from experience has been selective and incomplete. In particular, leading central bankers have drawn very different lessons from history, each haunted by a past trauma of his own institution, and this has shaped how they have responded to the present crisis.

NOTES

1. Furthermore, central banks have experienced difficulty in reducing the effective, as distinct from the official, nominal overnight rate to near-zero, because of the rise in risk premiums. Thus the Toronto-Dominion Bank's TD Effective Measure of Monetary Policy showed an effective rate of 2.30 percent in March 2009 compared to the Bank of Canada's official rate of 0.50 percent, because reductions totaling 400 basis points in the Bank of Canada's target overnight rate had been offset by a 212 basis point rise in credit spreads (Lascelles and Pollick, 2009).
2. Even as sharp-eyed a critic of investment bankers as Philip Augar (2005, pp. 44–5) discusses Kidder Peabody's downfall solely in terms of Joe Jett, without mention of the much larger problem of illiquid mortgage-backed bonds.
3. But see Lo (2012, p. 175) [Note added in proof].
4. In 1995, a budget deadlock between President Bill Clinton and House Speaker Newt Gingrich forced the US Treasury to reassure a delegation from the Brazilian Finance Ministry that the US was not about to default on its national debt, a conversation said to have been greatly enjoyed by the Brazilian visitors, but this was seen just as an incident of US politics, not as a crisis of the US economy. See Alan Greenspan (2007) to savor the view of financial crises as something afflicting the rest of the world, which the US would sort out.

REFERENCES

Ahamed, L. (2009), *Lords of Finance: The Bankers Who Broke the World*, New York, Toronto and London: Penguin Books.

Andrews, E. (2009), "Fed's minutes reveal shock at intensity of downturn", *New York Times*, January 7, pp. B1, B4.

Augar, P. (2005), *The Greed Merchants: How the Investment Banks Played the Free Market Game*, London: Penguin.

Babad, M. and C. Mulroney (1995), *Where the Buck Stops: The Dollar, Democracy, and the Bank of Canada*, Toronto: Stoddart.

Bernanke, B. (1981), "Bankruptcy, liquidity, and recession", *American Economic Review: AEA Papers and Proceedings*, **71** (2) (May), 155–9.

Bernanke, B. (1983), "Nonmonetary effects of the financial crisis on the propagation of the Great Depression", *American Economic Review*, **73** (3) (June), 257–76.

Bernanke, B. (1995), "Money, credit and banking lecture: the macroeconomics of the Great Depression: a comparative approach", *Journal of Money, Credit and Banking*, **27** (1) (January), 1–28.

Bernanke, B. (2000), *Essays on the Great Depression*, Princeton, NJ: Princeton University Press.

Bernanke, B. and A.S. Blinder (1988), "Money, credit and aggregate demand", *American Economic Review: AEA Papers and Proceedings*, **78** (2) (May), 435–9.

Bernanke, B. and M. Gertler (1989), "Agency costs, net worth and business fluctuations", *American Economic Review*, **79** (1) (March), 14–31.

Bernanke, B., T. Laubach, F.S. Mishkin and A.S. Posen (1999), *Inflation Targeting: Lessons from the International Experience*, Princeton, NJ: Princeton University Press.

Bragues, G. (2009), "Ben's blunders: no one seemed to notice that the more the U.S. Fed Chairman did, the worse things got", *Financial Post*, January 28, p. FP19.

Bresciani-Turroni, C. (1937), *The Economics of Inflation*, with an introduction by Lionel Robbins, London: George Allen & Unwin.

Cargill, T. (1992), "Miscellany: Irving Fisher comments on Benjamin Strong and the Federal Reserve in the 1930s", *Journal of Political Economy*, **100** (6) (December), 1273–7.

Carmichael, K. (2008), "Europe's inflation fighter turns gaze to rate cuts: central bank leaves benchmark unchanged but concedes that growth is a bigger concern than price increases", *Globe and Mail*, October 3, p. B3.

Carmichael, K. and H. Scofield (2008), "Europe, U.S. at odds over approach to interest rates: Canada and Britain have slashed rates along with the U.S., but the European Central Bank refuses to follow suit", *Globe and Mail*, April 11.

Davidson, P. (1991) "Is probability theory relevant for uncertainty: a Post Keynesian perspective", *Journal of Economic Perspectives*, **5** (1) (Spring), 29–43.

Dimand, R. and R.H. Koehn (2008), "Central bankers in the Minsky moment: how different central banks have responded to the threat of debt-deflation", *Journal of Economic Asymmetries*, **5** (1) (June), 139–48.

Dodge, D. (2008a), "Central banking in a time of crisis and beyond", Benefactors Lecture, C.D. Howe Research Institute, November, available at: www.cdhowe.org (accessed February 13, 2012).

Dodge, D. (2008b), "Rebuilding the global financial system", Thomas d'Aquino Lecture on Leadership, Toronto Club, Toronto, November, available at: www.ceocouncil.ca (accessed February 13, 2012).

Economist, The (2007), "Leader: the bank that failed: the governor of the Bank of England is the biggest casualty of a financial fiasco – far from the only one", September 22, p. 16.

Economist, The (2008a), "Charlemagne: don't play politics with the euro – the lessons of German history haunt the single currency", March 8, p. 62.

Economist, The (2008b), "Fuld of experience: by learning from past mistakes, Dick Fuld has brought Lehman Brothers back from the brink", April 26, p. 86.

Economist, The (2008c), "A decade in the sun: the ECB has had a good credit crisis and a solid first decade. That was the easy bit", June 7, pp. 79–81.

Economist, The (2009a), "The monetary policy maze", April 25, pp. 74–6.

Economist, The (2009b), "Rating agencies: the wages of sin – the Fed is perpetuating a discredited oligopoly", April 25, p. 80.

Economist, The (2009c), "Don't blame Canada: a country that got things right", in "Special report on international banking: Rebuilding the banks", May 16, p. 7.

Ferguson, N. (2009), "Diminished returns: why we never learn the right lessons from financial crises", *Sunday New York Times Magazine*, May 17, pp. 19–20.

Fisher, I. (1932), *Booms and Depressions*, New York: Adelphi.

Fisher, I. (1933), "The debt-deflation theory of great depressions", *Econometrica*, **1** (3) (October), 337–57.

Fitzgerald, P. (2008), "U.S. bankruptcy law reform urged", *Financial Post*, September 24.

Friedman, M. and Anna J. Schwartz (1963), *A Monetary History of the United States, 1867–1960*, Princeton, NJ: Princeton University Press for the National Bureau of Economic Research.

Goodhart, C.A.E. (2008), "Money and default", in M. Forstater and L. Randall Wray (eds), *Keynes for the Twenty-First Century*, New York and Basingstoke: Palgrave Macmillan, pp. 213–23.

Gordon, H.S. (1961), *The Economists versus the Bank of Canada*, Toronto: Ryerson Press.

Greenspan, A. (2007), *The Age of Turbulence: Adventures in a New World*, New York: Penguin.

Greenspan, S. (2008), *The Annals of Gullibility*, New York: Praeger.

Halberstam, D. (1979), *The Powers That Be*, New York: Dell.

Hughes, J. and L.P. Cain (2007), *American Economic History*, 7th edn, Boston, MA: Pearson Addison-Wesley.

Keynes, J.M. (1923), *A Tract on Monetary Reform*, London: Macmillan.

Keynes, J.M. (1925), *The Economic Consequences of Mr. Churchill*, London: Hogarth Press.

Keynes, J.M. (1931a), "An economic analysis of unemployment", in Q. Wright (ed.), *Unemployment as a World Problem*, Chicago, IL: University of Chicago Press, as reprinted in Keynes (1973).

Keynes, J.M. (1931b), "The consequences to the banks of the collapse in money values", in Keynes, *Essays in Persuasion*, London: Macmillan.

Keynes, J.M. (1936), *The General Theory of Employment, Interest and Money*, London: Macmillan.

Keynes, J.M. (1973), *The Collected Writings of John Maynard Keynes*, Vol. XIII, ed. D.E. Moggridge. London: Macmillan and New York: Cambridge University Press, for the Royal Economic Society.

Kindleberger, C.P. (1978), *Manias, Panics, and Crashes*, New York: Basic Books.

King, M. (1994), "Presidential address: Debt-deflation: theory and evidence", *European Economic Review*, **38**, 419–45.

Labaton, S. (2008), "Agency's '04 Rule let banks pile up new debt, and risk", *New York Times*, October 3, pp. A1, A23.

Lascelles, E. and I. Pollick (2009), "Monetary reality: a new gauge shows that the real cost far exceeds the Bank of Canada's overnight rate of 0.50%", *Financial Post*, March 13.

Lo, A.W. (2012), "Reading about the financial crisis: a twenty-one book review", *Journal of Economic Literature*, **50** (1) (March), 175.

Lowenstein, R. (2008), "Triple-A Failure", *Sunday New York Times Magazine*, April 27, pp. 36–41.

MacArthur, G. and J. McNish (2009), "Canada's dirty subprime secret", *Globe and Mail*, March 14, pp. A8–A9.

Marche, S. (2008), "Man of the Year: for staying cool during the bubble – our derided ex-PM set a fiscal course that could save Canada from the worst of the meltdown", *Toronto Star*, December 27, p. ID3.

Minsky, H. (1975), *John Maynard Keynes*, New York: Columbia University Press.

Minsky, H. (1982), *Can "It" Happen Again? Essays on Instability and Finance*, Armonk, NY: M.E. Sharpe.

Moggridge, D.E. (1972), *British Monetary Policy, 1921–31: The Norman Conquest of $4.86*, Cambridge: Cambridge University Press.

Morgenson, G. (2008), "As good as cash, until it's not: auction-rate notes were fine when they could be sold", *New York Times*, March 9.

Nocera, J. (2009), "Risk mismanagement: were the measures used to evaluate Wall Street trades flawed? Or was the mistake ignoring them?", *Sunday New York Times Magazine*, January 4, pp. 24–33, 46, 50–51.

Norris, F. (2008), "Plan B: flood banks with cash", *New York Times*, October 10, pp. B1, B8.

O'Boyle, T.F. (1998), *At Any Cost: Jack Welch, General Electric, and the Pursuit of Profit*, New York: Vintage Books.

Overbye, D. (2009), "They tried to outsmart Wall Street: the story of the Quants", *New York Times*, March 10, pp. D1, D4.

Porter, E. (2008), "Ponzi schemes never change: Madoff's fraudulent scheme actually underscores how stable the institutions of finance truly are", *International Herald Tribune*, December 29.

Posner, R.A. (2009), *A Failure of Capitalism: The Crisis of '08 and the Descent into Depression*, Cambridge, MA: Harvard University Press.

Rosenkranz, R. (2009), "Let's write the rating agencies out of our law", *Wall Street Journal*, January 2.

Raphael, A. (1994), *Ultimate Risk: The Inside Story of the Lloyd's Catastrophe*, London: Bantam.

Rubin, R.E. and J. Weisberg (2003), *In an Uncertain World: Tough Choices from Wall Street to Washington*, New York: Random House.

Schwartz, A. (2009), "Don't let judges fix loans", *New York Times*, February 27.

Scofield, H. (2009), "Bank of Canada breaks from the pack: many central banks are having their money-printing presses run around the clock – not Canada", *Globe and Mail*, May 20.

Shaikh, F. and M. Jones (2009), "BoE slashes interest rates to record low", *Financial Post*, March 6, p. FP10.

Shermer, M. (2009), "The art of the con: how we can avoid falling prey to con men such as Bernard Madoff", *Scientific American*, March, p. 28.

Shiller, R.J. (2000), *Irrational Exuberance*, Princeton, NJ: Princeton University Press.

Shiller, R.J. (2009), *The Subprime Solution: How Today's Global Financial Crisis Happened, and What to Do About It*, Princeton, NJ: Princeton University Press.

Spotton Visano, B. (2006), *Financial Crises: Socio-economic Causes and Institutional Context*, London and New York: Routledge.

Taleb, N.N. (2007), *The Black Swan*, New York: Random House.

Tobin, J. (1980), *Asset Accumulation and Economic Activity*, Chicago, IL: University of Chicago Press, and Oxford: Blackwell.

8. Central banking in a systemic crisis: the Federal Reserve's "credit easing"

Robert Guttmann

1 A STRUCTURAL CRISIS

The current crisis, which began in mid-2007 and has yet to run its full course more than four years later (February 2012), is not just a normal cyclical downturn of the kind last encountered in 1990/91 and 2000/01. Those two recessions caused temporary pain, but were inherently self-correcting. What we have today, in contrast, can be more accurately characterized as a "structural crisis", the result of a longer-term accumulation of imbalances (for example, leverage ratios in the private sector) and asymmetries (for example, US trade deficits) which have gathered sufficient force to explode into the open and cause massive disruption of economic activity. Such crises are obviously deeper and last longer than normal recessions. And they can in all likelihood only be overcome with institutional reforms and new policies that address the underlying imbalances.

If we look back at previous structural crises, notably 1873–79, 1929–39, and even 1979–82, each one of these was triggered by a severe bout of financial instability which paralyzed the banking system, caused credit to dry up, and so forced severe cutbacks in spending. Such a historical account would suggest that there is a direct relationship between the intensity of the financial instability at the onset of the crisis and the depth of subsequent declines in production, employment, and trade. This link obviously continues to hold. We have had a very serious financial crisis, especially in the aftermath of Lehman's collapse in mid-September 2008, and as a result we have seen near-depression levels of decline on a global scale.

The principal imbalances underlying this last structural crisis have been the growing centrality of finance, manifest in the extraordinary expansion of financial assets and income sources over the last quarter of a century (relative to non-financial measures), and increasingly large external disequilibria among the world's major economies.[1] The incredible growth of financial institutions and markets in recent years was nourished by a growing reliance on debt financing among many sectors of the economy, increasingly complex connections between different financial instruments (loans, securities, derivatives), and a tendency for these intertwined and highly leveraged funding channels to feed ever-larger speculative bubbles. With regard to the external imbalances referred to above, we are talking in particular about growing US trade deficits which have been matched by equally large trade surpluses of China and, to a lesser extent, other export-dependent industrial nations (for example, Japan, Germany) or emerging-market economies (for example, Brazil, India). Of course, these two forces are connected directly to the extent that large and chronic current-account imbalances require (and fuel) commensurate cross-border flows of financial capital. But their connection also has a more complex and institutionally specific dynamic, centered on the dollar-based international monetary system first put into place at the end of the Second World War.

The role of the dollar as world money has meant that the United States is in a position of being able to run chronic balance-of-payments deficits, which supply the rest of the world with needed new supplies of dollars thereby transferred into international circulation, and have those automatically financed by the rest of the world. This advantage, which I have referred to earlier as "global seigniorage" (see Guttmann, 1994), translated during the first post-war decades – until 1971 – into US capital exports large enough to outweigh chronic US trade surpluses (by means of foreign aid and assistance programs, overseas military expenditures, and direct investments of US multinationals). Ever since 1985, however, the composition of US balance-of-payments deficits shifted to ever-larger US trade deficits that came to be matched by chronic US capital imports from the world's major surplus nations. These cross-border capital flows helped feed dollar-based financial markets from which emerged three consecutive US-based speculative bubbles – the tidal wave of leveraged buyouts launched by corporate raiders in the 1980s, the dot-com boom of the 1990s, and the housing bubble of the 2000s.[2]

2 AMERICA'S HOUSING BUBBLE

That last bubble, the one fueling an unprecedented boom in US home-ownership and housing prices, is the one at the core of the structural crisis we are facing today. Like all the other bubbles, this one too was driven forward by a financial innovation which fed its debt-financed expansion by exploiting sustained conditions of "easy credit". We are talking here specifically about the repackaging of loans into tradable securities which began to take root in earnest during the mid-1990s. Banks bundled together mortgage loans and then issued securities against those loan pools. Those "mortgage-backed securities" (MBS), whose income stems from the debt-servicing charges of mortgage borrowers in the pool, allowed banks to turn over funds much more quickly for added lending power, earn additional service fees from their issue, and transfer default risks to the buyers of those bonds. This practice was initially launched in the 1980s by Fannie Mae and Freddie Mac, two government-sponsored lenders specifically authorized by the US Congress to develop and maintain a secondary market for mortgages in order to encourage the financing of home ownership among Americans.

Their success in launching this innovation had two consequences, which first manifested themselves in the late 1990s and then took off after 2003. The first was that a rapidly growing number of commercial banks got into the act of issuing their own MBS, turning this practice within a decade into a major profit center. Attracted by the relatively high yields of these securities, especially during a period of historically low yields on other types of bonds, more and more investors all over the world began to invest their excess dollars in these MBS. Second, with MBS thus becoming a globally traded instrument, US banks had growing amounts of funds to lend out to potential and actual homeowners. Banks thus had every incentive to loan more, which they did by developing new sources of mortgage demand. For instance, banks made it increasingly easy for their clients to *refinance* existing mortgages, a practice rendered especially attractive for Americans during periods of lower interest rates (for example, mid-1990s, 2001–05). Typically, US consumers ended up borrowing more when refinancing, using the increase in the appraised value of their home serving as collateral to qualify for higher levels of debt. During the 2000s, millions of US homeowners took out so-called "home-equity loans", which they could also secure with their homes even those that were already mortgaged, thereby finding another convenient way to draw cash from their capital gains. Finally, banks pushed *non-traditional* mortgages which carried much more lenient conditions in terms of eligibility. Most important among those were the so-called "subprimes" offered to Americans with low credit scores. Many of these higher-risk loans offered initially very low interest rates during the first couple of years, which would then at a certain date be re-set to much higher levels and so leave intrinsically vulnerable debtors with significantly larger monthly interest payments.

The spread of subprimes and other high-risk mortgages (for example, Alt-As, piggybacks), which by 2007 amounted to 40 percent of all US mortgages, prompted a major extension of the securitization infrastructure which started to take off in 2004. Mixing a growing proportion of high-risk mortgages into the underlying loan pool threatened the investment-grade ratings of MBS without which these securities would not sell nearly as well across the globe. The banks responded to this challenge by bundling MBS with other asset-backed securities (ABS) and loan pools into so-called "collateralized debt obligations" (CDOs), splitting the latter into high- and low-risk tranches (depending on their position in the payoff pyramid), and creating a network of special-purpose entities and hedge funds to help make a market for these instruments. By engaging these off-balance-sheet partners to absorb the higher-risk junior tranches and buying the highest-risk equity tranches from each other, the banks were able to sell the large (typically 80 percent-sized) senior tranches as AAA-safe to the rest of the world.

The successful launch of this "shadow-banking system", which had grown to a $2 trillion market in a matter of a few years (by 2007), mobilized huge sums for an unprecedented housing boom in the United States. The boom-induced appreciation in housing prices fueled a borrowing spree among American homeowners able to borrow growing amounts as their homes became more valuable. These so-called "home equity withdrawals" boosted the US growth rate by 2–3 percent per annum while also contributing to a collapse in American personal savings.[3] With such large capital gains (as housing prices doubled over five years), Americans did not feel a need to save and could focus on excess consumption instead. Driven by this *wealth effect* the household sector ended up with a negative savings rate of 2 percent in 2007. The country's excess spending translated into a steadily growing US trade deficit, exceeding $850 billion (or 6.5 percent of GDP) by mid-2007. Serving thus as the world's "buyers of last resort", American consumers sustained the export-led growth strategies of other industrial nations (for example, Japan, Korea, many EU countries), emerging-market economies (for example, China, India, Brazil), and commodity-producing nations (for example, the Organization of Petroleum-Exporting Countries (OPEC), Russia). Those countries then would lend a large portion of their surpluses back to the United States to finance its current-account deficits, a recycling mechanism which perpetuated the global growth dynamic for years.

That connection between US excess spending and export-driven growth in the rest of the world established itself first during the early 1980s, in the wake of Ronald Reagan's huge tax cuts and military-spending increases which soon turned the United States into a net debtor nation (in 1985). The pattern was reinforced during the subsequent leveraged-buyout and dot-com bubbles of the late 1980s and 1990s. US-led stimulation of the global economy enabled scores of developing countries to emerge out of a decade-long debt crisis and hitherto communist societies to manage a difficult transition to market regulation. The housing bubble of the 2000s, with its ingenious funding machine of loan securitizations and home equity withdrawals, pushed this pro-growth dynamic to new heights, with the world economy expanding during those boom years at its fastest clip in over four decades. While we rightfully pinpoint structural changes in finance – notably the combination of financial deregulation, globalization, and innovation – as a key engine feeding this growth pattern, it owes its longstanding presence also to the specific institutional arrangements of the prevailing international monetary system. Based on the US dollar as world money, that system requires chronic US external deficits to supply the rest of the world with needed dollar-denominated liquidity. It is, after all, only through US balance-of-payments deficits that dollars, created initially within the US domestic banking system, flow from their country of issue to the rest of the world. These US deficits are then automatically financed by anyone outside the United States using the dollars as international reserve asset or medium of exchange. The United States is thus in the advantageous position of being able to borrow cheaply and automatically from the rest of the world in its own currency. That so-called global seigniorage advantage of the US from the international use of its currency is at the center of the global growth pattern described in this section, one fueled by US-generated debt-financed asset bubbles.

3   THE PHASES OF A SYSTEMIC CRISIS

Bubbles burst, once they have generated unsustainable imbalances. Slowed down by 17 consecutive interest-rate hikes of the Fed over a two-year period, the US housing bubble finally came to an end in late 2006 when sales peaked and prices reached a ceiling nationwide. The first major wave of interest-rate re-sets among subprimes brought a spike in loan defaults during early 2007 which soon began to create problems among mortgage banks and funds heavily invested in MBS (for example, two funds of Bear Stearns in July 2007). Increased incidences of downgrades cast doubt on the underlying assumptions driving the valuation of MBS and CDOs.

The crisis exploded into the open on 9 August 2007 when the French bank BNP Paribas announced that turbulent market conditions no longer allowed it to value accurately three of its funds specializing in US-issued MBS. This announcement triggered a first panic, as investors realized that potential losses among US subprime loans endangered the viability of MBS and could even spill into the senior tranches of CDOs. Since securitization instruments were opaque, worried investors had no way of figuring out how many impaired subprimes there were in the underlying pool and what damage they might cause. This made it impossible for them to figure out how to readjust prices for MBS and CDOs downward. Without price, no trade! The entire infrastructure of MBS and CDO markets simply disintegrated literally from one day to the next, including the crucial market for asset-backed commercial paper (ABCP) which had become the primary funding source for the different components of the shadow-banking system (for example, special-investment vehicles, hedge funds). The paralysis of the ABCP spilled right away into the commercial-paper market whose perturbations in turn triggered massive calls on standby credit lines kept open precisely for such emergency situations. These calls, of course, triggered a spike in loan demand in the interbank market where banks, no longer trusting each other in terms of the equity and mezzanine CDO tranches they had bought from one another, now suddenly were reluctant to lend short-term funds to each other. That same day, August 9, the European Central Bank (ECB) injected the then-unheard sum of €95 billion into the system to deal with this sudden explosion of tensions in the interbank market. The crisis had finally broken full blast into the open![4]

The disintegration of the MBS–CDO–ABCP securitization layers not only cut off a key funding pipeline for new loans, but it also left banks with potentially huge losses from devalued securities and defaults among their off-balance-sheet entities. Forced by mark-to-market accounting rules to recognize market losses right away, the banks were at first ironically lucky to have no functioning market, hence no price recovery. They could thus estimate new prices of impaired securities, adopting in the process in effect "mark-to-model" accounting. While their loss recognition practices varied widely, the world's leading banks all adopted more or less the same gradualist strategy of declaring a certain limited amount of write-down losses in line with their ability to beef up their capital base each quarter. This worked for a short while, but became progressively more difficult as losses mounted while new capital became increasingly difficult to tap.[5] In the face of repeated loss declarations, investors (including other banks, private equity funds, and sovereign wealth funds) became more and more hesitant to supply banks with more capital. This was especially true after the Fed-arranged takeover of defunct Bear Stearns in March 2008 by JPMorgan Chase for $2 a share, which effectively wiped out the former's shareholders. Now investors had good reason to worry that any bank, especially those with high levels of leverage and a small (or non-existent) deposit base, could collapse and take them with it.

The Bear Stearns débâcle, the first systemic bank failure of the subprime crisis, created massive market anxiety about the health (or lack thereof) of banks. As such it marked the emergence of a new type of run on banks. Any loud market rumor about the imminent collapse of major financial institutions would now trigger a spike in the premium of that firm's credit default swaps (CDS), a new derivative contract providing investors with default insurance. Various CDS-centered trading techniques had made this new tool a very attractive means with which to place speculative bets on the future of individual firms and share in trading gains without actually owning the underlying items in the portfolio. Any rumor-fed jump in a troubled bank's CDS premium would signal to the rest of the world that trouble might be brewing in the institution concerned, setting off sell-offs of the company's bonds and stocks. This kind of bank run would intensify during the summer of 2008 and reach fever-pitch intensity after the government takeovers of Fannie Mae and Freddie Mac on 7 September 2008. Those bank nationalizations set off an absolutely amazing chain of events, culminating in the bankruptcy of Lehman Brothers a week later, followed by Bank of America's takeover of Merrill Lynch, the bailout of AIG, and the failures of Washington Mutual as well as Wachovia – all in the last two weeks of September.

Lehman's collapse was a turning point towards a full-blown global credit crunch, due to its terrifying impact on the money-market funds (after the oldest among them, Reserve Primary Fund, "broke the buck" in the wake of large Lehman-induced losses) and enormous losses in the markets for corporate debt (commercial paper, corporate bonds). The interbank market froze up, making it impossible for nearly every bank to refinance itself. The risk premiums on everything except US Treasuries shot into the stratosphere. Cut off from access to borrowed funds, debtors were slashing spending and selling off assets to hoard cash and bring down excessively high debt levels ("deleveraging"). These widespread spending cutbacks threw the entire world economy into the worst downturn since the Great Depression, with surprisingly large reversals in all the globalization vectors – trade, direct cross-border investments, portfolio investments, aid and assistance, as well as remittances – providing further fuel to the contraction of all the world's major economic regions.

4   THE DANGERS OF DEBT-DEFLATION

As already argued so convincingly by Hyman Minsky (1982, 1986), financial instability is inherent to modern capitalist economies, the result of increasing financial fragility of overextended debtors being squeezed by sharply rising debt-servicing burdens at a time of declining incomes.[6] In recent years we have had recurrent bouts of financial instability, but none of those had the force and reach of the post-Lehman panic. This one was a systemic crisis, in the sense that it paralyzed the entire globally integrated system of financial markets and institutions all at once. The collapse of securitization and the shadow-banking system sustaining it did a lot of damage to the banking system. As a result the monetary transmission mechanism of lending and spending has been severely disrupted, with both money multiplier and the velocity of money sharply lower. As credit dried up, overextended debtors had to sell off assets and cut spending to lower their debt levels. This process, now often referred to in the rather neutral term of "deleveraging", is characterized by collapsing asset prices which eventually spread into product and resource (including labor) markets to drive down prices there as well. A sufficiently large financial crisis, which disrupts the normal level of lending, thus typically threatens to set off deflationary pressures across the entire economy. It is this downward spiral of falling prices and lower spending, famously analyzed by Irving Fisher (1933) as a "debt-deflation spiral", which brings us to the brink of a long and painful depression, a crisis far deeper and longer than your normal cycle-bound recession.

Deflation is dangerous. It is arguably more dangerous than inflation, even though the public tends to worry more about the latter on the basis of more recent experience. There are several powerful reasons why Fisher's debt-deflation spiral has such devastating potential and thus needs to be avoided or contained at all costs before it will have pushed our economy into depression:

- Deflationary forces have even more powerful multiplier effects than inflation. That is so, because price declines amount to direct income losses for all actors selling objects whose prices have gone down. Such income losses cause spending cutbacks which push prices downwards more. And the number of objects subject to such deflationary pressure tends to spread in accelerating fashion. This acceleration is due to asset deflation feeding excess capacity in industry which in turn causes falling output prices that depress demand for (and hence also prices of) resource prices, in particular labor. To the extent that such deflationary spirals typically only get triggered in the wake of major financial crises when debt levels in the private sector have grown dangerously high, the pressure from high (fixed) debt-servicing costs to lower spending in line with income declines (or even more so) is intense. This acute need to lower debt burdens gives the debt-deflation spiral such enormous virulence.

- Once deflation has settled in, there is a growing tendency for economic actors to anticipate that prices concerned will go down further. They will then become inclined to postpone purchases until later when prices of the object desired will have come down. This attitude turns the expectation of lower prices in the near future into a self-fulfilling prophecy and so renders the deflationary more powerfully entrenched.

- Fisher's interaction between debt and deflation, from whence the notion of the debt-deflation spiral, also works the other way around inasmuch as deflation obliges debtors to pay back their debts with higher-valued dollars. Their debt burden thus rises with deflation, and does so cumulatively thanks to the power of compounding (especially during periods of high "real" interest rates). The de facto increase in debt-servicing burdens caused by deflation feeds defaults and bankruptcies, thereby deepening the underlying financial crisis which drives the deflation process.

- Deflation renders traditional monetary policy rapidly ineffective. Once central bankers have pushed the short-term interest rates under their control (for example, discount rate, refinancing rate, deposit rate on reserves) down to zero, they cannot go any further. The problem then is that nominal rates at zero still translate into positive "real" interest rates when you have deflation, thereby making a recovery of investment activity (and, more generally defined, all debt-financed spending) that much harder to come by.

- The great British economist John Maynard Keynes (1930, 1936), who developed a unique understanding of money and banking under pressure, identified two other limits to monetary policy during deflationary spirals which led him to emphasize fiscal policy, specifically massive deficit-spending initiatives, as the better policy response to counter a potential or actual depression. One limit is the contractionary force of a shrinking monetary base, as more rapidly repaid or defaulting loans literally destroy the money supply. The other limit pertains to the difficulty of stimulating the economy through additional bank reserves when everybody is hoarding cash out of precaution and fear, a mass-psychological barrier he referred to as a "liquidity trap". Both of these factors played a crucial role in the Great Depression of the 1930s, the background of Keynes's analytical work, and will still prove relevant during any systemic financial crisis capable of triggering a debt-deflation spiral of the Fisher type.

The key challenge for central bankers facing such a systemic crisis is to contain its nefarious dynamic before it can unleash a full-blown debt-deflation spiral. The monetary policy response must thus be massive and rapid. Luckily, the current head of the Fed, Ben Bernanke, understands this better than most. Having made his career in academe as a historian of the Great Depression and specialist on deflation (see Bernanke, 1983,

2002, 2005), Bernanke is well aware of the traumatic events surrounding the banking crisis of 1931 that turned a serious recession into a worldwide depression.[7] As he faced the post-Lehman panic, Bernanke – the right man at the helm of the world's leading central bank for this kind of once-in-a-lifetime crisis – was determined not to repeat the Fed's mistakes eight decades earlier and to heed the lessons of Keynes.

5 EXTENSION OF TRADITIONAL MONETARY POLICY TOOLS

In response to the worst crisis since the Great Depression, the Federal Reserve has undertaken a series of different policy measures. These can be divided into two response categories. The first, discussed in this section, consists of extensions of traditional monetary-policy tools, which have had to be adjusted and/or ramped up to scale in the face of an unprecedented financial crisis. The second, analyzed in the next section, involve entirely new channels of liquidity provision designed to revive or replace financial markets that no longer work properly following their breakdown in the crisis.

Among the extensions of traditional monetary-policy tools, we can count six different initiatives.

Interest-rate Cuts

Soon after the onset of the crisis in August 2007 the Fed began an aggressive round of interest-rate cuts, pushing those rates from over 5 percent to 0 percent in little over a year. The idea here was to forestall deflation by offering the economy negative "real" interest rates, which relieve the pressure on banks and overextended debtors. The unprecedented and decisive action on interest rates went hand in hand with massive injections of liquidity designed to unclog the clogged-up US banking system. It should be noted in this context that central banks have arrived at a point where they are even contemplating how to implement possibly negative nominal interest rates, as evidenced by the recent decision (August 2009) of Sweden's Sveriges Riksbank to charge its domestic banks 0.25 percent for their reserve deposits.

Rescuing Systematically Important Financial Institutions

The Fed also took its lender-of-last-resort function a lot more seriously this time than in the Great Depression. Already in March 2008 it helped sell off Bear Stearns to JPMorgan Chase. Later on it aided the bailouts of Washington Mutual, Wachovia, and Merrill Lynch with emergency loans and loss-stop guarantees. It also allowed investment banks Goldman Sachs and Morgan Stanley to turn themselves into bank holding corporations so that these companies could benefit from access to the Fed's payments services and funding support. And, in its most dramatic bailout intervention, it provided an $85 billion credit facility to the world's leading insurance company AIG.

Where the Fed failed in its bailout function was during the fateful bankruptcy of Lehman Brothers. The Fed and the US Treasury have insisted that at the time they did not have the legal authority to save Lehman. This is at best arguable, given emergency lending to other non-bank financial institutions (for example, Bear Stearns, AIG). Under Section 13(3) of the Federal Reserve Act of 1913 the Fed has the power to provide emergency assistance to any borrower under "unusual and exigent circumstances", the same authority it has subsequently used to launch new lending programs on an unprecedented scale (see Section 6, below). The Fed's claim that Lehman did not have sufficient and adequate collateral to back such a loan rings hollow in light of other, comparable interventions, but cannot be verified independently and must therefore be taken at face value. Less clear is why the Fed could not provide a temporary stop-gap support for a few days until British bank Barclays would have had enough time to win shareholder approval for its proposed takeover of Lehman. The US could also have prevented the Lehman bankruptcy by giving Bank of America enough sweeteners to swallow the failing institution. Given that at the time there were two potential suitors of Lehman, its bankruptcy was clearly more the result of a political choice by the Bush administration to "set an example" of market failure and so counteract the moral-hazard problem.[8]

Be that as it may, in the aftermath of the Lehman débâcle, US government officials dramatically expanded existing lender-of-last-resort tools and intensified their cooperation to make sure that such a disaster would not repeat itself. The key extension was the $700 billion support given to the US Treasury by Congress, the so-called "Troubled Asset Relief Program" (TARP). These TARP funds were initially designed for an effort to buy up the banks' toxic assets, but were later used instead to recapitalize the 19 leading financial institutions of the United States (and even to help bail out the car-makers General Motors and Chrysler). The Federal Deposit Insurance Corporation (FDIC) temporarily expanded its deposit insurance from $100,000 to $250,000 per deposit and introduced a new program, the so-called "Term Liquidity Guarantee Program" (TLGP), to guarantee senior unsecured corporate debt issued by banks, thrifts, and certain holding companies.[9] At the same time the US Treasury tapped $34 billion from its Exchange Stabilization Fund to insure money-market funds which got hit with a panic run after the Lehman collapse amidst large losses by the Reserve Primary Fund.

Even though the Lehman débâcle has demonstrated the dangers of letting a systemically important institution fail, the American public has become increasingly angry at the government bailouts of banks. Part of this anger, which taps into a longstanding populist tradition of mistrusting the power of Wall Street, comes from Americans comparing the hardships they encounter in the form of job losses and home foreclosures with the royal treatment afforded government-assisted bankers whose follies caused the crisis (and subsequent hardships) in the first place. That anger was fueled to the point of hysteria in March 2009 when it became clear that government-saved bankers were continuing to pay themselves outrageously high bonuses irrespective of their performance and presumably now with the support of taxpayer funds at a time of exploding government deficits. Public anger at banks, bailouts, and the cost of the crisis did not spare the Fed, whose aggressive behind-the-scenes interventions in several bailout operations, especially in the Merrill Lynch and AIG rescues, created a large outcry in Congress once details surfaced in July 2009.

Paying Interest on Reserve Deposits

On 9 October 2008 the Fed decided to pay interest on the banks' reserve deposits, a step which Congress had authorized under the Financial Services Modernization (Gramm–Bliley–Leach) Act of 1999 and which the ECB has had in its toolbox ever since its inception that same year (1999). The Fed had initially not seen any need to put this measure into effect until the virulence of the crisis obliged it to revisit the issue. Pumping hundreds of billions of excess reserves into a paralyzed banking system after Lehman's collapse in mid-September, the Fed did not want these huge injections to drive the interbank or discount rates down to zero too fast. By setting a floor on interest rates, such a new deposit rate would enable the Fed to maintain positive short-term money-market rates in the face of massive liquidity injections and so buy some time before it would have to think of more radical new measures once it had exhausted its policy of cutting interest rates progressively. Of course, the Fed reached this zero-interest limit anyway a few months later out of its own volition. And it is also likely that the introduction of a positive deposit rate gave weary banks an additional incentive to park all that extra liquidity in their reserve accounts with the Fed rather than loaning them out, thereby making the liquidity trap worse.[10] On the other hand, the deposit rate will have the eventual benefit of greatly aiding the Fed's "exit" strategy when sufficient indication of a sustainable recover will prompt the central bank to reverse all these huge liquidity injections lest it wants inflationary pressures to intensify. Raising the deposit rate should prove a powerful tool with which to mop up the banks' excess reserves.

Money Auctions (TAF)

The Fed has also overhauled another major monetary-policy tool of long standing, the provision of short-term lending to commercial banks in dire need of funds. Such emergency lending in the Fed's discount window used to be done on an individual basis, to cover reserve deficiencies of this or that bank. The very onset of the crisis in August 2007, however, made it immediately clear that such ad hoc lending would not suffice in the face of a paralysis of the interbank market depriving hundreds of banks of usually available funds. Let us not forget that when that crisis hit on 9 August 2007, the ECB pumped €95 billion into the banking system, with other central banks following suit with somewhat smaller, but still-massive liquidity injections to unblock clogs in their segments of the global interbank market. During the following months it became clear that such money-market seizures could occur all of a sudden at any time, thanks to severely impaired balance sheets of many banks making the global investment community very nervous. So central banks developed a new, possibly permanent extension of their emergency-lending facility for funding-impaired banks, the so-called "term auction facility" (TAF), which now all the world's major central banks have adopted or are giving serious consideration to. In this procedure the central bank offers a fixed (and typically very large) amount of funds, which it auctions off to the highest bidders. In this way any bank can get the funds it needs, provided it is willing to pay for those (and has the collateral in excess of loaned amounts demanded by the Fed). Another major advantage is that by reporting TAF-based lending only in the aggregate (and conducting the auctions over the telephone and spread over the entire country), the Fed consciously does not expose details about individual banks and so avoids the "stigma" attached to going to the central bank for emergency help of the last resort. Of course, this lack of transparency concerning to whom the Fed is lending money has fueled the anger of politicians, stirred up by public outrage against billion dollar bailouts for banks, to the point of endangering the Fed's traditional political autonomy.[11]

Purchases of Government Bonds

Another monetary-policy innovation concerned the so-called "open-market operations" whereby central banks trade government securities to alter desired levels of bank reserves, the raw material of the money supply (whereby a certain level of such reserves gives rise to a supposedly stable multiple of money supply in circulation). When the central bank buys such paper, it pays for their acquisition by adding the equivalent amount to the reserves of the bank involved as counterparty (or intermediary when buying from the non-bank public). When it sells such securities, the central bank achieves the opposite – a shrinking of bank reserves and, correspondingly, the money supply as well. While it does both, your typical central bank all over the world typically buys more securities than it sells, thereby assuring a gradual expansion of its stock of government securities, which facilitates an equally steady increase in the money supply to support economic growth at a sustainable level. Of course, a side consequence of this policy is the automatic *monetization* of government debt by the central banks whose net purchases of the government's debt instruments cover a portion of its excess spending and so make it that much easier to finance budget deficits.

Central banks have until now focused exclusively on the short span of the term structure, buying and selling mostly Treasury bills with a maturity of 90 days or less. In early 2009, amidst an explosion in government deficits (amidst automatic fiscal stabilizers kicking in and adoption of massive stimulus packages), the Fed decided it was also time to buy longer-term bonds, announcing a $300 billion purchase program to that effect. The primary policy objective here was to push up the prices of these Treasury notes and bonds, which translates automatically into lower yields. Getting long-term interest rates lower in turn should stimulate business investment, construction, and household spending on large-ticket consumer items (homes, cars, and so on) all of which depend on debt financing and hence on long-term interest rates.[12] Securities purchases by the central bank had also been at the core of the so-called "quantitative easing" of the Bank of Japan during its fight against deflation in the 1990s, a series of steps to pump up bank reserves in the face of a stubborn debt-deflation spiral. Now, in the face of yet another deflation threat, the central banks of Japan, England, the European Union, and others have resumed bond-purchase programs. The Fed ended up buying far fewer bonds than expected, in effect terminating this program within six months during the summer of 2009. What prompted this reversal was the Fed's realization of the symbolic importance of such bond purchases. Aware that all great bouts of hyperinflation (for example, Germany during the early 1920s, Hungary after the Second World War) were triggered and nourished by increasingly aggressive central bank buying of government debt, international investors soon began to fear the inflationary potential of having the Fed progressively getting more involved with debt monetizing, especially when looking at a decade or so of extremely high budget deficits. The Fed really does not want such expectations! Announcing the end of its bond-purchase policy has had the added advantage of allowing the Fed to show that it was getting ready to initiate an exit strategy at a time when the first "green sprouts" sign of imminent recovery warranted preparing for such policy reversal, lest the Fed ends up being seen as encouraging a new bubble or overheating down the road.

Currency Swap Lines

A final policy extension concerns "currency swaps lines" (CSL) among the world's leading central banks through which these institutions furnish each other their respective currencies. Those are needed to meet foreign-exchange demand of financial institutions under their respective jurisdictions. Operating in a globally integrated credit system, transnational banks run balance sheets and income flows in a large variety of currencies, with currency mismatches a major source of profits from arbitrage, hedging, speculation, or intermediation activities. Borrowing cheaply in low-yield currencies and then loaning out those funds at much higher yields in the local currency is a favorite game of banks, as is more generally currency speculation which has become one of the three most significant profit sources for the largest ones among them.[13] Central banks have maintained a mutual-support system of currency swaps for half a century, ever since the General Agreement to Borrow (GAB) concluded in 1960 in response to the first incidence of generalized financial stress hitting the post-war dollar-based international monetary system known as Bretton Woods.

These CSL enable central banks to have the foreign currencies on hand which financial institutions under their control may need when unwinding assets or refinancing liabilities denominated in those different monies. The US dollar plays a particularly important role in those arrangements as the principal vehicle currency which absorbs even today a >50 percent market share in the international monetary system (measured in terms of official and private reserves, debts, invoicing of commodities, and so on). Most CSL therefore involve the dollar, obliging the Fed to cooperate closely with other central banks. This time around it was no different, except for the unprecedented scale and scope of the Fed's CLS commitments since the onset of systemic crisis in August 2007. At the center of the world's money markets is the eurocurrency market, in particular the interbank portion of it which the multiplying stressors during September 2008 hit to the point of paralysis. This blockage at the strategic epicenter of global finance suddenly deprived many non-US banks of access to short-term borrowings of dollars just at a time when these very institutions faced a spike in dollar redemptions of their clients and short-term loans coming due in dollars, both of which forced them then to unwind dollar-based assets. The CSL assured that non-US banks could survive such a crisis-induced squeeze on their dollar positions. Since the first round of crisis-induced, multi-billion CSL in late 2007 (with the ECB, the Bank of England, the Bank of Japan, and Swiss National Bank) the Fed has on several occasions opened up new CSL with additional central banks (of Canada, Mexico, Brazil, Norway, Sweden, South Korea, Singapore, Australia, New Zealand) and/or raised the sums involved in the various swap lines.

These arrangements mark an important extension of the mutual-assistance ties of the world's leading central banks, organized under the auspices of the Bank for International Settlements (BIS) based in Basel (Switzerland), and may as such herald a significant step toward greater cooperation among them. That is important when facing a globally trans-mitted crisis and may play an indispensable role in containing tensions arising from a systemically volatile international monetary system.[14] We also note in this context that China's central bank has since March 2009 also launched a variety of swaps (with Hong Kong, Malaysia, Singapore, South Korea, Indonesia, Belarus, Argentina), basically as a means to accelerate the international use and circulation of its hitherto-inconvertible currency known as yuan or also renminbi. Such internationalization, a process of catching up monetarily and financially with where China is already industrially and commercially, would create yet another chal-lenger to the dollar's predominance, together with the European Union's single currency known as the euro. Any emerging tri-polar (multi-) currency system will need a modicum of central bank coordination lest the centrifugal forces built into such a triad of monetary fragmentation are allowed to fester and come to dominate the world economy.

6   THE FED'S NEW MARKET-SUPPORT PROGRAMS

In the course of his crisis management, Bernanke soon discovered that he had underestimated its destructive force early on and that he needed to catch up to its edge sooner rather than later. Since then he has plunged ahead with a series of new programs through which the US central bank has tried to revive the broken-down credit system. These programs, of which the Fed has launched nearly two dozen since October 2008, are not very much in the public eye or under Congressional scrutiny. They have come to take the place of other, more transparent and democratically controlled crisis-management strategies which neither the White House nor Congress have the will or ability to pass into law in the face of growing public opposition. In that sense it is fair to say that the Fed is uniquely privileged, and hence politically advantaged, as the only governmental organization in the United States to spend at will without need for *ex ante* authorization by another political body. Put at the head of such an all-powerful institution an economic historian whose studies of Fed mistakes during the Great Depression convinced him of the need for innovative and unorthodox policy responses in the face of unprecedented crisis, and you have the recipe for major initiatives. Bernanke's new lending programs have evolved, one by one, in the face of exigencies. Facing a step-by-step disintegration of our credit system, punctuated by failing banks and collapsing financial markets, the Fed chair decided ad hoc, at different points of time, that this or that segment of our credit system needed a revival scheme.

Before looking in greater detail at the individual lending programs launched by the Fed since August 2007, we should keep in mind that in the context of this major crisis the traditional monetary policy course soon found the limits of its effectiveness. Once you have nominal interest rates at or near zero and the crisis is sill raging, you will need to move toward unorthodox monetary policy measures that are not usually in your repertoire. The Fed and other central banks had recent precedents for such a situation, notably the crisis-management strategies of Japan's central bank, known as "quantitative easing". In the face of a decade-long deflation the Bank of Japan flooded the banking system with unlimited amounts of bank reserves. It soon became clear, however, that Bernanke would choose a different, ultimately more far-reaching strategy of liquidity injection which he has come to characterize as "credit easing". That strategy does not rely so much on expansion of bank reserves *per se*, but focuses instead more on central bank support for purchases of financial assets in otherwise pressured or impaired markets so that the latter can revive or at least continue to function at an above-minimal level of operations. The idea was to help rebuild the broken-down credit system one step at a time by addressing concrete bottlenecks as they arose in the course of the crisis. These have included help for the mortgage market, the primary dealers, money markets, and commercial paper in particular.

Help for Mortgages

Continuing a long US tradition of promoting homeownership, policy makers soon responded to the depression hitting the US housing sector in the aftermath of the collapse of securitization following a wave of defaults among subprimes during 2007/08. Given the importance of the real-estate sector for the US economy and of the home as largest asset among a majority of American families, it also soon became evident that any sustainable US recovery would only come about with an end to the collapse of housing (prices, sales, construction). The US government increased its role in that sector's revival when it nationalized both Fannie Mae and Freddie Mac in September 2008 after having forestalled their imminent collapse in a massive rescue operation two months earlier. These two government-sponsored enterprises (GSEs) fund a large portion of housing finance in the United States and hold or guarantee more than half of all US mortgages. They are therefore an effective tool with which to counteract the tightening of credit among private lenders.[15]

In November 2008 the Federal Reserve announced that it intended to purchase up to $100 billion of direct obligations of housing-related GSEs, meaning Fannie Mae, Freddie Mac and the Federal Home Loan Banks, as well as $500 billion of MBS backed by Fannie Mae, Freddie Mac, and mortgage guarantor Ginnie Mae. This massive purchase program had the desired effect of lowering US mortgage rates by over 150 basis points to just below 5 percent within six months. In March and April 2009 these historically low mortgage rates set off a boomlet in refinancings and, by handing millions of US homeowners doing so a windfall gain, gave rise to the first signs of revival of US consumer spending after its horrific slide in late 2008 and early 2009. Encouraged by these positive signs, the Fed increased its purchase program of mortgages and MBS to $1,450 billion in March 2009, of which it had spent about half six months later.

Primary Dealers

The MBS purchases mentioned in the preceding paragraph have been organized through the Fed's network of so-called "primary dealers", a network of the world's largest financial institutions which the Federal Reserve uses to conduct its open-market operations of buying and selling securities.[16] These institutions are chosen by the Fed because of their capital size, global market presence, and wide range of services, all key comparative advantages to carry out large-scale market operations on behalf of the US central bank. Given the world-money status of the US dollar, these institutions and their operations have an innately global reach. Primary dealers are therefore the world's most-privileged, best-positioned, and strongest financial institution. Reflecting the rapidly progressing centralization and concentration of the financial sector, its numbers have declined steadily over the last couple of decades – from a high of 46 institutions in 1988 to only 18 two decades later (among which there was quite a bit of reshuffling in 2008 as some of them disappeared as independent enterprises, with new additions expected soon). They are, as of August 2009, BNP Paribas, Bank of America, Barclays,

Cantor Fitzgerald, Citigroup, Credit Suisse, Daiwa, Deutsche Bank, Goldman Sachs, the Hong Kong Shanghai Banking Corporation (HSBC), JPMorgan Chase, Jefferies & Co., Mizuho, Morgan Stanley, Nomura, the Royal Bank of Canada (RBC), the Royal Bank of Scotland (RBS), and Union Bank of Switzerland (UBS).

Among these firms are not just America's leading institutions, but also the largest British, French, German, Swiss, Japanese, and Canadian banks. And this group comprises both commercial as well as investment banks (in their function here as brokers and dealers of securities). Within the context of a rapidly globalizing and widely deregulated financial sector, these distinctions have lost much of their significance. Today's transnational bank, a characterization befitting all of these market leaders, is globally organized beyond national boundaries and combines the full gamut of financial services under one organizational "universal bank" umbrella. But from the point of view of government policy toward finance, the distinctions between national versus global and commercial-banking versus investment-banking functions still matter. The Fed deals far more extensively with national (rather than foreign) and commercial (rather than investment) banks in terms of monetary policy, access to payments services, lender-of-last-resort assistance, and regulatory restraints. The recent crisis brought this contradiction between market structure and government policy to a head, as the United States faced above all the collapse of major US investment banks (Bear Stearns, Lehman Brothers, Merrill Lynch) to the point where even the two remaining ones (Goldman Sachs, Morgan Stanley) transformed themselves into bank-holding companies with a commercial-bank license to gain access to the Fed's support channels. Keenly aware of the need to break down these outdated and increasingly artificial institutional distinctions, the Fed found that one efficient way of doing this was to target primary dealers, a group of globally organized universal banks, for special support programs.

Already in an earlier crisis, the hit to the payments systems from the 9/11 terrorist attack, the Fed launched (in October 2001) a securities lending program aimed at the primary dealers. This program offers eligible institutions securities on loan from the Fed's System Open Market Account (SOMA) on an overnight basis, with possible multiple extensions. In effect a bond-for-bond swap, whereby primary dealers can exchange their toxic assets for liquid, safe assets held in the Fed's portfolio, it is based on competitive bids and has a $5 billion limit per bank.[17] At the height of the most recent crisis, in October 2008, daily borrowing by the primary dealers through the SOMA swaps peaked at $27 billion. That activity has calmed down greatly and progressively since then, indicating an improved liquidity position for the world's leading banks.

Following the collapse of Bear Stearns, the Fed realized that its existing tool-kit *vis-à-vis* investment banks (and, to a lesser extent, foreign banks as well) was inadequate. Targeting primary dealers for further assistance would at least take care of the liquidity and solvency constraints afflicting the world's leading financial institutions, thereby shoring up the core of the world's dollar-based international monetary system and protecting the center of global finance. On 11 March 2008, the Fed dramatically expanded the existing arrangements for SOMA swaps, both in scope and length, by launching the Term Securities Lending Facility (TSLF) whereby it would lend primary dealers up to $200 billion in Treasuries for up to 28 days (rather than just overnight) and in exchange for a much larger variety of bank assets, including top-rated MBS.[18]

Five days later, on 16 March 2008, the Fed opened yet another liquidity-supply channel for primary dealers, the so-called "Primary Dealer Credit Facility" (PDCF), consisting of overnight loans, secured by eligible collateral, at the discount rate (currently at 0.5 percent) which could be rolled over indefinitely (but at a penalty rate after 45 days). Following the Lehman collapse, the range of eligible collateral was widened considerably beyond investment-grade paper, and borrowings from this facility peaked at an amazing $150 billion. The qualifying banks liked the anonymity of this facility, with the Fed publishing only aggregate data but not divulging details about individual borrowers (hence avoiding the stigma associated with seeking last-resort help from the Fed). Of course, as already mentioned earlier, this secrecy has fueled political criticism of the Fed in Congress and by the media, arising amidst intensifying public anger about banks being given such generous help. Much of that anger, as understandable as it is, does not address the tricky issue of what consequences may arise from the eventual collapse of "too-big-to-fail" institutions (a question of acute importance in the aftermath of the Lehman débâcle). Nor does that anger address the important question about which regulatory constraints and supervisory standards the primary dealers should be subjected to now that they have been given full access to the support net of the Fed.

Money-market Mutual Funds

One of the most important triggers of global panic paralyzing the world's financial markets was the declaration, on 16 September 2008, by the $60 billion Reserve Primary Fund, that heavy Lehman-related losses had pushed its net asset value below the normally guaranteed $1 level. This announcement of "breaking the buck" by the oldest money-market mutual fund (MMMF) made it clear to the global investor community that these funds, hitherto considered essentially free of risk, might not survive this extremely virulent phase of the crisis. During the next two days frightened investors withdrew $150 billion (or 4.3 percent of total MMMF assets in the United States) from MMMF, forcing the latter into massive selloffs to meet this unprecedented wave of withdrawals. As MMMF dumped assets and stopped supplying funding support, crucial money markets ceased to function normally and cut off an array of financial institutions and corporate borrowers relying on short-term borrowings. In the face of enormous money-market stress, the US government immediately began to revive those essential financial markets by backstopping the MMMF at their center.

On 19 September 2008 the US Treasury promised that it would insure MMMF deposits over the next year and set aside $50 billion from its Exchange Stabilization Fund for that purpose. On the same day the Fed introduced the so-called "Asset-Backed Commercial Paper Money Market Mutual Fund Liquidity Facility" (AMLF) through which it would lend to banks so that those could buy asset-backed commercial paper from MMMF facing heavy redemptions (in excess of 5 percent of net assets on a single day or of at least 10 percent over a week). This channel, meant to last initially for 18 months, allowed the Fed to pump emergency funds into MMMF via banks, using high-quality paper as collateral. A month later the Fed set up an additional facility, the so-called "Money Market Investor Funding Facility" (MMIFF), whereby it would fund five special-purpose vehicles (SPVs) so that those could in turn buy a large range of eligible money-market instruments with maturities ranging from 7 to 90 days (for example, commercial paper, negotiable certificates of deposit, bank notes). This backstop was designed to move MMMF and other money-market investors away from just doing overnight business and inducing them to re-engage with term instruments as a prerequisite for the revival of money markets. To the extent that those calmed down, not least due to these support measures, the MMIFF never lent any money to any SVPs before it was allowed to expire in June 2009.

Reviving Broken Financial Markets

Among the arguably most ambitious credit-easing programs launched by the Fed have been sustained and large-scale efforts to revive key money markets which had disintegrated in the wake of the Lehman collapse. The first effort in this direction targeted the crucial commercial-paper market, affecting the most widely used money-market instrument issued by a large number of financial and non-financial firms. As that market became strained, interest rates on longer-term commercial paper shot up while new issues stopped and the overall volume of outstanding paper declined. A growing percentage of outstanding commercial paper had to be refinanced daily, depriving banks and other lenders of the means to meet the credit needs of businesses and households. In early October 2008, three weeks into the full-blown credit crunch, the Fed reacted to this dire situation by introducing the so-called "Commercial Paper Funding Facility" (CPFF). Under this facility the Fed set up an SPV managed by bond trader PIMCO and provided it with funds to finance purchases of newly issued (unsecured and asset-backed) commercial paper from the issuers themselves. The CPFF has been judged a success, especially during the transition from 2008 into early 2009, when it ostensibly helped to increase the volume of new issues and drive rates lower.[19]

Six weeks later, on 25 November 2008, the Fed decided to tackle the defunct market for securitized instruments in support of consumer loans by launching its most ambitious credit-easing program as of yet, the so-called "Term Asset-Backed Securities Lending Facility" (TALF). This funding facility makes available cheap Fed loans, with a maturity of up to five years, to investors for purchases of eligible ABS. Those funds are non-recourse loans backed by thereby purchased ABS serving as collateral. This is a good deal for the investors, since their losses are limited to the payments already made on the loan in case the ABS defaults. The risk of loss, on the other hand, is bigger for the Fed, since it has no recourse to the investors it finances other than getting their (potentially much devalued) collateral. To compensate for that risk, the Fed asks its TALF borrowers to provide collateral whose current market value exceeds substantially the amount of the loan – an arrangement known as a "haircut".

By financing thereby a network of potential buyers on attractive terms, TALF facilitates the issue of new top-rated ABS. Initially, in December 2008, the Fed sought to help primarily ABS backed by consumer and business loans (that is, student loans, auto loans, credit card loans, loans to small businesses guaranteed by the Small Business Administration). In early February 2009, with TARP funds exhausted and Congress hostile to further taxpayer bailouts of banks amidst a public outcry over AIG's post-rescue bonus payments, the Fed took the politically expedient step of expanding TALF fivefold to $1 trillion and widening its eligibility to new ABS backed by commercial mortgages, (non-agency) residential mortgages, business equipment leases, leases of vehicle fleets, floor-plan loans, and mortgage servicing advances. Further extension occurred in March 2009, when TALF funds were made available to buyers of *previously* issued securities (so-called "legacy securities"). At this point the facility gained new purpose, becoming in effect a complement to the Treasury's initiative known as the Public Private Investment Program

(PPIP) whereby the Obama administration sought to help banks rid themselves of their toxic assets.[20] Most of these were MBS that had been rated AAA at the time of their issue, but were now worth a lot less than initially thought. As the relentlessly deepening real-estate crisis spilled over into commercial real estate, the Fed decided in May 2009 to include both old and new commercial mortgage-backed securities (CMBS) as collateral for TALF loans.

TALF has proven a powerful tool with which to rebuild the broken markets for loan-securitization instruments that had been hit hard by the subprime crisis and then the Lehman collapse. That crucial part of the credit system had ceased functioning in September 2008, after a year-long decline. For instance, new issues of ABS backed by consumer loans had peaked in late August 2007 at $296 billion (the total during the first eight months of the year), then fallen to $122 billion over the same period in 2008, only to collapse after the Lehman débâcle to a mere $8.2 billion issued during the final quarter of 2008. This asphyxiation of the ABS market forced banks to curtail car loans, become less generous about credit cards, and make student loans more difficult to get. All this contributed to a dramatic intensification of credit-crunch conditions, throwing the world economy off its rails in the final months of 2008 and early 2009. In the wake of this disintegration once-ready buyers of seemingly safe, yet high-yielding ABS disappeared literally from one day to the next – especially foreign banks (for example, UBS) and the structured-investment vehicles (SIVs) used by large US banks to fund securitization off their balance sheets. After Lehman the first group withdrew, and the second group simply collapsed.

The TALF experiment has revived securitization by funding a whole new group of investors willing to buy ABS, notably hedge funds. Signs of this revival abound. For instance, about $100 billion in new bonds backed by car loans or credit-card debt were issued between March and August 2008, a sixfold increase over the level issued in that ABS category during the last quarter of 2008 and not much below the $122 billion issued during the second and third quarters of 2008. TALF financed 77 percent of these new 2009 issues. Another sign of how much TALF has helped is the decline in risk premium associated with these consumer-loan ABS from 3.5 percent above LIBOR, the global benchmark for short-term borrowing, before the launch of this Fed facility to just 1.25 percent in early September 2009.[21] The TALF tranches dealing with residential and commercial mortgages or small-business loans have performed less spectacularly, not least because underlying loan pools are much more complicated and currently prone to greater losses from defaults. But even there we can see positive signs of revival. The jury is still out on TALF-funded bank efforts to unload their toxic legacy assets.

7 THE FED'S EXIT STRATEGIES

The Fed's aggressive response to the greatest financial crisis in eight decades has succeeded in pulling the economy back from the brink, in conjunction with large fiscal-stimulus packages and extensive bank-recapitalization support. The worst seems to be over. A year after the Lehman collapse we can see "green shoots" abound, even firming signs of imminent rebound in the United States and elsewhere. This raises the question of "what now" for the Fed, specifically what it needs to do in support of sustainable recovery, how to do it, and when to start doing it. These questions have no easy and obvious answers, since the central bank is operating in entirely uncharted territory. Facing options and constraints of unprecedented complexity, its choices over the next couple of years will have as much of a decisive impact as the crisis-fighting measures it took to get us here.

The Fed's Bloated Balance Sheet

Bernanke's asset-purchase and market-support programs in the face of an extremely dangerous crisis have transformed the US central bank, notably increasing its size threefold:

- This increase did not happen right away. In the initial phase of the crisis, from August 2007 to March 2008, neither size nor composition of the Fed's balance sheet changed much. It remained pegged at $800 billion, with over 95 percent in Treasuries.
- During the second phase of the crisis, from March 2008 to September 2008, the Fed's size still stayed stable. But its composition changed in the form of a major asset swap, replacing about $300 billion in Treasuries with an equivalent combination of cash reserves (through TAF), repurchasing agreements, and CSL.
- The collapse of Lehman on 15 September 2008, the catalyst for the virulent panic phase of the crisis, was followed by an extraordinary three-month expansion of the Fed from an asset base of $820 billion to a peak of $2.34 trillion by year-end. This sudden tripling in size resulted from Bernanke's rapid-fire introduction of new solvency-support and liquidity-injection channels described above (in Sections 5 and 6), notably dramatic expansion of direct bank lending through TAF or PDCF (to a peak of $550 billion in March 2009) and of CSL (all the way to $582 billion in December 2009), plus the "Maiden Lane" bailout loans for Bear Stearns and AIG (totaling $100 billion). In addition, newly launched commercial

paper/money-market facilities (MMIFF, AMLF, CPFF) grew rapidly from zero to a peak of $358 billion at the end of 2008.

- Once acute credit-crunch conditions began to subside six months after the Lehman disaster, all these emergency facilities became less important. What came to the fore instead during that fourth phase of the crisis, from March 2009 to September 2009, were the Fed's purchases of government bonds, agency debt, and MBS to drive long-term rates lower. These totaled $1 trillion over that short period of just six months.
- The gradual expansion of TALF signaled perhaps yet another phase, stretching from mid-2009 to mid-2010, when the Fed brings securitization back to life and so enables banks finally to get rid of their toxic assets. In the meantime the Fed's balance sheet continues to hover around $2 trillion; it may even grow further as TALF kicks in to full scale and the Fed's MBS purchases continue abreast.[22]

The Fed's tripling in size during the last quarter of 2008 compensated in proportional fashion for the equally dramatic declines in the money multiplier (as bank lending shrank) and money velocity (as the pace of spending slowed), much like the explosion of the US budget deficit (from 3 to 12 percent of GDP during the two-year crisis) counteracted the sharp increases in household and business savings amidst declining consumption and investment activities. It is therefore accurate to say that both expansionary fiscal policy and extremely accommodating monetary policy were the right policy prescriptions at the time. At the center of the Fed's bloated size, funding its huge lending volumes and asset purchases, are $800 billion worth of bank reserves kept with the Fed (down from a post-Lehman peak of $950 billion, but still way higher than the $100 billion norm before Lehman's failure). At some point, if and when the finance sector will have continued its healing to allow a broad-based and solid recovery take hold, the Fed will no longer need to be that large. Then all this liquidity support, which the Fed pumped into the system during the crisis, will become more problematic. While it is not clear how rapid inflationary pressures will reappear on the horizon upon recovery, excess reserves may feed new bubbles. They also pose a threat inasmuch as they may feed inflationary expectations among financial investors and other economic actors long before any signs of actual inflation, thereby threatening new rounds of instability that could endanger any fledgling recovery. This risk is acute in the face of America's super-large budget deficits and weakening dollar in connection which the large base of bank reserves may be seen as a potentially dangerous facilitator of inflationary pressures. The Fed will therefore have to execute a carefully timed and effectively planned exit strategy winding down its extraordinary support operations.

Timing of Exit

The Fed, and to a somewhat lesser extent also the other leading central banks (ECB, Bank of Japan, Bank of England, and so on), will have to be careful about when to start implementing whatever exit strategy they have decided to pursue. If they do it too early, they may choke off a still-fragile recovery and perhaps trigger enough instability among financial institutions and markets to cause a double-dip recession – a very dangerous prospect. For this type of policy mistake we have two historic precedents worth remembering: the premature tightening by the Roosevelt administration in 1937 throwing the US economy back into a sharp downturn, and the Bank of Japan's fateful tightening during the 1999–2001 period allowing sustained deflation to take hold amidst renewed recession. On the other hand, if the Fed waits too long, it may very well end up having created conditions for a resumption of inflation – surging commodity prices, cheap credit feeding too much speculation, overheating of key emerging-market economies (for example, China, Brazil), heavy monetization of large structural budget deficits, a consistently weakening dollar, and so forth. Even during 2010 and 2011, when the economy was still operating far below its potential, we saw signs of these conditions taking hold. Still, it is not likely that inflation is around the corner. The crisis has sobered much of the excess behavior of inflation-prone actors and left us with huge amounts of surplus capacity limiting the scope for higher prices. Then again, the Fed waited too long after the last two downturns (1990/91, 2000/01) to prevent ultimately dangerous bubbles from taking root. And who is to say that it will not make the same mistake again in the face of a much deeper crisis.

The Fed is mindful of this challenge, especially as pertains to expectations which tend to shape behavior that make them self-fulfilling prophecies. These depend not least on how central bankers communicate their intentions, prompting the Fed and others facing similar dilemmas to discuss openly the "when" and "how" of their exit strategies so as to reassure the public. In this context central bankers need to be mindful that loose talk among Japanese policy makers in the mid-1990s about the need to tighten actually sooner rather than later undermined the effectiveness of earlier policy stimulation aimed at countering deflationary forces.

The timing of any monetary-policy switch will surely also depend on the shape of whatever recovery takes hold. It makes quite a difference in terms of monetary-policy conduct whether the recovery is strong (V-shaped), or gradual (U-shaped), or prone to break down after the inventory cycle and fiscal stimuli have run their course (W-shaped), or too weak to carry the world economy out of its deflationary doldrums (L-shaped). Which of these outcomes we shall face is still too early to tell. In the meantime the central bankers have to prepare for any recovery pattern, a difficult task since they all require very different policy prescriptions.[23]

Operational Challenges

Our discussion of the different crisis-fighting steps taken by the Fed in the preceding two subsections indicates quite clearly that the various facilities and programs it has set up are each an innovation, thus without precedent, and uniquely constructed in their design. There is no one-size-fits-all recipe for how to scale them back or phase them out. Much depends here on the pattern of a specific program's continued purpose, as manifest in the recent evolution of demand for its services and what kind of long-term role it may have in a reconstructed finance system, if any. Depending on the answers to these two questions the Fed will have to decide which to terminate, which to scale back, and which to push harder. Some programs will just not be renewed when their expiration date comes up, as is already beginning to happen (for example, two programs for money-market mutual funds). Others will be phased out, but left open for emergency situations (as may be planned for the FDIC's debt guarantee program, for instance). Still others, especially those of a longer-term nature and/or those that have not yet come off the ground sufficiently, may actually have to be scaled up. This is the case for TALF support of residential and commercial MBS, old or new.

Where possible, the Fed may opt for a gradualist strategy of slowly making the terms of its assistance in this or that program less attractive (for example, through higher borrowing rates, larger fees, and tougher collateral restrictions). As market conditions improve, such tightening of assistance conditions makes potential users less willing to use the Fed's programs at the same time as they are also becoming more able to do without those. The kinds of adjustments depend on how the Fed sees any program over the long run. Among the two dozen or so new initiatives launched by the Fed some were clearly of an emergency nature and as such of limited duration. Their short life cycle endures for the duration of the panic, but need not persist beyond that. Most of the exceptional liquidity facilities fall under this category, other than those the Fed may wish to make permanent. For instance, if we have meaningful financial reform that includes new receivership procedures for the orderly removal of many hitherto systemically important institutions, then it might make sense for the Fed to keep the PDCF for assistance to primary dealers as the only important institutions still "too big to fail".

Similar differentiation of time horizons applies to the asset-swap programs. The Fed, for instance, was smart to cut off its program to purchase long-term government bonds after just a few months, before its continued presence would come to be seen by a skeptical global investor community as a dangerous extension of automatic debt monetization at a time of super-high US budget deficits. Such belief is fodder for fears of future inflation, and this would have made the recovery much more difficult to come by successfully. But the same question is less clear with regard to the Fed's purchases of agency debt, given the political pressures in favor of helping with mortgages as well as the transformation of Fannie and Freddie into government-controlled lenders, or with housing-related ABS where the Fed faces the difficult (and more long-term) tasks of re-creating a destroyed market structure and taking care of the banks' toxic assets otherwise still on their books. The latter may also be hard to sell without the Fed taking a significant loss, in which case it might be better for the Fed to keep impaired securities just on its own books until they mature. TALF in particular has a long way to go. It is a pathbreaking program that has just started to get off the ground, has yet to make its presence felt in several strategic areas of the credit system (MBS, equipment-lease financing, small-business lending), and will draw in a steadily widening circle of institutions as borrowers of its TALF funds, such as hedge funds, private equity funds, or pension funds. To the extent that there is a global consensus concerning the need for systemwide supervision and regulation, all financial institutions of importance will come into the orbit of the Fed's reach. And as a systemic-risk regulator, a central bank may want to have an asset-funding machine like TALF in place for more effective counter-cyclical management of bubbles (contained) and crashes (buffered).

The most important aspect of the exit strategy may well be the challenge of reining in the huge quantities of bank reserves in place and figuring out how to raise interest rates, if needed, while there may still be exceptional quantities of liquidity in the system. These objectives require complex interventions. The Fed, of course, has a large arsenal of well-tested instruments in place to drain the system of excess bank reserves, notably raising reserve requirements, accelerating asset sales, or calling back more loans. Still, its most important tools will be applied in entirely different institutional contexts than before the crisis. The new Term Auction Facility, having largely crowded out the discount window as the main channel for emergency loans to reserve-deficient banks, has yet to be tested during periods of tightening. A crucial mechanism, the reverse repurchasing agreements the Fed sets up with banks, will have to be used massively while the repo market gets revamped in the aftermath of its malfunction during the Lehman collapse. An interim measure, in the form of a credit facility for securities companies (TSLF), is set to expire in February 2010. At that point the Fed plans to replace the traditional system of clearing banks in the repo market with a new utility pledging collateral and transferring cash for borrowers. This change has proven necessary, since clearing banks have innate conflicts of interest that come to the fore during times of stress in money markets and make tensions there worse. Finally, and most importantly, the Fed has a new reserve-draining tool, the interest it pays on bank reserves, which elsewhere has worked as an effective floor. This mechanism is still very new, and the Fed has yet to learn fully how to control it best (as evidenced by some difficulties it had to absorb the lower-rate borrowing of Fannie and Freddie after their nationalization). But it is already clear from comments by Bernanke and other leaders of the Fed that it intends to put great emphasis on using deposit rates actively for management of bank reserves, much like the Bank of England, the Bank of Japan, and above all the ECB are already doing.[24]

Losses and Gains

The crisis-induced tripling of the Fed in size has so far been quite a profitable undertaking. Calculating the difference between fees and interest earned from the various liquidity facilities (for example, TAF, CSL, CPFF, TALF) it has launched since August 2007 (that is, $19 billion) and the interest it would have earned from investing the same funds in Treasury bills (that is, $5 billion), the Fed estimates that it has turned a $14 billion profit on these crisis loans. This figure is neither official (subject to audit) nor adjusted for risk. The latter is a controversial task. In the midst of the crisis, when the Fed launched these lending channels, risk premiums reached extreme levels. Under those conditions the Fed can make loans at rates lower than those demanded by panicky private lenders, but still much higher than the private market rates prevailing before the crisis for taking on the same risks. The Fed thus stands to earn enough from emergency lending during the crisis to cover any eventual losses, ending up with a likely profit even when adjusted for risk.

The $14 billion profit estimate does not give us the full picture of the impact its crisis-fighting measures have on its income statement. Let us not forget that the Fed, apart from its liquidity facilities, has also launched a $1,750 billion asset purchase program. While this huge expansion in its portfolio of Treasuries and MBS has earned the Fed an ongoing stream of interest income, the central bank could face significant losses if it ever has to sell those securities when interest rates are higher than when it purchased them. Many of the MBS on the books of the Fed are toxic assets it has taken on from eligible banks in order to relieve their burden, and those impaired assets may eventually cause the Fed some default and market losses. And it could face even more pronounced losses from its Maiden Lane loans extended during bank bailouts. Even though the US Treasury has made a nice bundle from its TARP investments in banks, earning $12.3 billion in additional income (interest, dividend, warrant sales) on $72 billion in preferred equity redemptions through which banks reimburse the Treasury for its capital injections (September 2009), it has had the benefit of getting money back from the strongest banks (for example, Goldman Sachs, JPMorgan Chase) able and willing to cut their ties to the US government. The Fed may not be so lucky. It has a $165 billion exposure from its bailout support of Bear Stearns and AIG, and these Maiden Lane loans carry a lot of default risk. If the Fed ever suffers large losses, it can get recapitalization help from the Treasury.

Long-term Questions of Institutional Context

All these facets of the Fed's exit strategy will unfold during a period of heightened uncertainty pertaining to its role, status, and modus operandi over the longer term. What does a return to "normal" mean when so much will have been changed by the crisis? Fed officials have to face this question from a variety of different angles.

First, even though the Fed under Bernanke has managed the crisis aggressively and played a major role in pulling back the US economy from the brink, its standing with the public has suffered a great deal. It is a far less respected institution than it used to be. The Fed's earlier permissiveness, both in terms of its support for deregulation and its initially benign view of asset bubbles, is seen as a major cause of the crisis. This justified blame also makes Congress hesitant to give the Fed more such powers. On the contrary, there is growing support for greater Congressional oversight of the Fed's decision making, including its conduct of monetary policy. This emerging threat to the Fed's long-cherished political independence feeds on the palpable public anger against banks and their bailouts with which the Fed is inevitably associated as well. All this plays out against a long-standing suspicion on both the Right and the Left against the Fed as one of most obscure, yet powerful levers of government encroachment in favor of elite interests. In the end the Fed's independence may be weakened in more surreptitious fashion, either by its growing engagement with other government agencies bringing their own agenda to bear (US Treasury, FDIC) or because its targeted boosting of certain sectors (for example, housing, cars, insurance) exposes it to private-sector lobbies and political pressure.

A second complication arises from the fact that the Fed's reach has dramatically expanded and will continue to do so. The Fed deals now with a far larger number of financial institutions than before (for example, hedge funds, foreign banks among primary dealers, insurance companies) and has dramatically expanded its role in many financial markets. These changes are unlikely to get reversed, and whatever regulatory reform is likely to get passed will indeed make the Fed's widened net permanent. The various reform plans under discussion right now also foresee a significant expansion of the Fed's different roles, most notably closer supervision of banks as well as systemically important non-bank financial institutions, enforcement of new banking regulations, and macro-prudential intervention capacity as "systemic-risk regulator" to identify and counteract worrisome trends in the credit system. It is not clear that the Fed has the resources to take on all these additional responsibilities effectively, beyond its conduct of monetary policy. To the extent that the Fed already had existing responsibilities in these areas, it definitely failed to use them so as to prevent the crisis we are currently living through. The Fed did not match comprehensive deregulation of banking in the 1980s and 1990s with improved supervision to see what these now-liberated bankers were up to. Its responsibilities for the protection of consumers in finance did not prevent widespread abuse and fraud in consumer banking (as in the case of sub-primes and other non-traditional mortgages). Finally, the Fed greatly facilitated, if not altogether fed, speculation-driven bubbles by keeping very lax monetary-policy conditions prevailing for too long – and made that same mistake three times in a row (1984–86, 1993–96, 2002–05). Given this consistently poor record of the Fed in crucial policy areas during recent years, one has to be skeptical as to how well the Fed can do these jobs going forward. But it is not clear that institutional alternatives to sole Fed power, such as having a group of regulatory agencies (for example, Fed, FDIC, the Securities and Exchange Commission (SEC), Treasury's Comptroller) manage systemic risk together or setting up new agencies for specific functions (for example, Barack Obama's proposed consumer finance protection agency), would work better. It makes sense to leave difficult intervention jobs to a single regulator, provided this organization is well prepared to do the job. Fed officials, from Bernanke on down, have indicated repeatedly, starting in late 2009, that they will have to make internal changes in the central bank's modus operandi as they assess the main reasons for past failure. Let us hope that the Fed knows how to learn from mistakes.

The Fed will have to make these learning-curve adjustments while its standing with the public and support from Congress has greatly eroded. As if this hostile environment does not make a difficult job even more challenging, the Fed also faces a new global environment in the aftermath of the crisis. Globally organized financial institutions need to be regulated and supervised on a transnational basis, with national regulators having to cooperate on a whole new level in terms of examining, restraining, and assisting banks together. They are building new mechanisms for such cross-border cooperation, including the BIS or the Financial Stability Board. At the same time the crisis has also demonstrated the dangers of letting global imbalances build up to the point of getting out of hand and so triggering crisis (for example, US trade deficits, surpluses and reserve build-ups among emerging-market economies, need for structural reforms in the European Union and Japan). Cooperation, probably within the new G20 network and in conjunction with a reorganized International Monetary Fund, will be required to act together in addressing the imbalances together in order to make individual adjustment paths of different countries easier to go through. The collective approach toward global imbalances will have to come about while the long-standing dollar standard gives rise to a tri-polar configuration as the euro and a fully convertible yuan challenge for the first time the dominance of the US dollar. This transition will create potentially destabilizing pressure points, forcing the Fed and other central banks to manage the tense confluence of financial centralization (fewer, larger banks) and monetary fragmentation (with three key currencies competing for global dominance).

How well the Fed will face these new challenges depends on its ability for new thinking. The crisis has exposed serious limitations in the way we conceive of the economy. A mainstream paradigm dominated by unrealistically optimistic insistence on the self-regulating stability properties of economies, efficiency of markets, and rationality of individual actors will have a hard time being prepared when the exact opposite happens – an economy riding cycles of bubbles and crashes; markets that are hardly efficient when object of speculative mania or swamped by panic; individual actors whose behavior in their social togetherness is anything but rational. These realities have to be accepted as too powerful to ignore. So we need policy makers who can anticipate cyclical behavior and the fragility of markets. And we need policy makers who have a sense of the interaction of tangible economic activity and the financial contracts supporting it.

Lastly, we would benefit from policy makers endowed with a sense that globalization creates qualitatively new interdependencies. Such thinking has to come not least also from the world of academe and research. Economists will have to do their share. We have to accept that our collective inability to foresee what was about to happen is no accident. We were blind to the presence of destabilizing forces. It is time for economists to come to grips with cycles, incorporate finance and its instability in models, and get a sense of the world economy as more than just the sum of its parts.

NOTES

1. Financial institutions' share in total US profits grew from a stable 16 percent share in the 1973–85 period to a range of 21 to 30 percent in the 1990s all the way to a peak share of 41 percent in 2007. Even more impressively, financial sector debt in the United States grew from 25 percent of GDP in 1982 to 49 percent in 1991 and an astoundingly high 121 percent in 2008. Several heterodox theories have recently focused on the broader implications of finance's centrality, as embodied in such key concepts as "financialization" and "finance-led capitalism". For Post Keynesian thinking along those lines, see Stockhammer (2004). The analysis of finance-led capitalism in Guttmann (2008) represents the tradition of the French Régulation school whereas Epstein (2005) or Tabb (2007) typify the approach taken by US radicals grouped around the URPE organization.
2. For more on America's post-Reagan transformation into a debt-fueled "bubble economy" and its three consecutive bubbles, see Guttmann (2009) as well as Guttmann and Plihon (2010). On that topic, see also Baker (2009).
3. In his only published empirical study as Fed Chair, Alan Greenspan (see Greenspan and Kennedy, 2005) provided data measuring carefully the size of home equity withdrawals and their wealth effect (impact on spending and saving patterns).
4. On collapse of securitization layers, see Dodd (2007), Guttmann (2007), and Dodd and Mills (2008).
5. Capital is crucial as a cushion against losses and hence protection against insolvency. Banks, by their very nature of financial intermediation services carrying much less capital (as a percentage of assets) than other types of businesses, met this crisis especially undercapitalized. A new global regime of self-regulation to determine risk-adjusted capital levels, known as Basel II and supervised by the Basel Committee for Banking Supervision of the Bank for International Settlements, allowed banks to underestimate systematically their capital needs and get away with it. For more on the BIS's Basel II regime, see Guttmann (2011).
6. Minsky (1992 [1993]), in his "financial instability hypothesis", distinguished between hedge borrowers whose income is at any time sufficient to pay off all debts, speculative finance where the debtor's income is large enough to cover current debt-servicing charges, and Ponzi debtors who need to borrow more to service the old debt and thus are on the way to unsustainable levels of leverage endangering their solvency. Over time the number of Ponzi debtors rises, as a prelude to the outbreak of acute financial crisis.
7. In the wake of the economic downturn following the stock-market crash of October 1929 the Fed failed to provide banks with adequate emergency funds, thereby letting them go under and failing to prevent a dramatic shrinkage of the money supply.
8. The "moral hazard" arises when banks, fully aware that they are too big to fail and will therefore be saved when facing failure, pursue excessive risks as a result. Such a course of action will reap large profits, if those risky strategies work out – and if not, then the government will step in to blunt the consequences of such failure. For more on the Bush administration officials' desire to take a hard line on Lehman out of moral-hazard concerns, see Van Duyn et al. (2008).

9. As reported by Paletta and Gongloff (2009), the FDIC's debt guarantee program helped banks issue new debt in greater volumes and lower costs at a time when their normal borrowing capacity had been seriously disrupted. The program covered over $300 billion in guaranteed debt during its first year, in exchange for banks paying the FDIC $9.3 billion in fees for this insurance.

10. The Fed's own data on the "aggregate reserves of depository institutions" shows that in the aftermath of Lehman's collapse the banks' excess reserves shot up from near zero ($1.5 billion to $9 billion on a weekly basis) to over $900 billion, where it stayed more or less for the next nine months. Consequently the M2 multiplier has declined sharply from just below 9 to barely above 5 in the course of 2009.

11. A bill, introduced in February 2009 by long-standing Fed foe Ron Paul (R-TX), to audit the Fed more aggressively and extend such audits to its monetary-policy conduct, already has 256 signatories in the House and 25 co-sponsors in the Senate.

12. This is not the first time the Fed has committed to open-market operations on the long end of the term structure of Treasuries. During the Second World War, all the way to the height of the Korean War (that is, 1951), it bought bonds to keep long-term yields below an artificially low ceiling. And in the so-called "Operation Twist" during 1960/61 the Fed sold short and bought long to deal with the simultaneous confluence of a weakening economy and a balance-of-payments crisis via a flattening of the yield curve.

13. At the center of global finance and feeding its huge currency trading (at a truly staggering volume of $2 trillion per day at its 2007 peak) are the so-called "Eurocurrency markets", a globally organized $10 trillion network of the world's leading banks offering deposits, loans, and securities in currencies outside their country of issue (for example, a dollar-denominated deposit account in London). It is extremely easy in this network to move funds across borders and from one currency into another, with a significant overlap between these euromarkets and the huge currency (that is, FOREX) market.

14. Depending on the counterparty's relative size, the Fed's currency swap lines with other central banks range from $2.5 billion to $30 billion as standing commitments. By end-2008 the Fed had a total of $554 billion of such CSL commitments with other central banks.

15. Besides channeling a lot of funds into housing through Fannie and Freddie, the Obama administration also pushed restructuring of mortgages in default and other foreclosure prevention measures financed by TARP funds while giving first-time buyers a significant tax credit of $8,000 as part of its stimulus package.

16. Primary dealers engage directly with the Fed as its counterparties whenever the central bank wants to buy or sell securities. They also engage in the auctions of the Fed as bidders. They are under obligation to cooperate in prescribed fashion with the Fed whenever the latter desires so.

17. The System Open Market Account consists of the Federal Reserve's domestic and foreign portfolios, in addition to reciprocal currency arrangements made with foreign central banks. SOMA's domestic portfolio involves US Treasury and Federal Agency securities held on both an outright and a temporary basis. The SOMA foreign currency portfolio is made up of investments denominated in euros and yen.

18. A related program launched at the same time, the Term Securities Lending Options Program (TOP), gave primary dealers an option to acquire short-term TSLF loans and so provided added liquidity during periods of heightened collateral market pressure (for example, end of quarters). TOP was suspended after only 15 months, in June 2009, indicating a return to calmer market conditions.

19. See Anderson (2009) for more on the CPFF and its likely impact.

20. Obama's PPIP initiative was originally (in March 2009) designed to provide generous government support for a network of five SPVs that would create a market for toxic bank assets, those previously mentioned legacy securities, by organizing auctions. This process would tackle the tricky problem of how to value impaired securities and provide

a means for banks to sell those off. PPIP has encountered a number of organizational start-up problems, which have prevented it so far from functioning properly.

21. See Shrivastava (2009) and Van Duyn (2009) for more details on TALF's impact on the consumer-loan tranche of the ABS market.

22. The Fed publishes its balance-sheet data weekly in a table called "Factors Affecting Reserve Balances" which is accessible through the "Economic Research & Data" link of the federalreserve.gov site.

23. See Atkins and Guha (2009) for a good discussion of the different likely recovery patterns and the implications of each for monetary policy.

24. Higher interest paid on reserves may well induce banks to hold more reserves rather than use them for lending (and money-creation) purposes. See Bernanke (2009) and Melloan (2009) for more details on the Fed's contemplations of various exit strategies

REFERENCES

Anderson, R. (2009), "The Success of the CPFF?", *Economic Synopses*, no. 18, Federal Reserve Bank of St. Louis, available at: research.stlouisfed.org/publications/es/09/ES0918.pdf (accessed April 16, 2009).

Atkins, R. and K. Guha (2009), "Comment: In search of the exit", *Financial Times*, June 29, p. 11.

Baker, D. (2009), *Plunder and Blunder: The Rise and Fall of the Bubble Economy*, Sausalito, CA: PoliPoint Press.

Bernanke, B. (1983), "Nonmonetary effects of the financial crisis in the propagation of the Great Depression", *American Economic Review*, **73** (3): 257–76.

Bernanke, B. (2002), "Deflation: making sure 'it' doesn't happen here", Remarks before the National Economists Club, Washington, DC, November 21, available at: www.federalreserve.gov/BOARDDOCS/SPEECHES/2002/20021121/default.htm (accessed July 7, 2009).

Bernanke, B. (2005), *Essays on the Great Depression*, Princeton, NJ: Princeton University Press.

Bernanke, B. (2009), "The Fed's exit strategy", *Wall Street Journal*, July 21, p. A15.

Dodd, R. (2007), "Subprimes: tentacles of a crisis", *Finance and Development*, **44** (4), IMF, Washington, DC, available at: www.imf.org/external/pubs/ft/fandd/2007/12/dodd.htm (accessed May 23, 2009).

Dodd, R. and P. Mills (2008), "Outbreak: U.S. subprime contagion", *Finance and Development*, **45** (2), IMF, Washington, DC, available at: www.imf.org/external/pubs/ft/fandd/2008/06/dodd.htm (accessed May 23, 2009).

Epstein, G. (ed.) (2005), *Financialization and the World Economy*, Cheltenham, UK and Northampton, MA, USA: Edward Elgar.

Fisher, I. (1933), "The debt-deflation theory of great depressions", *Econometrica*, **1** (4): 337–57.

Greenspan, A. and J. Kennedy (2005), "Estimates of home mortgage originations, repayments, and debt on one-to-four-family residences", Finance and Economics Discussion Series 2005-41, Federal Reserve Board, Washington, DC.

Guttmann, R. (1994), *How Credit-Money Shapes the Economy: The United States in a Global System*, Armonk, NY: M.E. Sharpe.

Guttmann, R. (2007), "The collapse of securitization: from subprimes to global credit crunch", La Lettre du CEPN 2, Centre d'Économie Paris-Nord, Villetaneuse, December, available at: www.univ-paris13.fr/CEPN/lettre_cepn_02.pdf.

Guttmann, R. (2008), "A primer on finance-led capitalism and its crisis", *Revue de la Régulation*, no. 3/4, December, available at: regulation.revues.org/document5843.html.

Guttmann, R. (2009), "Asset bubbles, debt deflation, and global imbalances", *International Journal of Political Economy*, **38** (2): 46–69.

Guttmann, R. (2011), "Basel II: a new regulatory framework for global banking", in C. Gnos and L.-P. Rochon (eds), *Credit, Money and Macroeconomic Policy: A Post-Keynesian Approach*, Cheltenham, UK and Northampton, MA, USA: Edward Elgar, pp. 145–73.

Guttmann, R. and D. Plihon (2010), "Consumer debt and financial fragility", *International Review of Applied Economics*, **24** (3): 264–82.

Keynes, J.M. (1930), *Treatise on Money*, London: Macmillan.

Keynes, J.M. (1936), *The General Theory of Money, Interest and Employment*, London: Macmillan.

Melloan, G. (2009), "Bernanke's exit dilemma", *Wall Street Journal*, August 4, p. A13.

Minsky, H. (1982), *Can "It" Happen Again?*, Armonk, NY: M.E. Sharpe.

Minsky, H. (1986), *Stabilizing An Unstable Economy*, New Haven, CT: Yale University Press.

Minsky, H. (1992 [1993]), "The 'financial instability' hypothesis", Working Paper 74, The Jerome Levy Economics Institute of Bard College, New York; published in P. Arestis and M. Sawyer (eds), *Handbook of Radical Political Economy*, Aldershot, UK and Brookfield, VT, USA: Edward Elgar.

Paletta, D. and M. Gongloff (2009), "Banks face loss of debt guarantee", *Wall Street Journal*, September 10, p. A02.

Shrivastava, A. (2009), "TALF helps revive securities", *Wall Street Journal*, September 3, p. A03.

Stockhammer, E. (2004), "Financialisation and the slowdown of accumulation", *Cambridge Journal of Economics*, **28** (5): 719–41.

Tabb, W. (2007), "The centrality of finance", *Journal of World-Systems Research*, **13** (1): 1–11.

Van Duyn, A. (2009), "Talf data point to improved loan outlook", *Financial Times*, 3 September, p. 4.

Van Duyn, A., D. Brewster and G. Tett (2008), "The Lehman legacy: catalyst of the crisis", *Financial Times*, 12 October, p. 9.

9. Monetary policy in a period of financial chaos: the political economy of the Bank of Canada in extraordinary times

Marc Lavoie and Mario Seccareccia*

1 INTRODUCTION

The events that have unfolded since August 2007 were no doubt of an extraordinary magnitude. There were many troubling signs before that date but, with the exception of those closely involved with financial markets, few seemed to care. Furthermore, we kept being told by chief economists and regulators that "the fundamentals" were sound. Then, as European investors became nervous when it became known that two large German banks were on the brink of bankruptcy because of their large holdings of US mortgage-backed securities, no one felt safe. Banks that were in a surplus position in the clearing and settlement system refused to lend on the interbank market to banks in a debit-clearing position. As a gridlock developed, the interbank interest rate shot up, forcing the European Central Bank to provide almost unlimited amounts of clearing balances to money markets in an effort to keep the overnight interest rate near its benchmark level and to make sure that clearing accounts would be settled.

In Canada, there was also a scare on the inter bank market, as the Bank of Canada was forced to engage in large repo operations on August 9 and 10, 2007, to keep the overnight rate at its target level, leaving nearly a billion and a half Canadian dollars in excess settlement balances on those two days, and hundreds of millions during the subsequent weeks, as shown in Figure 9.1. But the greatest impact was on the market for asset-backed commercial paper (ABCP). Back in 1998, a little-known company – Coventree – had started a profitable business, funding purchases of US mortgage-backed securities and mortgage derivatives by issuing short-term debt – the ABCP. Coventree was soon to be imitated by banks and other

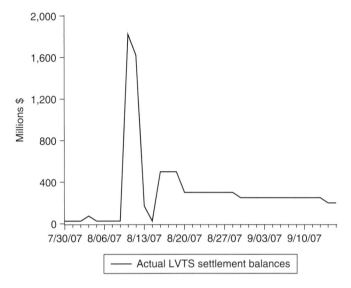

Source: Bank of Canada (http://www.bank-banque-canada.ca/en/rates/interest-look.html).

Figure 9.1   Actual LVTS balances, July–September 2007

non-bank conduits. But as the European conduits based on US mortgage-backed securities and derivatives were going down or were freezing with-. drawals, a sufficiently large number of investors were declining to rollover their take in ABCP, and hence on the morning of August 13, Coventree could not deliver. The foreign banks that were supposed to provide liquidity refused to extend a credit line, and so did the Bank of Canada which declined to participate at a meeting that was called during the previous weekend. Other non-bank ABCP issuers at first rejoiced at the difficulties that Coventree was experiencing, believing that a rival had been knocked over, but then within a few hours they realized that they were about to suffer the same fate. The entire non-bank ABCP market froze. Meanwhile the ABCP market sponsored by Canadian banks nearly shut down.

The crisis seemed to subside, however. As early as September 6, 2007, only three weeks after having decided to expand its list of collateral eligible for repo transactions so that banks could offer asset-backed commercial paper in exchange for liquidity-creating Special Purchase and Resale Agreements (SPRAs), the Bank of Canada rescinded its decision. As similar events unfolded elsewhere, once more observers were led to believe that central bankers had cleverly avoided further financial trouble. It seemed that the self-regulating forces of the financial system were

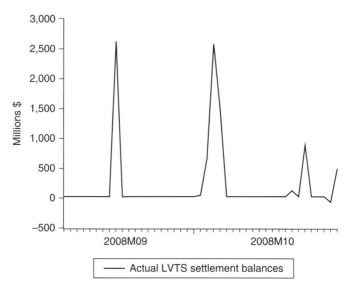

Source: Bank of Canada (http://www.bank-banque-canada.ca/en/rates/interest-look.html).

Figure 9.2   Actual LVTS balances, September–October 2008

sufficiently strong to make it resilient enough to face large losses, and that these would have no impact on the real economy. This illusion was about to persevere for another year or so, with some hiccups in financial markets and the stock market, but then, in the Fall of 2008, the financial storm was everywhere, with one piece of shocking news following another. The US government-sponsored agencies Freddie Mac and Fanny Mae had to be rescued, Wall Street banks tumbled one after the other, two large US banks – Washington Mutual and Wachovia – had to be acquired, and the giant insurer AIG had to be bailed out by the US government, as were then a string of large European banks, including the whole Icelandic banking system. It then became clear to all, especially following the refusal of the American government and the Fed to rescue the Lehman Brothers bank, that the financial crisis would spread to the real economy in a serious way. As a consequence of all this turmoil, on September 19, 2008 the Bank of Canada started weekly auctions for term repos, called "term PRAs", based on 28- or 91-day operations. Despite these term repos, the Bank of Canada was forced once more to engage in standard one-day repo operations to keep the overnight rate near its target level in September and October 2008, also leaving extra settlement balances in the payment system, as shown in Figure 9.2.

2 INFLATION AUTISM

Amusingly, while the rest of the world was crumbling into financial chaos and depression, officials at the Bank of Canada were going around making speeches about how best to measure inflation (Murray, 2008) and about whether the Bank should adopt lower inflation targets or move towards price-level targeting (Duguay, 2007; Jenkins, 2007).[1] At a time when one would have thought that financial stability would become the main concern of the Bank, its officials are still persuaded that "low, stable, and predictable inflation is the best contribution that monetary policy can make to the economic and the financial welfare of Canadians" (Bank of Canada, 2009a, p. 25). This comes as a leitmotiv in exactly, or nearly exactly, the same terms in all the speeches of Bank officials, before, during or after the crisis. Indeed, Bank officials have gone so far as to say that "an inflation-targeting regime is the best monetary policy regime for reducing the probability that asset-price bubbles will develop in the first place" (Selody and Wilkins, 2004, p. 6), being seemingly unaware that direct financial regulation would most likely do a much better job. Instead the Bank seems to be worried about both cassandras – namely the belief that prices are about to drop continuously and rentiers thinking that inflation will soon take off when problems miraculously disappear. To quash these fears, Deputy Governor Murray (2009, p. 5) has reiterated that "any unconventional action initiated by the Bank must have as its primary objective the achievement and maintenance of the Bank's 2 percent inflation target". So if any action is taken, it is not to stop the economy from reaching double-digit unemployment rates; rather it is to bring back the inflation rate towards its target.

When assessing the action that it must take to do so, Bank officials claim that they are looking at least 18 months in the future. Indeed the new consensus model which is now the bread and butter of central bankers, known as ToTEM at the Bank of Canada, is based on the assumption that the entrepreneurs form forward-looking expectations with regard to inflation. In the past, the Bank was using some measure of the NAIRU (non-accelerating inflation rate of unemployment) to estimate future inflation, but with the rate of unemployment being a rather politically sensitive variable and with a poor forecasting record, this was changed to the rate of capacity utilization in the 1990s. Then, as the so-called "Taylor rule" came to the forefront, output potential became the fashionable variable bound to produce a correct estimate of the path to be followed by inflation in the future, with the lag being estimated to be something like 18 or 24 months. While the Bank of Canada is pretty transparent in most of what it does, its measure of potential output and its associated output gap is quite obscure.

Table 9.1   *Realized real GDP quarter-over-quarter percentage change,*
            averaged per semester, versus base-case projections of the Bank
            of Canada

Year	2006		2007		2008		2009	
Semester	I	II	I	II	I	II	I	II
Realized rates	2.2	1.4	2.9	2.1	0	−1.4	−5.9	3.1
Forecast 12 months ahead	*	2.9	2.9	2.7	2.8	2.5	2.7	2.2
Forecast 6 months ahead	2.9	3.2	2.5	2.6	2.1	1.8	0.4	0.7

Note: * Not shown in April 2005 *Report.*

Sources: Various April and October issues of the *Monetary Policy Report* of the Bank of Canada; and Statistics Canada, *National Income and Expenditure Accounts.*

Ironically, most recently, the Bank has provided a somewhat more explicit definition of its output gap, relating it to the discrepancy between the growth rate of the economy and its natural rate, tied to productivity growth and the growth of the labor force (Bank of Canada, 2009a, p. 12). This, however, is not reassuring in the least, as the Bank forecasters seem to be quite unable to predict future rates of real growth, even only 12 or 6 months in advance. Table 9.1 compares the actual semester growth rates of real GDP, as measured by the national income and expenditure accounts, with the forecasts of the Bank, 12 or 6 months before the middle of the semester in question. The table shows that the Bank can err on both sides. Also, obviously, as most private forecasters, those at the Bank of Canada have completely underestimated the negative impact of the financial crisis on the real economy. In any case, as long as the Bank is unaware of a major shift, its 12-month GDP growth forecast seems to oscillate around 2.8 percent.

Still, even more amusing is the fact that the Bank of Canada is getting into a web of contradictions. Research being carried out at the Bank and elsewhere seems to indicate that the economy would benefit from any of the three alternatives being advocated by the very best of the economics profession: setting a price-level target, setting an inflation rate target closer to zero percent, and setting a deflation rate target (a *negative* inflation rate target), equal to the rate of growth of productivity so that the target interest rate is zero, as in Milton Friedman's celebrated but widely ignored essay on the optimal quantity of money. Although this research is based on abstract neoclassical theorizing about allocative efficiency, the models manage to provide numerical estimates of the potential welfare gains of moving inflation rates from 2 to 0 percent, but the estimates vary from 1 percent of GDP to as little as 0.1 percent of GDP (Amano et al., 2009).

If the Bank believes that such gains are worth going after and that the scholars advocating such alternatives have anything to say about the real world, it would seem that 2009 was the best time to put into practice any of these three alternatives. As of June 2009, the rate of inflation/deflation based on the consumer price index (CPI) was at a 15-year low of –0.3 percent on a 12-month basis, that is to say, the rate was essentially at zero. Since the main objection against lowering the inflation target is the short-run cost endured during the transition to the lower inflation rate, such costs would be avoided if the target was being changed then. One could object that while the overall inflation rate was zero in 2009, the core inflation rate was still somewhat high. Indeed, the core inflation has barely been below 2 percent during the first half of 2009. But then, if the core inflation rate is right on target, why is it that the target interest rate has been set at 1 percent or below since January 2009?

The answer naturally is that the Bank cannot ignore what is going on in financial markets or in the rest of the world when setting the target overnight rate. With the Canadian economy being in a recession and with unemployment rates quickly rising, and with banks and other financial institutions still being provided with help by the central bank and the Canadian government, it is clear that all these academic discussions about zero inflation targeting need to consider another problem, often highlighted by some Bank officials in the past, that of the zero lower bound on nominal interest rates. It is often claimed, on the basis of the new consensus model so popular among central bankers, that price-level targeting would help to alleviate the problems of the zero lower bound in achieving contra-cyclical monetary policy. However, such claims are hard to swallow when more realistic assumptions are entertained, such as inflation expectations being based on past rates, the presence of large commodity and energy shocks, and the frequency of wild fluctuations in the exchange rate, as experienced by Canada over the last couple of years, with the Canadian dollar moving up to US$1.09, then free-falling to US$0.77 less than a year later, only to move back up to US$0.90.

Whatever happens to the debate on the proper inflation target, or even whether there should be inflation targeting, "the significance of the zero lower bound has increased significantly in the aftermath of the 2007 subprime-mortgage meltdown" (ibid., p. 9). Zero interest rates are no longer a remote possibility associated with the case of Japan; it has become

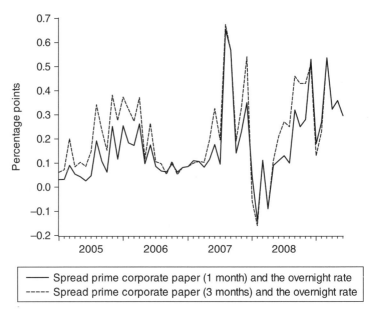

Source: Statistics Canada, CANSIM II, Series V122491, V122509, and V39050.

Figure 9.3   Evolution of spreads between prime corporate paper rates and the overnight rate, Canada, 2005–2009

a reality for the US and Canada. And with inflation rates quickly reaching zero, it is clear that the Fed and the Bank of Canada are now unable to set negative real interest rates to boost their economies, as seems to be needed to crank up the economy. Thus the standard monetary instrument of central bankers, based on Wicksellian rules, has reached its limits, making the central bank unable to pursue a more expansionary monetary policy. These difficulties associated with the zero lower bound on nominal interest rates have been extended by the rising spreads between the overnight and market rates. The spreads since the beginning of the crisis have become highly volatile and have now been much higher than what they were before the crisis, thus reinforcing the difficulties in achieving negative real rates of interest when needed, as shown in Figure 9.3.

Furthermore, all these problems are being compounded by the more stringent credit conditions. As can be seen in Figure 9.4, loan officers have been tightening lending conditions since the third quarter of 2007, when the crisis erupted, and nearly two years later, these credit conditions were still being tightened. Thus monetary policy is even more restrictive than a strict reading of the values taken by the real overnight rate.

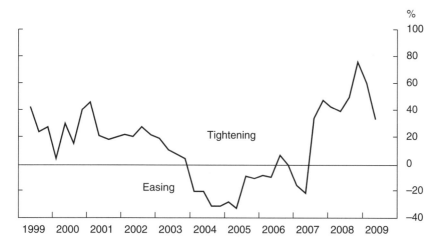

Source: Bank of Canada website, Senior Loan Officer Survey, 13 July 2009.

Figure 9.4   Overall business-lending conditions: balance of opinions

3   ZERO INTEREST RATE POLICY (ZIRP)

What else then has the Bank of Canada been able to do, or what does it intend to do in the future? In a recent document, the Bank of Canada (2009b) outlined a non-conventional approach to monetary policy, which is supposed to go beyond the currently helpless features of the so-called "conventional approach" based on interest rate targeting, inspired by a Wicksellian framework, which some authors associate with a reaction function akin to the Taylor rule. Since this approach is powerless under the zero lower bound on nominal interest rates, the Bank of Canada has devised a new framework – a zero interest rate policy (ZIRP), based on four pillars:

1. a conditional promise to keep the target overnight rate where it is for more than a year;
2. a deposit rate on bank balances equal to the target overnight rate;
3. credit easing: the Bank purchases certain private sector assets in certain credit markets, to ease pressures on these markets; and
4. quantitative easing, or unsterilized operations, designed to increase bank reserves.

The Bank of Canada makes announcements about future target overnight interest rates, promising as it did on April 21, 2009 that it would

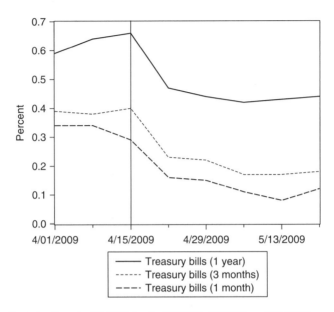

Source: Statistics Canada, CANSIM series V121777, V121778, and V121780.

Figure 9.5   Yields on Canadian government bills after promise to keep
            interest rates down on April 21, 2009 (April–May 2009,
            weekly observations)

keep the target interest rate at low levels, in this case at 0.25 percent for
more than a year, until June 2010. By so doing the Bank hoped to change
expectations about future interest rates, thus bringing down medium-term
rates. The announcements were conditional on the future behavior of
inflation rates, so as to tame fears about future high inflation rates, and
thus ensuring that medium-term rates fall relative to the overnight rate. If
interest rates were set without any consideration of possible inflationary
pressures, the announcement might lead instead to rising medium-term
rates. The Governor of the Bank of Canada, Mark Carney (2009, p. 3),
has claimed that this first unconventional feature has been quite successful, since, as a result of the conditional statement, "interest rates across the
maturity horizon of the commitment fell", as can be verified with the help
of Figure 9.5.

The second unconventional feature of ZIRP was the decision to set
the deposit rate on bank settlement balances at the target overnight rate.
Normally, as shown in Figure 9.6, the rate on central bank advances to
private banks is set 25 basis points above the target overnight rate, while

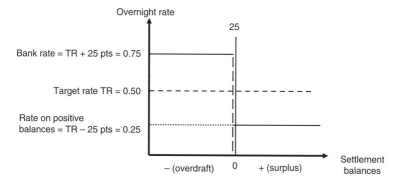

Figure 9.6 The standard corridor framework of the Bank of Canada

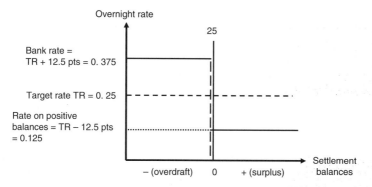

Figure 9.7 An alternative corridor framework

the rate on positive balances (that is, the deposits of banks at the central bank) is set 25 basis points below the target rate. The Bank then ensures that the overall amount of settlement balances in the system be exactly equal to zero, or nearly zero, as shown in Figure 9.6, so that the actual overnight rate stands right in the middle of the corridor, at or nearly at the target overnight rate. However, under the current circumstances, where the target rate was brought down from 0.50 to 0.25 percent, this would have meant a rate of interest on bank balances at 0 percent. We would have been back to the old situation where bank reserves were not remunerated. An alternative would have been to shrink the corridor between the Bank rate on advances and the rate on bank balances from 50 basis points (as shown in Figure 9.6) to 25 points, as suggested in Figure 9.7. The Bank could have kept the target overnight rate at 0.25 percent while remunerating the deposit balances at the Bank at some positive rate, here 0.125

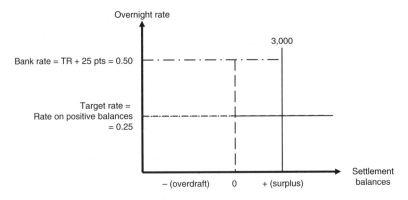

Figure 9.8   The new ZIRP floor framework of the Bank of Canada

percent. Past experience has certainly demonstrated that it is possible for the Bank to narrow the corridor to 25 basis points.

The Bank decided otherwise, however, opting for a third scheme, outlined in Figure 9.8, where the target overnight rate and the rate on positive balances are equal to each other at 0.25 percent, while the Bank rate on advances stands at 0.50 percent. Had the Bank of Canada kept the other part of its implementation tool, setting the overall amount of settlement balances at zero as usual, the actual overnight rate would have trended around the middle of this corridor, around 0.375 percent. To avoid this, the Bank decided to set on a daily basis an excess amount of settlement balances in the system, to the tune of 3 billion dollars. By doing so, there are always more banks in the clearing and settlement system that find themselves in a surplus position than there are in a deficit position. In other words, within the Canadian main clearing system – the Large Value Transfer System (LVTS) – the amount of positive LVTS balances is always larger than the amount of negative LVTS balances. As a result, the overnight rate is being pushed down to 0.25 percent, because banks in a surplus position know that they are unlikely to find a counterparty and hence have no choice other than depositing their surplus balances at the Bank of Canada at 0.25 percent.

4   QUANTITATIVE EASING

The 3 billion dollars daily excess settlement balances is a form of quantitative easing since, in the standard lingo of textbooks, banks hold 3 billion dollars of excess reserves every day. The only difference between the

Table 9.2   Quantitative easing in a mild form: excess settlement balances

Assets	80.4	75.3	Liabilities		
	March 2009	May 2009		March 2009	May 2009
Bills	13.8	13.1	Notes	51.2	52.0
Bonds	31.5	32.5	Govt deposits	28.1	19.1
PRA	34.8	29.4	Bank reserves	0	3.0

situation of bank reserves at 3 billion dollars and the standard interpretation of quantitative easing is that the excess settlement balances are being provided by moving around government deposits – actually through auctions – whereas the strict definition of quantitative easing as defined by the Bank of Canada would see the excess reserves being provided by open market operations. In reality, central banks have to conduct defensive operations on a daily basis, and the amount of reserves left in the monetary system has very little correlation with the size or even the sign of open market operations being conducted (Eichner, 1985). This is because whenever the central bank and the government enter into financial transactions with the rest of the economy, a surplus or a deficit of settlement balances is created. The central bank thus needs to neutralize the effects of these operations, as long as it wishes to achieve a given interest rate target. These neutralizing operations are no different from the sterilizing operations that need to be conducted when a country operates on a fixed exchange rate regime and desires to keep interest rates at a given level.

One may wonder why the floor system described by Figure 9.8 would apply instead of the corridor of Figure 9.7. It may be because of rising pressures from old-style monetarists at the Bank of Canada. Ever since the Bank moved to a Wicksellian approach, there have been pressures within and outside the Bank to reintroduce some monetarist elements in policy implementation (Engert and Selody, 1998; Laidler, 1999). Providing the banks with a large amount of positive settlement balances – what used to be called "excess bank reserves" – is a move which seems to follow the strictures of monetarism, according to which an increase in bank reserves would generate an increase in the money supply and in the rate of inflation. It might be just the kind of compromise that would keep peace within the Bank and that would stall criticism from monetarist-friendly academics. Table 9.2 shows the introduction of these bank reserves in the balance sheet of the central bank.

There is a lot of irony with the current situation. What is now called "conventional monetary policy" is a slightly modified version of the kind of policy implementation advocated since the late 1950s by heterodox and

Post Keynesian economists such as Nicholas Kaldor (1964) and Richard Kahn (1972) and that was put forth by Bank of England officials to the Radcliffe Committee. It has become conventional policy once more since the early 1990s, after the demise of monetarism in the mid-1980s. By contrast, unconventional monetary policy, in particular quantitative easing, is the kind of monetary policy implementation that can be found in nearly every neoclassical textbook and that central bank economists pretended to pursue in an effort to appease their academic colleagues and as a response to both politicians and an outraged public (Bindseil, 2004; Tucker, 2004). Officials at the Bank of Canada are quite aware of this paradox, and are obviously uncomfortable with it, as the following statement shows.

> Although quantitative easing is now referred to as an unconventional monetary policy tool, the purchase of government securities is, in fact, the conventional textbooks approach to monetary policy. . . . In practice, most central banks have chosen to conduct monetary policy by targeting the price of liquidity because the relationship between the amounts of liquidity provided by the central bank and monetary aggregates on the one hand, and between monetary aggregates and aggregate demand and inflation on the other, are not very stable. (Bank of Canada, 2009b, p. 26)

The Bank of Canada thus feels compelled to recall that monetary aggregates are very badly correlated with price inflation, and that base money is also very badly correlated with the money supply. To provide excess bank reserves, as recommended by monetarists, central banks must decline to sterilize their liquidity-creating financial operations or must conduct open-market operations by purchasing assets. As pointed out by Deputy Governor John Murray (2009), "All quantitative easing is, by definition, 'unsterilized'. Although this is correctly viewed as unconventional, it closely resembles the way monetary policy is described in most undergraduate textbooks, and is broadly similar to how it was conducted in the heyday of monetarism". Murray misleadingly insinuates that such a technique has been implemented before, namely during the 1975–82 monetarist experiment in Canada. What can really be said is that quantitative easing is an attempt to put into practice what academics have been preaching in their textbooks for decades from their ivory towers. It is merely monetarism but in reverse gear. While monetarist policy of the 1970s was implemented to reduce the rate of inflation, current monetarist quantitative easing is being applied to generate an *increase* in the rate of inflation.

As a result, the claims of quantitative easing are just as misleading as the claims of monetarism of the 1970s and early 1980s. Bank of Canada officials claim: "The expansion of the amount of settlement balances available to [banks] would encourage them to acquire assets or increase the supply of credit to households and businesses. This would increase the supply of deposits" (Bank of Canada, 2009b, p. 26), adding that quantitative easing injects "additional central bank reserves into the financial system, which deposit-taking institutions can use to generate additional loans" (Murray, 2009). In our opinion, these statements are misleading and indeed completely wrong. They rely on the monetarist causation, endorsed in all neoclassical textbooks, which goes from reserves to credit and monetary aggregates. It implies that banks wait to get reserves before granting new loans. This has been demonstrated to be completely false in the world of no compulsory reserves in which we have lived since 1994. In any event, even before 1994, as argued by a former official at the Bank of Canada, the task of central banks is precisely to provide the amount of base money that banks require (Clinton, 1991). Banks do not wait for new reserves to grant credit. What they are looking for are creditworthy borrowers.

Quantitative easing is an essentially useless channel. It assumes that credit is supply constrained. It assumes that banks will grant more loans because they have more settlement balances. Both of these assumptions are likely to be false, at least in Canada. With the possible exception of its impact on the term structure of interest rates, the only effect of quantitative easing might be to lower interest rates on some assets relative to the target overnight rate, as these assets are being purchased by the central bank through its open-market operations. It is doubtful that the amplitude of these interest rate changes will have any impact on private borrowing or on the exchange rate. Indeed, in Japan, which has had experience with zero interest rates for many years, quantitative easing was pursued relentlessly between 2001 and 2004, but with no effect, as "the expansion of reserves has not been associated with an expansion of bank lending" (MacLean, 2006, p. 96). Indeed, officials at the Bank of Japan did not themselves believe that quantitative easing could on its own be of any help, but they tried it anyway as a result of the pressure and advice of international experts. As Ito (2004, p. 27) notes in relation to the Bank of Japan, "Given that the interest rate is zero, no policy measures are available to lift the inflation rate to positive territory . . . The Bank did not have the tools to achieve it".

5 CREDIT EASING

Whereas quantitative easing targets the liability side of the balance sheet of a central bank, credit easing – the only other tool left – targets the asset side. In a sense, this is the tool that has been most pursued in Canada, but not necessarily or exclusively by the Bank of Canada. In fact, credit easing has shown that central bank independence is an illusion. Once again, at

Table 9.3   Evolution of some assets of chartered banks, August 2008 to March 2009

Chartered bank assets	August 2008	March 2009
Mortgages	487	434
Corporate securities	168	116
T-bills	28	53
Canadian govt bonds	126	211
Total	1,733	1,787

least to some extent, this has been recognized by officials at the Bank of Canada:

> Just as the boundary between monetary stability and financial stability becomes increasingly blurred in the midst of a financial crisis, so too does the boundary between monetary and fiscal policy actions. It isn't uncommon for both central bank and governments to initiate credit-easing measures, and it is important that the two work together. (Murray, 2009)

Indeed, while the size of the balance sheet of the Bank of Canada moved up from $53 billion in August 2008 to $80 billion in March 2009, the total amount of Government of Canada securities outstanding jumped from $402 billion to $497 billion during the same time period. This increase in the amount of gross debt of the Canadian government is totally unrelated to government deficits, since the 2008–09 fiscal year showed a nearly balanced budget. Thus, all of this, or nearly all of this, occurred before the Canadian government started racking up large deficits as a result of the economic recession. The increase in the outstanding gross debt must therefore be (nearly) entirely attributed to the efforts of the Canadian government to conduct credit easing in collaboration with the Bank of Canada.

Where did the $100 billion or so of additional Canadian government securities go? To a large extent, they ended up on the balance sheet of the banks. This is shown in Table 9.3, where the major assets of Canadian banks are shown as of August 2008 and March 2009. The amount of T-bills and Canadian government bonds held by banks has risen by $110 billion during these seven months, while banks managed to get rid of corporate securities and mortgages, reducing the sum of these assets by a combined nearly similar amount. But then, where did the mortgages go? They were purchased by the Canada Mortgage and Housing Corporation (CMHC) to the tune of $51 billion as of March 2009, through the Insured Mortgage Purchase Program launched in September 2008 (Government of Canada, Department of Finance, 2009, p. 117). Indeed $125 billion

Table 9.4   The CMHC acquires mortgages with loans from the federal government

Banks		CHMC	
Assets	Liabilities	Assets	Liabilities
Mortgages −$50 B		Mortgages +$50 B	Loans from the
Govt bonds +$50 B			federal govt +$50 B

Federal government	
Assets	Liabilities
Claims on CMHC +$50 B	Government bonds +$50 B

has been set aside for this program ($25 and $50 billion in the September 2008 and November 2008 announcements, and another $50 billion in the January 2009 budget), although the program later stalled as banks were more reluctant to give out their mortgages.

But then, how did the CMHC acquire the mortgages? They acquired them by obtaining loans from the federal government. Credit easing through the Insured Mortgage Purchase Program may thus be understood through Table 9.4, which provides a series of balance sheets. The federal government makes a loan to the CMHC, which allows the banks to offload their mortgages onto the CMHC. The federal government loan is financed by the issue of securities. These securities in turn are sold to banks, which purchase them with the proceeds of the sale of their mortgage assets to the CMHC.

Credit easing can be understood through two processes. We have already outlined the first one, which does not involve the central bank. The second process corresponds to the term PRA facility, that is, the various term purchase and resale agreements conducted by the Bank of Canada since mid-September 2008. As is well known, these repo operations are equivalent to making a collaterized loan, but with the collateral being legally in the hands of the lender. The Bank was then agreeing to purchase for one month or three months various public or private assets. The composition of these assets has varied through time, as shown in Table 9.5, with banks and primary dealers offering as collateral either long-term securities or less liquid assets, such as asset-backed commercial paper issued by conduits that had been sponsored by banks, the market of which, as explained earlier, had been nearly collapsing for a lack of customers. Still, about 50 percent of the collateral backing term PRAs is systematically made up of federal government securities. Pure credit

Table 9.5   Composition of the term purchase and resale agreements conducted by the Bank of Canada ($bn)

	2008		2009			
	November	December	January	February	March	April
Government of Canada securities	16.0	20.7	20.6	18.2	18.7	14.5
Provincial securities	9.8	8.0	11.1	13.1	11.1	10.6
Municipal securities	0	0.1	0.2	0.2	0.2	0.1
Corporate securities	5.7	5.6	3.7	3.9	4.8	4.7
ABCP	2.9	3.2	2.5	1.5	1.1	0.9
Total	34.4	37.7	38.2	37.0	35.9	29.4

Note: All numbers are rounded.

Source: Supplementary information of balance sheet loans and receivables, Bank of Canada, various months (http://www.bankofcanada.ca/about/corporate-governance/bank-of-canada-statement-financial-position/?page_moved=1).

easing, however, involves neutralizing operations. Neutralization occurs when the Bank of Canada sells its holdings of Treasury bills to the banks or the primary dealers. That the Bank conducts such outright sales to neutralize the effect of the repo operations associated with credit easing is quite obvious in the notice that announces these sales for "balance sheet management purposes". The Bank explains that "this transaction will partially offset the temporary increase in assets associated with the term purchase and resale transactions" announced the previous day (Bank of Canada, 2008).

During the first two weeks of October 2008, the Bank of Canada was selling the Treasury bills that it held on its own balance sheet. The increase of term PRAs on the asset side of the balance sheet of the Bank of Canada were thus being compensated by a fall of an almost exactly equal amount of Treasury bills also on the asset side. In other words, the central bank was exchanging advances to the private sector in lieu of advances to the public sector. Thus, in this case and during the period from July 2008 to mid-October 2008, the size of the balance sheet of the Bank of Canada did not change by much.[2]

However, as happened with the Fed, from mid-October on, the Bank of Canada started to follow a different approach in its efforts to provide more liquidity to term credit markets. From then on, the size of the Bank's balance sheet grew very quickly, as the Bank was acquiring Treasury bills newly issued by the Government of Canada, providing the Canadian government

Table 9.6   Impact of term PRA operations on LVTS balances when the size of the balance sheet of the Bank of Canada is rising

Banks		Bank of Canada	
Assets	Liabilities	Assets	Liabilities
Long-term securities –$30 B LVTS balances +$30 B		Term RPAs +$30 B LVTS balances –$30 B	
		T-bills +$30 B	Government deposits +$30 B
T-bills +$30 B LVTS balances –$30 B		T-bills –$30 B LVTS balances +$30 B	
Long-term securities –$30 B T-bills +$30 B		Term RPAs +$30 B	Government deposits +$30 B

with deposits at the Bank in return. The acquired Treasury bills were then sold in turn to the banks as a way to neutralize the effects of the liquidity-creating term repo operations. In so doing, the Bank managed to keep its stock of Treasury bills at an approximately constant level, while the size of its balance sheet grew by the sum of the granted term advances and term PRAs. Table 9.6 outlines the sequence of monetary operations conducted by the Bank of Canada and their impact on LVTS balances, with the last row of the table representing the final result of the previous three operations.

The term PRA operations have a double impact. On the one hand, they tend to reduce interest rates on the assets acquired as collateral by the Bank of Canada, as their supply in private portfolios gets reduced. On the other hand, banks wind up with a more liquid balance sheet, as they can easily sell their newly acquired Treasury bills or use them for their own repo operations to obtain cash. To sum up, term repo operations can be understood as transactions that remove less liquid assets from the balance sheets of banks – mainly long-term federal, provincial, municipal and corporate securities as well as asset-backed corporate paper – putting in their place the highly liquid treasury bills.

Figures 9.9 and 9.10 illustrates the two variants of the credit easing mechanism involving the central bank, by showing the evolution of the balance sheet of the Bank of Canada from July 2008 to June 2009. The size of the balance sheet reached its peak on April 1, 2009. At that time, the Bank's holdings of T-bills had fallen by about $8 billion relative to July 2008, while the amount of PRAs had increased by $34 billion, for a net addition of about $26 billion. As a counterpart, on the liability side, the government deposits had also increased by about $26 billion. During

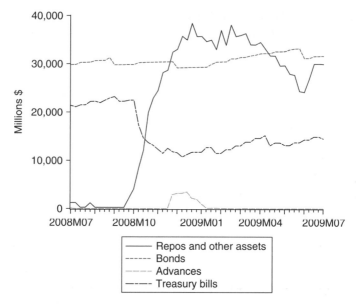

Source: Statistics Canada, CANSIM Series V36612, V36613, V36634, V36635, and V44201362.

Figure 9.9 *Evolution of the assets of the Bank of Canada, July 2008 to June 2009*

both periods, there was hardly any change in the size of the monetary base (notes plus bank reserves). More recently, as can be seen from Figure 9.9, the credit easing operations have tended to go into reverse gear, perhaps an indication that tensions on term financial credit markets are not as severe as they were in the last quarter of 2008 and the first quarter of 2009.

Table 9.7 describes, in a very rough and approximate way, what has been going on at the level of the entire economy between August 2008 and March 2009. We use a matrix based on the quadruple entry principle, first outlined by Copeland (1949), where by definition, the sum of each row and of each column must be zero, so that there is no black hole. As a result, any change in one cell induces at least three other changes, since each row and each column must sum to zero. A liability carries a negative sign, and thus –100 then means an increase of 100 in this liability, while +100 would imply a reduction in that liability. An asset carries a positive sign, and thus –45 then means a decrease of 45 in the holdings of that asset. The table supposes that the economy can be divided into six sectors: the federal government, the central bank on its own, banks, non-bank

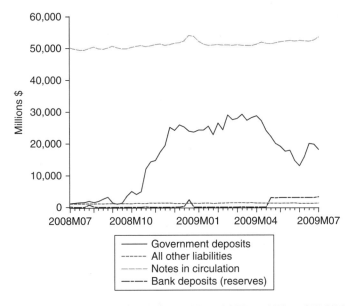

Source: Statistics Canada, CANSIM Series V36625, V36628, V36632, and V36636.

Figure 9.10 Evolution of the liabilities of the Bank of Canada, July 2008 to June 2009

Table 9.7 Indicative evolution of various balance sheets from the recognition of the existence of a financial crisis (August 2008) to its peak (March 2009)

	Govt	B of C	Banks	NBFI	FGBE	House-holds
T-Bills	−100	−10	+110			
Mortgages			−45	−30	+75	
Deposits at B of C	+25	−25				
Deposits at banks			−50	+20		+30
ABCP				+30		−30
Bank loan			+20	−20		
PRA		+35	−35			
Claims	+75				−75	
Total	0	0	0	0	0	0

Note: B of C: Bank of Canada; NBFI: non-banking financial institution; FGBE: financial government business entity (here in particular the CMHC).

financial institutions or the shadow banking sector, financial government business entities (essentially the CMHC), and households. Changes in the balance sheets of firms have been left out.

The changes that are represented illustrate what we consider to be stylized facts. The changes in the balance sheet of the central bank are nearly exactly those given by the actual data of Figures 9.9 and 9.10. Changes in the balance sheet of the government are also quite close to reality, with the government issuing 100 billion dollars worth of new securities, the counterpart of which are their deposits at the Bank of Canada and advances to government agencies. In the case of banks, changes in holdings of government securities, in mortgages and in repos also reflect actual numbers. Other changes are essentially illustrative, with the assumption that households and the shadow banking system (say mutual funds) hold more banking deposits. It is also assumed that banks make more loans to non-bank financial institutions, essentially because households hold less asset-backed corporate paper previously issued by the shadow banking sector. The last two changes thus force this sector to borrow funds from the banking system and to sell part of its mortgage portfolio to financial government business entities. This sector, as pointed out earlier, holds more mortgages thanks to advances from the government.

6 CONCLUSION

The ongoing financial crisis since the summer of 2007 has revealed the underlying structural weakness of the monetary policy system put in place since the early 1990s when the Bank of Canada officially adopted a hybrid Wicksellian policy of inflation targeting via interest rate setting. In a deep recession in which the forces of deflation are present, the zero lower bound on nominal interest rates prevents the central bank from conducting discretionary interest rate policy much as it did during the 1930s. In ensuring that interbank settlement balances remain persistently positive, the Bank of Canada has de facto pegged the overnight rate at approximately zero for about a year. The conventional monetary policy view, in which the "maestro" at the central bank conducts discretionary interest rate policy and the fiscal authorities sit as mere spectators, has been shattered by the current financial crisis.

What has come to predominate in this new ZIRP environment is a set of unconventional policy measures – quantitative and credit easing – affecting both the asset and liability sides of banks' balance sheets. These policy choices may be considered as offshoots of the critical role of central banks as purveyors of liquidity. However they are now being justified within a policy framework that bring us back to the heydays of monetarism. This is particularly so with quantitative easing which, according to its advocates, is conceived of as something more than a measure that pins down the settlement balances of banks in a positive position in order to ensure that the overnight rate remains at its minimum level. Positive LVTS settlement balances are now seen as the supply-side infusion that would sustain bank lending in times of crisis. Credit easing, on the other hand, affects the composition of bank assets through term repo operations by transforming less-liquid into more-liquid bank assets.

As we pointed out, none of these measures can *per se* generate bank credit expansion since banks are not liquidity constrained but rather face a scarcity of creditworthy borrowers. The abandonment of discretionary interest rate policy and the replacement of the latter with ad hoc tinkering on the supply side imply that central bankers have not yet learned the fundamental lessons of the 1930s as crystallized in the central bank metaphor of "pushing on a string". During times of deep recession, the monetary emperor has no clothes. Central banks can only be a useful appendage to expansionary fiscal policy, with the latter doing the important work of reversing the downward trajectory of the private sector.

NOTES

*   This chapter was finalized in July 2009, less than a year after the worst of the financial crisis had passed in both Canada and internationally. Our analysis, with the supporting data, pertains exclusively to the two-year period immediately before the time of writing. Since June 2010, the Bank of Canada returned to a semblance of normality by reverting back to its pre-2007 era of inflation targeting, with zero settlement balances and a standard corridor system. No effort has been undertaken to update the chapter, except for Table 9.1.
1. To be fair, the Governor of the Bank, David Dodge, did make a speech identifying the main causes of the financial crisis as early as September 12, 2007. Still, this was one month after the gridlock on interbank markets. Subsequently, as one would expect, there have been many other speeches by various Bank officials about the financial crisis.
2. Although there was a $4 billion increase in the last two weeks of September, along the same line as the subsequent $10 billion increase of the last two weeks of October.

REFERENCES

Amano, R., T. Carter and D. Coletti (2009), "Next step for Canadian monetary policy", *Bank of Canada Review*, Spring, 5–18.
Bank of Canada (2008), "Notices and announcement; Bank of Canada to sell Treasury bills for balance sheet management purposes", 15 October available at: http://www.bankofcanada.ca/en/notices_fmd/2008/not151008_tbill.html (accessed 13 February 2011).

Bank of Canada (2009a), *Monetary Policy Report*, April.

Bank of Canada (2009b), "Framework for conducting monetary policy at low interest rates", Annex to the *Monetary Policy Report*, April.

Bindseil, U. (2004), *Monetary Policy Implementation: Theory–Past–Present*, Oxford: Oxford University Press.

Carney, M. (2009), "Opening statement to the Standing Senate Committee on Banking, Trade and Commerce", Bank of Canada, 6 May, available at: http://www.bankofcanada.ca/2009/05/speeches/opening statement-67 (accessed 13 February 2011).

Clinton, K. (1991), "Bank of Canada cash management: the main technique for implementing monetary policy", *Bank of Canada Review*, January, 3–32.

Copeland, M.A. (1949), "Social accounting for moneyflows", *The Accounting Review*, 24, July, 254–64.

Duguay, P. (2007), "The Bank of Canada's research agenda and the future of inflation targeting", speech to the Canadian Association for Business Economics in Kingston, Bank of Canada, 27 August, available at: http://www.bankofcanada.ca/en/speeches/2007/sp07-15.html (accessed 13 February 2011).

Eichner, A.S. (1985), "The demand curve for money further reconsidered", in Eichner, *Toward a New Economics: Essays in Post-Keynesian and Institutionalist Theory*, Armonk, NY: M.E. Sharpe, pp. 98–112.

Engert, W. and J. Selody (1998), "Uncertainty and multiple paradigms of the transmission mechanism", Working Paper 98-7, Bank of Canada.

Government of Canada, Department of Finance (2009), *Canada's Economic Plan: A First Report to Canadians*, tabled in the House of Commons by James M. Flaherty, 10 March, available at: http://www.plandaction.gc.ca/grfx/docs/ecoplan_e.pdf (accessed 13 February 2011).

Ito, T. (2004), "Inflation targeting and Japan: why has the Bank of Japan not adopted inflation targeting", Working Paper 10818, NBER working paper series, available at: http://www.nber.org/papers/w10818.pdf (accessed 13 February 2011).

Jenkins, P. (2007), "Modern central banking: a Canadian perspective", presentation to the HEC Montréal, Bank of Canada, 20 October, available at: http://www.bankofcanada.ca/2007/10/speeches/modern-central-banking-canadian-perspective (accessed 13 February 2011).

Kahn, R.F. (1972), "Memorandum of evidence submitted to the Radcliffe Committee", in Kahn, *Selected Essays on Employment and Growth*, Cambridge: Cambridge University Press, pp. 124–52.

Kaldor, N. (1964), "Monetary policy, economic stability and growth", in *Essays on Economic Policy*, vol. 1, London: Duckworth, pp. 128–53.

Laidler, D. (1999), "Passive money, active money, and monetary policy", *Bank of Canada Review*, Summer, 15–25.

MacLean, B. (2006), "Avoiding a great depression but getting a great recession: the Bank of Japan and Japanese macroeconomic policy, 1991–2004", *International Journal of Political Economy*, 35 (1), Spring, 84–107.

Murray, J. (2008), "Measuring inflation: methodology and misconceptions", speech to the Certified General Accountants of Ontario in Toronto, Bank of Canada, 18 September, available at: http://www.bankofcanada.ca/2008/09/speeches/measuring-inflation-methodology-misconceptions (accessed 13 February 2011).

Murray, J. (2009), "When the unconventional becomes conventional: monetary policy in extraordinary times", speech to the Global interdependence center in Philadelphia, Bank of Canada, 19 May, http://www.bankofcanada.ca/2009/05/ speeches/unconventional-becomes-conventional-monetary-policy (accessed 13 February 2011).

Selody, J. and C. Wilkins (2004), "Asset prices and monetary policy: a Canadian perspective on the issues", *Bank of Canada Review*, Autumn, 3–14.

Tucker, P. (2004), "Managing the central bank's balance sheet: where monetary policy meets financial stability", *Bank of England Quarterly Bulletin*, Autumn, 359–82.

10. The euro and its guardian of stability: fiction and reality of the 10th anniversary blast

Jörg Bibow*

1 INTRODUCTION

As the tenth anniversary of the euro's launch neared, European Union (EU) policy makers felt they deserved to be in celebratory mood. Economic growth in the core of Europe had finally picked up in 2006 and the dark clouds that had appeared in the seemingly bright blue sky since August 2007 were believed to pass by Europe's "zone of stability" thanks to diligently pursued "stability-oriented" macroeconomic policies that had steered the union away from "global imbalances" elsewhere in the world economy. EU Commissioner for Economic and Monetary Affairs Joaquín Almunia (2008) probably captured the mood of European pride about being a "pole of stability for the global economy" well when he declared in a foreword to the official *EMU@10* success story volume that must have been written early enough in the year:

> A full decade after Europe's leaders took the decision to launch the euro, we have good reason to be proud of our single currency. The Economic and Monetary Union [EMU] and the euro are a major success. For its member countries, EMU has anchored macroeconomic stability, and increased cross-border trade, financial integration and investment. For the EU as a whole, the euro is a keystone of further economic integration and a potent symbol of our growing political unity. And for the world, the euro is a major new pillar in the international monetary system and a pole of stability for the global economy. As the euro area enlarges in the coming years, its benefits will increasingly spread to the new EU members that joined in 2004 and 2007.

As party time arrived on 1 January 2009, the European economy was in free fall and speculations about an imminent breakup of "Euroland" (officially: euro area, the group of EU countries that have adopted the euro) soared in financial markets. Somebody must have taken the punch bowl away all too early, but who? While one set of illusions concerning

Euroland as an island of stability in a stormy sea were brutally shattered, another set of illusions still prevails among key European policy makers: the view of Europe as the victim of external shocks, unfairly pushed off track by reckless policies pursued elsewhere.

This chapter sets out to question and demolish these unfounded beliefs. It argues that Europe had not only contributed handsomely to the build-up of global imbalances since the 1990s and came to experience their implosive unwinding as an internal crisis from the beginning, but had also nourished its own homemade intra-Euroland and intra-EU imbalances, the simultaneous implosion of which further aggravated Europe's predicament – striking as a "triple whammy" perfect storm. Contrary to the naive idea of quickly returning to proven pre-crisis stability-oriented policy wisdom, the analysis in this chapter suggests that those stale ideas which inspired the EMU policy regime agreed upon in Maastricht in the early 1990s (the "Maastricht regime") should better be trashed to avoid a continuation of malperformance. Apart from the paramount problem of leaders who are the slaves of defunct spirits whose thoughts are wholly unsuitable for Europe today, one complicating factor is that the legacies of intra-European imbalances will make a fresh start so much more difficult. Another is that the global environment may be less favorable than during the first 10 years, and provide head- rather than tailwinds.

The focus of the analysis will be on the role of the European Central Bank (ECB) and the "Eurosystem", that is, the decentralized central bank system including the ECB and the national central banks (NCBs) of EU member states that have adopted the euro, as the guardian of the euro's stability. The analysis starts in Section 2 with an overview of the policy regime underlying Europe's EMU, highlighting the regime's peculiarities and crucial deficiencies while focusing on the pivotal role of the Eurosystem. The regime's historical origins in German ideas and Bundesbank mythology are then explored in Section 3. The analysis of Euroland's performance under the Maastricht regime prior to the global crisis is the subject of Section 4, while Section 5 investigates how Europe has coped in its aftermath. Section 6 concludes.

2 THE MAASTRICHT REGIME OF EMU AND THE EURO'S GUARDIAN OF STABILITY

Some 11 years after its launch on 1 January 1999, Europe's "single currency" was shared by only 16 of the 27 EU member states. Some old (that is, pre-2004 enlargement) EU members either by law (that is, "opt-out clause", the UK and Denmark) or practice (Sweden), continue to hold on to their national currencies. While four of the new EU members have adopted the euro (Slovenia, Malta, Cyprus and Slovakia), the majority has yet to meet the entry conditions to be admitted to the select euro club. Suffice to say that not all European countries are EU members, and may not even currently aspire to become such, with prominent non-members including Switzerland and Norway. Meanwhile the euro has come to play a significant international role in the union's neighboring region (including Russia).

In discussing the political economy of central banking in Europe, two questions need to be asked. One is whether a common currency may or may not make sense in principle for Europe or particular countries. Another – related but distinct – issue is whether the particular regime of EMU chosen as the foundation of the euro is likely to foster its members' economic fortunes in sustainable ways, even if the first question were answered in the affirmative. My focus in what follows will be on the latter issue: to highlight the peculiarities of the Maastricht regime of EMU in guiding economic policies, foremost in those countries that have already adopted the euro, but to a degree also in countries that aspire to do so; and also with wider regional and global ramifications, for regime flaws rather than the idea of a common European currency as such are to blame for Europe's malaise.

The Maastricht regime is truly special and unique in featuring a federal supranational monetary authority paired with national fiscal authorities. Reflecting the fact that the EU is not a proper political union, there is no common federal budget (to speak of) and, in fact, no European state standing behind the common currency over which member states agreed to share control. In other words, member states agreed to surrender their monetary, but not their fiscal, sovereignty. This divorce between money and the state (and public finances) has always seemed alien and troublesome from a Chartalist perspective (see Goodhart, 1998), contrasting with optimum currency area theorists' preoccupations with market rigidities that are held to hinder the smooth functioning of a common market sharing a common money (money being associated with the market rather than the state from this mainstream perspective).

The designers of the Maastricht regime underwent considerable difficulty in conceiving safeguards that would really ensure this peculiar divorce and the envisaged watertight separation between monetary and fiscal policies. In particular, the ECB as well as the NCBs of (all) EU member states – together forming the European System of Central Banks (ESCB), as distinct from the Eurosystem – are prohibited from "monetizing" public debt through direct purchases of public debts. To further protect "the printing press", constraints were put on public debt financing too. In particular, budget deficits exceeding 3 percent of GDP are generally deemed "excessive" and offenders will normally face penalties under the Excessive Deficit Procedure (EDP) unless they can claim special circumstances for erring from the prescribed path of fiscal virtue. The principles of fiscal virtue laid out in the Maastricht Treaty were further underscored by the Stability and Growth Pact (SGP), which requires members to attain a budget "in balance or in surplus" over the cycle. Finally, to protect the national partners from each other's fiscal failings a "no bailout" clause was included in the Maastricht Treaty, supposedly containing any national solvency issues at the respective national level at which they might arise.

All this was held to make the euro currency super sound and protect its guardians of stability – central bankers – from any conceivable political interference, including fiscal pressures. Given all this revealed distrust of (elected) politicians, it is of course quite ironic that Europe's (unelected) central bank politicians are not facing any effective discipline at all – a situation I dubbed the "Maastricht paradox" (Bibow, 2002). As no effective check was put in place to balance the ECB's authority (or whim), it is probably fair to say that the ECB is the world's most unconstrained (that is, independent and unaccountable) central bank. The bank publishes reports, holds regular press conferences, and its president engages in a "Monetary Dialogue" with a subcommittee of the European Parliament, but none of this publicity has any "bite" in the sense that the bank might face any real consequences for its own (mis)conduct.

Essentially the euro is managed by a federal supranational central bank that is not properly accountable to either national or European political authorities. The guardian's mandate as laid down in the Treaty is to "maintain price stability" and, without prejudice to this *primary* objective, to contribute to the achievement of other objectives pursued by the union (such as growth and employment). No doubt this mandate offers central bankers an enormous degree of independence, that is, *discretion*, in interpreting "price stability" and how to attain it, and in deciding what may constitute risks to this primary objective (and thus circumscribe the bank's support for any other goals). Moreover, and perhaps most importantly, the ECB's peculiar form of central bank independence is enshrined in the Treaty, which means that the ECB also enjoys the virtual absence of credible threats to have its constitution changed.

By purposeful design there is thus a clear dominance of central bankers and monetary policy within the Maastricht regime. In fact, not only does it lack a federal euro treasury, there is not even any proper coordination of national fiscal policies beyond the asymmetric constraints placed on national policies arising from the SGP and the "multilateral surveillance" process conducted under the auspices of the European Commission and the EU's Council of (Economics and Finance) Ministers (Ecofin).[1] As a result, "Euroland's overall fiscal stance is not deliberately set – so as to help stabilizing domestic demand in Euroland as a whole – but essentially the random outcome of national budget plans" (Bibow 2007c: 303). Asymmetrically constraining national fiscal policies by deficit ceilings also compromises member states' only remaining policy instrument for dealing with *asymmetric shocks*. And a further implication is that, beyond the working of the built-in stabilizers (and even more so if the stabilizers are not actually allowed to work automatically), monetary policy has to shoulder the main burden in countering *common shocks*. In line with the supposed dominance of monetary policy over fiscal policy and primary concern with central bank independence, the macro policy mix is left to the central bankers. In essence, the Maastricht regime has no-one "minding the store" (that is, stabilizing domestic demand and employment) unless central bankers – as benevolent dictators – choose to do so.

Relations between the monetary and fiscal/political authorities also concern exchange rate policy *vis-à-vis* non-EU members, an area in which the Maastricht regime has left a peculiar vacuum. The possibility of "general orientations" to be laid down by finance ministers under certain conditions is mentioned in the Treaty, but in practice any political influence on the euro's exchange rate is largely left to the actual interaction of the players involved. By words both the ECB and the Eurogroup have laid claim to their primacy. The ECB seems to have gained the de facto upper hand in an area which elsewhere is clearly under the control of the political authorities. First, the vacuum of legal responsibility and resulting ambiguity in practice may jeopardize one of the euro's key original motivations, namely that of acting as a protection shield against external developments. Second, this ambiguity also undermines Europe's part in global policy coordination. At the regional level the exchange rate issue also matters greatly to aspirants of euro adoption, as one of the entry criteria is two-year participation in the revised (euro-centered) exchange rate mechanism (ERM2).

A no less critical issue for Euroland members actually concerns intra-Euroland "exchange rates". For while *nominal* exchange rates between members have of course ceased to exist with the euro, competitiveness positions (or *real* exchange rates) are still liable to change, namely when wage and/or productivity trends diverge within the union. Like fiscal and social policies, wage policies in Euroland too remain a national affair, since wages are agreed by *national* "social partners" (and perhaps under the guidance of national policy makers). Effectively, national wage trends – by determining relative unit labor costs – have become the equivalent of intra-Euroland exchange rates. It is thus quite ironic that coordination is conspicuous in its absence in this area given that intra-area exchange rates were supposed to be a "matter of common concern" since the beginnings of European integration.

Instead, Europe's policy makers cherish the romantic idea that "liberalized" and "flexible" markets would generate any required adjustments on their own and without any further policy interferences with market forces. So guided by the "principles of an open market economy" and to raise and unleash Europe's growth potential in full, the whole focus of the EU's policy agenda has been to foster market flexibility. Ever since the Single Market Program of the 1980s and no less with the Lisbon Agenda, (and later Europe 2020) the EU Commission has been the champion of Europe's peculiarly one-sided "structural reform" policy orientation. In conjunction with the ECB's "stability-oriented" (price-stability only) policy focus, micro reforms are apparently held to deliver not only micro efficiency, but macro stability too. Market liberalization and integration are of course two sides of the same coin. But while creating a common European market has indeed made great progress since the 1980s in many areas, including financial integration, policy integration (or harmonization or even coordination), in some areas – including prudential supervision of pan-European financial institutions – is still peculiarly lacking today.

Prudential supervision has remained foremost a national prerogative, just as ultimate responsibility for financial stability in general also rests at the national level, too. This reflects the fact that in the absence of a fiscal union, solvency problems of European financial institutions can only be addressed at the national, rather than the union, level. This has left vital union-wide systemic questions unanswered, and the ECB once again fits oddly into the overall governance system. In monetary policy matters the politically unchallengeable ECB stands supreme as the supposed cockpit of the Eurosystem. By contrast, regarding financial stability policy, while the NCBs may play varying roles in their respective national financial system realms, the Treaty merely asks the ESCB to "contribute to the smooth conduct of policies pursued by the competent authorities relating to prudential supervision of credit institutions and the stability of the financial system", mentioning almost in passing that "specific tasks concerning policies relating to the prudential supervision of credit institutions may be conferred upon the ECB". In the absence of more explicit responsibilities regarding financial stability policy, it has once again been left to the ECB to decide whether and how to fill the systemic void, should such need arise, using the monetary policy instruments and powers at its disposal.

Additional complexity in this area arises from the fact that the UK, hosting Europe's foremost global financial center in London, remains outside Euroland to this day (and for the foreseeable future), so that the Bank of England, while not part of the Eurosystem, is bound to feature prominently in the ESCB (depending on whatever responsibilities the British authorities may assign to the bank in the financial stability arena). Further scope for ambiguity once again relates to the fiscal issue; given the general practical difficulty of distinguishing liquidity and solvency problems, the ECB's position as a "lender of last resort" is inevitably a particularly delicate one. If emergency liquidity provisions to individual institutions were to haunt the bank as "solvency support turned sour", that is, central bank losses, the ECB could find itself negotiating its own recapitalization with national finance ministers – the very nightmare of compromising the ECB's independence that the designers of the Maastricht regime were so keen to rule out completely. Perhaps too firmly believing that price stability cum liberalized markets would guarantee both macro stability as well as financial system stability, the regime designers overlooked that Europe's supposedly integrated financial system would be made especially vulnerable at the systemic level for all those fiscal "safeguards", lacking both integrated financial supervision and a lender of last resort with a guaranteed fiscal backstop, that is, "deep (Treasury) pockets".

After highlighting that the Maastricht regime of EMU with the Eurosystem at its core features important peculiarities, it is now time to emphasize that the euro's guardian of stability has interpreted its special role in rather peculiar ways. In fact, from its inception the ECB, the Eurosystem's cockpit, has expressed rather idiosyncratic views on monetary policy. In particular, the ECB has been adamant in emphasizing that it was not in the business of inflation targeting. Instead, the ECB offered its "definition" of price stability as "a year-on-year increase in the Harmonized Index of Consumer Prices (HICP) for the euro area of below 2 percent" to be maintained "over the medium term" (ECB, MB, 1998), a definition later "clarified" as the aim of maintaining inflation "below but close" to 2 percent over the medium term. The ECB devised a "two-pillar stability-oriented" policy strategy which in its revised form includes an "economic analysis" of a variety of fairly conventional short-term economic indicators to be "cross-checked" by a "monetary analysis" featuring the broad monetary aggregate M3.[2] Together the two pillars are supposed to enable the ECB to assess the medium-term outlook and risks to price stability and to communicate its assessments and policy decisions to interested observers.

The more obvious contrasts to conventional inflation (forecast) targeting are to be seen in the fact that the ECB has failed to provide an explicitly symmetric price stability definition and that policy makers refuse to own what the bank publishes as its regular "staff projections". These differences provide revealing hints concerning the ECB's notorious asymmetry in approach and preference for retaining its scope for discretion. It would be only fair to add here though that at least the latter characteristic is broadly shared by the US Federal Reserve, which, moreover, until recently did not provide any definition of price stability either. In any case, the crux of the matter is rooted in contrasting policy mandates and their respective interpretations. Whereas the Fed was given a "dual mandate" that makes it very hard for it to deny responsibility for rising US unemployment in the case of recession, the ECB's mandate, by clearly prioritizing price stability, opens the door for the bank to deny any such responsibility if risks to its primary objective are believed to exist.

This leads us to the less obvious difference between the ECB's "stability-oriented" approach and inflation (forecast) targeting. Given that the latter approach prioritizes the attainment of the inflation target over other objectives, the key contrasting feature only emerges when policy makers' understanding of the relationship between price stability (or inflation) and other objectives is taken into account. In inflation targeting, the base case relationship is of a Phillips curve type, which at least by enlightened mainstream researchers and policy makers is acknowledged to be rather flat at low levels of inflation (see CEPR, 2002, for instance). The situation is very different at the ECB, which professes an acute dislike for any "output gap" measure. At issue is much more than just difficulties of measurement which undoubtedly exist in this regard – at issue is an outright rejection of "fine tuning" the economy. A "medium-term approach" to maintaining price stability by a "non-activist" policy is what the ECB claims to aspire to. From the ECB's perspective any concern for stagnant output, apart from its potential relevance for maintaining price stability "in the medium term", would be wholly misguided (see Bibow, 2004 for further discussion).

The ECB has therefore presented an "elegant" solution to fulfilling its official Treaty obligation to contribute to objectives other than price stability, namely that by maintaining price stability the ECB quite simply fulfills its job in total since, on the ECB's view, "maintaining price stability *in itself* contributes to the achievement of output and employment goals" (ECB, MB, 1999: 40; emphasis added). On the occasion of a Monetary Dialogue session, at which supposedly the ECB is "held to account", the ECB's first president Wim Duisenberg, who also used to refer to price stability as the ECB's "sole" objective, explained: "we always maintain – and we still do – that the best contribution that monetary policy can give to fulfill that second task is to maintain price stability" (Duisenberg, 2001). Similarly, the ECB's second president Jean-Claude Trichet later reiterated that "there is one needle in our compass and it is price stability" (Reuters, 2008).

Mainstream researchers have yet to come to grips with what lies behind the ECB's approach and mindset. A Center for Economic Policy Research report of 2002 provides a telling example:

> In this remarkable interpretation of the Treaty, the ECB fulfills its double mandate by reducing it to a single responsibility, a focus solely on price stability. All other objectives are then realized automatically. In this view the ECB cannot be held responsible for what happens in the real economy. We consider that this view is not just narrow, but mistaken. (CEPR, 2002: 12)

I shall have more to say on this vital issue below. Here we summarize that essentially, on the ECB's view, price stability somehow *causes* growth. If the economy refuses to grow while price stability is maintained, this cannot possibly constitute any additional responsibility for monetary policy. Instead, potential sources behind such malperformance include structural problems, ill-guided fiscal policies, or irresponsible policies and shocks originating in the rest of world.

To a large extent, the ECB's view is also Europe's official view, with the European Commission representing the other proponent of the policy wisdom that a sound combination of confidence-boosting structural reforms and "stability-oriented" macro policies will deliver the best of all possible worlds. In fact, key officials profess sufficient confidence in this peculiar wisdom to announce that the world at large would be best served by following Europe's model. For instance, just days before the Lehman collapse, EU Commissioner Joaquín Almunia announced: "I would be very happy if other central banks would follow the same criteria as the ECB in preserving price stability" (FT.com, 2008a). In July 2008, a year after the outbreak of the global crisis, the ECB implemented its "stability-oriented" wisdom by hiking interest rates – alone among the world's leading central banks. The next section investigates the historical origins behind the ECB's guiding principles and Europe's official view.

3   HISTORICAL ORIGINS OF THE MAASTRICHT REGIME: THE BUNDESBANK "SUCCESS STORY"

Put briefly, the historical intellectual origins behind the ECB's guiding principles and Europe's official view today are all German, just as the Maastricht regime is of German design and the ECB is modeled on the Bundesbank. So what we are really investigating are the historical roots of "the German view" and Bundesbank price stability mantra, and why the German view prevailed in Europe when the EMU regime was designed.

The first thing to note is that the Bundesbank's acclaimed independence arose as historical accident. The supposed independence of the

Bank deutscher Lander (BdL, the Bundesbank's forerunner) was neither imposed upon (West) Germany by the Allies, nor was it really intended in its actual form by the first federal government led by Konrad Adenauer, nor can it claim any theoretic grounding in the ordoliberal tradition of Walter Eucken (Bibow, 2009a).

The next thing to note is that in aspiring independence, the BdL/ Bundesbank developed its political instincts quickly and played its cards rather well. That central bankers were blessed with a head start *vis-à-vis* (West) Germany's first federal government was probably important. Over the years, the bank successfully self-stylized itself in the public's view as the guardian of stability and host of unchallengeable economic wisdom in the country. In achieving this position, orchestrated public conflicts with the government of the day formed an important aspect in its public relations strategy (see Katzenstein, 1987; Marsh, 1992; Johnson, 1998). Rather than serving as a politically accountable team-player in any government's economic program, German central bankers took it upon themselves to play the role of opponent or even referee *vis-à-vis* other political actors; promoting the idea that an independent central bank would somehow be directly accountable to the general public.

Another important aspect in the public relations strategy was the nourishing of hyperinflation fears by rewriting Germany's history. Johnson (1998: 199) refers to the Bundesbank's "orchestrated efforts to reinsert memories of the hyperinflation of the 1920s into Germany's postwar political mythology". It is true that Weimar Germany suffered severe hyperinflation in 1922–23. Yet, it is also true that Germany was brutally hit in the Great Depression.[3] While in the US the national crisis led to the New Deal under Franklin Roosevelt, across the Atlantic it delivered the death blow to Weimar Germany and paved the way for the rise of Adolf Hitler and Nazi Germany – with known consequences for Europe and the world. The very real consequences of Hitler for Germany itself, apart from millions of deaths and considerable destruction, included the fact that Germany ceased to exist in May 1945, to be re-established under Allied control as two countries in 1949, which followed a currency reform in the three western zones in 1948 that had given birth to the deutschmark – the stability-oriented guardianship for which the Bundesbank (established in 1957) would become reputable. Financially the Federal Republic of (West) Germany started with a fresh balance sheet, a new currency, a cleaned-up banking system, and little public debt.

It is surely remarkable that while memories of the Great Depression are still haunting US policy makers today, the Great Depression seems to have been deleted from the collective German memory – despite the fact that Germany was hit as hard as the US. Instead, German history – as propagated by independent central bankers – apparently featured *two* hyperinflations. First, there was the actual one that I referred to above, but then there allegedly was a second one following Hitler – suppressed while he was still inflicting his mass destructive lunacies – which then hit German savers with a lag; they thereby lost their savings, yet again in one generation. The picture of inflation, deflation, war, and losses is becoming seriously distorted. In view of the unspeakable monstrosities and immeasurable grief that Nazi Germany brought upon mankind, it is surely nothing short of embarrassing that German public figures should even mention those "poor" German savers who tragically lost their savings, of all things material or breathing, in those events. Just imagine someone who, say, as a car driver killed three children sitting in the backseat through "experimental driving" to then mention to the surviving father (who happens to be his neighbor and still tries to be his friend and partner), how very tragic it was, from the driver's perspective, that his favorite tie got ruined in that event. What a shameful tribute to German savers to declare Nazi Germany's "Total War" a monetary phenomenon!

But I can also see whom this kind of disgraceful historical fiction might have served rather well. In this conveniently redrafted history it was the Weimar hyperinflation which led straight to Hitler and another (suppressed) hyperinflation, with the Great Depression written out of the picture. It may then appear as if Germans might really have some justification in feeling neurotic about inflation, and every reason to adore the stability-oriented guardian who defends them against yet another hyperinflation, the threat of which is apparently ever-present.[4] German policy makers are notorious for seeing inflation risks everywhere while showing no concern whatsoever about threats of deflation and a repeat of the Great Depression experience. Only one thing is on the German mind, it seems: (hyper) inflation.

This leads me to the key peculiarity about German-style monetary policy: a conspicuous asymmetry in mindset and approach. The ECB may be portrayed as a driver who is quick to slam on the brakes, but highly reluctant to ever use the accelerator, with this asymmetric driving style giving rise to an "anti-growth bias". Historically, this peculiar policy style may be traced back to Germany's acclaimed independent central bankers. Start with Wilhelm Vocke, for instance, member of the Directorate of the German Reichsbank, 1919–39, president of the Directorate of the BdL, 1948–57, who then became the first Bundesbank president in 1957. In his memoirs, Vocke (1973) categorically declared that "every inflation starts in public finances as public expenditures get inflated". While Vocke seems to have distilled all his wisdom from Germany's notorious hyperinflation past, Otmar Issing, chief economist of the Bundesbank from 1990 to 1998 (who then went on to hold that position at the ECB in its critical formation years from 1998 to 2006), was also fond of recalling the lessons from the 1970s, observing: "Artificially stimulating the economy by large budget deficits and/or inflationary monetary policy is no viable option. In fact, history tells us that such policies can only provide temporary straw fires, with potentially damaging long-term consequences" (Issing, 2003).

Issing's point concerns fine tuning and the supposedly superior non-activist medium-term approach he favors. Note, however, that there appears to be nothing artificial about choking the economy, which becomes quite naturally necessary whenever "stability-oriented" central bankers believe inflation risks to require such activist policy reaction. The real question then becomes how this kind of asymmetry could possibly *not* give rise to an anti-growth bias.

To address this conundrum and understand why Germany's monetary anthem of "price stability above all else" actually worked for both the country and the Bundesbank, we need to account for international and regional monetary arrangements and the behavior of Germany's trading partners. (Western) European reconstruction and recovery following the Second World War started out within the Bretton Woods regime of exchange rates pegged to the US dollar. It did not take long for Europe to start thinking about alternatives that would make exchange rates within Europe even more stable, while making Europe less dependent on the United States. The interwar experience of "beggar-thy-neighbor" competitive devaluations provided the background to this craving for stable exchange rates. While earlier initiatives did not come to much, the establishment of the European Monetary System (EMS) in the late 1970s marks the starting point of the process that led to Europe's Economic and Monetary Union as we know it today.

Within German "stability culture", the Bundesbank's part was to enforce discipline, both budgetary and wage discipline. The result was not only low inflation, but inflation *lower* than that of Germany's trading partners. And that is an important factor within any system of pegged nominal exchange rates. For, over time, a country with relatively low inflation gains in competitiveness which is boosting its export performance. Stability-oriented policy worked well under the Bretton Woods regime, establishing both Germany's export-oriented growth strategy and the Bundesbank's claim to fame as inflation fighter.

Essentially, the establishment of the EMS then recreated the same conditions within Europe in the 1980s. As Europe pegged its currencies to the deutschmark while still having significantly higher inflation, rising competitiveness again fired Germany's export motor and the country ran up a 5 percent of GDP current account surplus over the 1980s.

Another factor is important here. In the late 1970s, Germany had for once bowed to international pressure and agreed to act as "locomotive" and applied fiscal stimulus. As inflation soared with the second oil price shock, the outcome was judged a policy failure. For instance, and typical for habitual references by German policy makers, Issing's "straw fire" remark refers to this episode, an experience never to be repeated. In fact, with the change in government in 1982, Germany officially ended any attempt at demand management, with balancing the budget attaining policy priority. The predictable result was domestic demand stagnation and rising unemployment. What rescued Germany in the first half of the 1980s was the Reagan expansion and strong US dollar. The export motor was then sustained in the second half of the 1980s as the competitiveness gains within the EMS came through. Germany ended the decade not only with a large current account surplus, but also with a balanced budget.

Bundesbank virtues of stability and discipline thus found all the support they needed within the German political elite when it came to laying down the right policy regime for Europe. What works for Germany will also work for Europe. In fact, they must have thought that if everybody were to adopt German stability culture, things would work even better for everyone. In Germany, price stability and fiscal discipline caused growth, it seemed, when actually it was *relative* price stability that did the trick.

Why did Europe accept the "made in Germany" Maastricht regime? I said above that the EMS provided the starting point of what became EMU. By intention and design, the EMS was supposed to be a "symmetric" system of equal partners, bestowing no special status on any particular country or currency to act as "anchor", but constructing the synthetic European Currency Unit as a basket of participating currencies instead. Ideals of equality were one thing; in reality, the EMS evolved into a larger deutschmark zone over the course of the 1980s, with the Bundesbank pulling the monetary shots in Europe.

It is easy to see that especially Germany's larger European partners did not really appreciate this outcome and came to see EMU as their best option to partly regain monetary sovereignty, namely by establishing shared control over a common European currency. German monetary hegemony in Europe was not a politically tolerable long-term solution, particularly after German unification – an event that may have accelerated EMU. Nor was it economically sound to have a central bank with the mandate to maintain price stability in Germany set monetary policy for Europe. Yet, given the deutschmark's anchor role within Europe, Germany was, de facto, the only country left to yet surrender its monetary sovereignty; and therefore in a strong bargaining position. For domestic political reasons, Helmut Kohl, German Chancellor at the time, had to make sure of having the Bundesbank "on board", as selling the euro to the German populace would hardly have been possible without public sanctioning by the trusted guardian of the beloved deutschmark. This meant that the Bundesbank could dictate the conditions of its own abdication of monetary rule over Europe. The conditions it laid down were such that probably even the Bundesbank itself considered it unlikely that Europe would swallow them. That Europeans did so after all is foremost a reflection of their yearning to overcome Bundesbank supremacy.

As a result, Euroland members today share sovereignty in monetary control, but much of Europe ended up operating under a central bank single-mindedly focused on maintaining price stability and national finance ministers who are constrained in making a balanced budget the primary goal of their policy making. The euro is a currency without a state or federal treasury backing it. In this regime, monetary policy has no role in stabilizing the economy apart from maintaining price stability; national fiscal policies have no such role to play either, apart from whatever support might come from built-in automatic fiscal stabilizers. It is not the economy, but policy itself, that needs to be stabilized. Germans like to speak of "stability" rather than "stabilization" policy. "Blinded by success", German policy makers failed to understand that they were asking for trouble by expecting others to follow the German model – the workability of which depends precisely on others behaving differently.[5]

4   EUROPE'S (MAL)PERFORMANCE UNDER THE MAASTRICHT REGIME

From a Keynesian vantage point, the conditions for the Maastricht regime to work at all for Euroland may be identified as follows: monetary policy would have to boost domestic demand sufficiently to prevent fiscal policy from becoming too much of a drag, the global environment and euro exchange rate needed to be benign, and wage trends and structural reforms had to be such as not to create serious intra-area imbalances either (Kregel, 1999; Bibow, 2001). In actual fact, these conditions have not been met consistently since the 1990s and Euroland's economic performance has proved correspondingly disappointing. Unsurprisingly, in view of its central role, the ECB bears the foremost responsibility for this outcome.

This section singles out three prominent cases of malperformance or policy blunders. The first concerns Euroland's business cycle, which features brief booms, long periods of stagnation, and astonishing export dependency. The second concerns the outstandingly counterproductive way of interaction between monetary and fiscal policies in the period of protracted stagnation between 2001 and 2005, producing a phenomenon which I dubbed "tax-push inflation" (Bibow, 1998, 2006). The third is that

Source: OECD, *Economic Outlook*, no. 85 (June 2009).

Figure 10.1   Economic growth since Maastricht in Euroland, Germany, and the US

the Maastricht regime and official view have not acted as a "glue" nour-ishing convergence among members, but actually amplified divergences within the union in rather dangerous ways.

To begin with, exporting the German model to Europe through the Maastricht regime meant that inflation would be low across Europe, while all countries would try to balance their budgets at the same time. When German stability policy was jointly applied across Europe in the early 1990s, the predictable result was domestic demand stagnation and rising unemployment. Even by 1996 it looked as though EMU was not going to take off because stagnation kept budget deficits above the 3 percent ceiling across the continent. Luckily, the US "new economy" boom and strong US dollar came to the rescue, and 11 countries qualified in the spring of 1998 to launch the euro in January 1999. In other words, laboring under the Maastricht constraints, Europe failed to generate sufficient homemade demand growth, but benevolent external forces allowed the euro to get off the ground just on time.

Figure 10.1 shows the recession in Euroland in the early 1990s fol-lowing the Bundesbank's tight money crusade in response to German

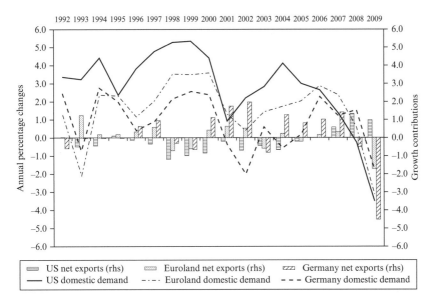

Source: OECD, *Economic Outlook*, no. 85 (June 2009).

Figure 10.2   German model features remarkable export dependence

unification – an asymmetric shock hitting the anchor country, the monetary policy reaction to which was transmitted throughout Europe through the EMS, once more convincing Germany's partners how useful it would be to get rid of Bundesbank supremacy. Both recessions in the early 1990s and early 2000s were followed by protracted domestic demand weakness, most pronounced in Germany itself, as Figure 10.2 reveals by separating domestic demand growth and net export contributions to GDP growth.

But Figure 10.2 also shows that the euro area actually experienced a brief period of stronger domestic demand growth toward the end of the 1990s (and again in 2006–07), even as the Asian crisis meant negative net export contributions in the earlier episode. A key driving force behind this burst of growth was "interest rate convergence". In the 1990s, as the introduction of the euro neared, interest rates in incipient member countries converged toward their lower German levels. This process provided an important temporary boost to asset prices and domestic demand in countries other than Germany, countries such as Spain and Ireland. The same kind of process was repeated in the 2000s around the time of entry of the new EU member countries in Eastern and Central Europe as the prospect

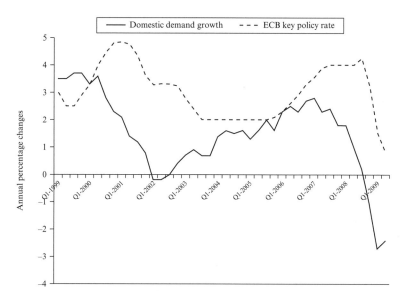

Note: Policy rate in percent; domestic demand (excluding inventories) as contribution to GDP growth in percentage points.

Source: Eurostat, ECB.

Figure 10.3   Quick to hike, slow to ease

of EU membership – to be followed by euro adoption – again encouraged markets to engage in "convergence play". Between 2003 and 2008 these countries were the recipients of massive capital inflows, leaving uncompetitive exchange rates, asset price bubbles and domestic demand booms, and huge current account deficits in their wake. It is important to note that this is a one-off adjustment in interest rates and asset prices, which runs its course – and may end in tears (see below).

It is instructive to take a closer look now at the 2001–05 period, during which "the eurozone was the sick giant of the world economy" (Wolf, 2007). Figure 10.1 shows that Germany and Euroland participated in the 2001 "global slowdown", while Figure 10.2 highlights that, in their case, this episode featured above all a collapse in domestic demand. The collapse in domestic demand followed the aggressive monetary tightening by the ECB that can be seen in Figure 10.3, which had the unfortunate side-effect of crashing the euro and thereby driving up inflation (see Figure 10.4).[6] With inflation pushed up in this way from its (too!) low starting level of just 0.8 percent in 1999 to *above* 2 percent, the ECB felt all too

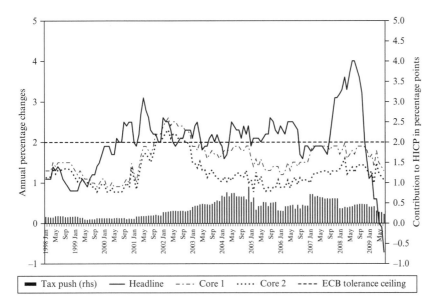

Source: Eurostat, ECB.

Figure 10.4   Headline inflation obsession backfires to ruin ECB's record

justified in sitting tight and adopting a "wait-and-see" approach while domestic demand stagnated.

Alas, this non-activist approach ("steadyhandedness") had rather predictable consequences for public finances. As ever more member states were facing "excessive deficit procedures" (or the threat thereof), among their widespread procyclical retrenchment measures increases in "administered prices" and indirect taxes came to feature rather prominently, pushing up headline inflation which, in turn, meant more "wait and see" from the ECB. Note the irony here: with central bankers single-mindedly focused on squeezing inflation "below 2 percent" and finance ministers single-mindedly focused on bringing the deficit "below 3 percent", by shooting each other in the foot and strangling domestic demand, the unintended consequences were to keep both inflation and deficits above their respective magical numbers. Figure 10.4 shows that "tax-push inflation" conspicuously contributed to headline inflation during these years of stagnation. When volatile energy and food prices are accounted for (core 1), and especially when the stagnation-induced fiscal policy ("tax-push") contribution is also excluded (core 2), underlying inflation pressures are seen to have stayed below 2 percent throughout. Note also that "market-determined underlying inflation" (core 2) reveals a clear decline over these years, despite allegedly all-pervasive structural rigidities which, according to myth, gave rise to inflation persistence. By design the Maastricht regime has monetary domination built into the system, but sound central bankers should still internalize fiscal policy though. As Euroland got stuck in a stability-oriented vicious circle, tax-push inflation emerged as the key symptom in a macroeconomic policy blunder that kept inflation persistently above 2 percent and domestic demand stagnant. Obsessively aiming at too much of the good thing may not pay off, but rather it may backfire.

Intra-Euroland divergence also took off during this period – marking the third key policy blunder. I mentioned the interest rate convergence process temporarily boosting asset prices and domestic demand in old EU members other than Germany (1990s) and later in the new EU members (2000s). Stimuli like these are quite inevitable when approaching a monetary union with a low inflation anchor, and can be met by appropriate fiscal policies in particular. They became a problem in EMU because the anchor, Germany, was stagnating for most of the time, thereby pulling interest rates across the union lower than would otherwise have been warranted, while inflicting weak German import growth on partner countries too. A possible reason why Germany was plagued by particularly stubborn stagnation emerges from the analysis above: the German model failed to work in its homeland as Germany's partners converged to the German norm, shutting off the valves of Germany's export engine by leaving Germany as part of that new common norm.

In fact, things were made far worse by Germany's reaction to its sputtering export engine. Starting in the mid-1990s, Germany prescribed itself a wage deflation strategy: diverging downward from its own previous, and Euroland's supposed new *common*, stability norm (see Figure 10.5). As a result, Germany has experienced a very sizable improvement in its competitiveness position within Europe, which over time did *not* fail to ignite the export engine, leaving Germany with a current account surplus of 8 percent of GDP by 2007. The problem is, of course, that such a policy of wage underbidding cannot work for Euroland as a whole, as one country's competitiveness gains come at partners' expense. Ironically, it was precisely this kind of "beggar-thy-neighbor" competitive devaluation that EMU was supposed to ban forever. (Note here that France and "Euroland excluding Germany" stayed very close to the stability norm, calculated as an ECB-compatible annual 2 percent rise in nominal unit labor costs.)

Figure 10.6 shows changes in real exchange rates relative to the euro area (in terms of unit labor costs) and changes in member states' current

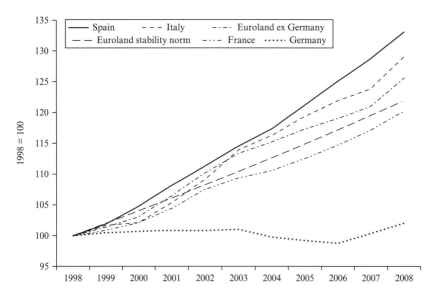

Sources: Eurostat Ameco database; own calculations.

Figure 10.5 Germany underbidding its partners

account balances since 1999, with changes in current account balances also providing a good indication of changes in bilateral trade balances within Euroland. As Euroland's overall current account position did not change much and remained roughly balanced during this period, this inspired Euroland's policy makers' belief that they had no business with "global imbalances". Yet, serious intra-area imbalances were caused in this way. All along, countries like Spain had to be grateful that German stagnation also pulled down interest rates, so that strong domestic demand growth would offset the net export drag they experienced thanks to their lead partner's betrayal. As a result, however, the structure of demand inside Euroland became seriously distorted, with soaring imbalances creating challenges that are not easily solvable in a monetary union.

At issue here is the supposedly *equilibrating* working of the "competitiveness channel" inside monetary unions. Official dogma has it that wage–price flexibility should move competitiveness positions in line with relative economic weakness or strength in the union, so that Germany would have seemed justified in having lower wage inflation than everyone else. Unfortunately this doctrine misconstrues a basic tenet of optimum currency area theory, overlooks that wages are also income and, as such, rather vital to domestic demand growth, and also ignores the destabilizing

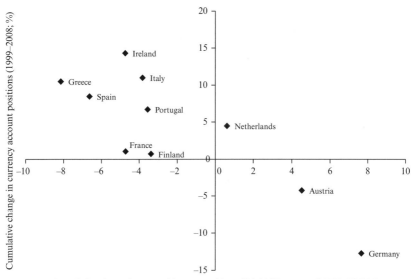

Cumulative change in competitiveness positions (Q4–2008/average of 1995–2007; %)

Source: Eurostat.

Figure 10.6   *Build-up of intra-Euroland imbalances: Germany versus the rest*

forces unleashed by the Maastricht regime when the competitiveness channel is relied upon to do a job that it cannot accomplish.

Recall that Mundell's (1961) point was that *asymmetric* shocks may require real exchange rates to adjust which, in the absence of nominal exchange rates, requires either factors and/or factor prices to be sufficiently mobile and/or flexible to bring this about. As a matter of fact, however, the "global slowdown" of 2001 was surely *not* an asymmetric shock. Rather, it was a common and largely symmetric shock, which – for failure of Euroland's macro policy regime – was not appropriately countered (see "tax-push" above). Yet, it is seriously flawed to interpret Germany's "cyclical weakness" as an asymmetric shock (see European Commission 2008b: 105–7) and thereby excuse its wage underbidding strategy when this very strategy *caused* Germany's cyclical weakness in the first place.[7]

Do not miss here how the Maastricht regime itself actually amplified divergences in the process. Start with Germany. By pushing its national wage–price inflation trend below everyone else's, with common nominal interest rates across Euroland, Germany ends up having higher real interest rates than its partners – turning Europe's pre-EMU world upside down! Further problems come from the SGP requiring budget austerity at a time when domestic demand is struggling anyway. As stagnation is supposed to depress wage growth even more, at least according to the official wage–price flexibility doctrine, this further reinforces domestic demand weakness most directly. Of course, except for small countries it is hard for net exports to dominate domestic demand. In Germany's case in the 2000s it took a historic global boom of five years to finally pull this off in 2006. Meanwhile a booming country such as Spain experiences the opposite: relatively low real interest rates, stronger wage growth, and a budgetary position that may even encourage tax cuts rather than austerity, for, given the SGP's inherent asymmetry, a country already in trouble is disciplined, while a country in a benign fiscal position is not. In short, the Maastricht regime *amplified* divergences and fed the build-up of imbalances – with *lasting* competitiveness distortions fatefully excused by the flawed official flexibility doctrine (Bibow, 2007a).

Germany has paid a heavy price for this policy blunder in terms of years of stagnating private consumption and protracted domestic demand weakness, pulling down interest rates, across Euroland. Following a long boom fired by falling interest rates, Spain is paying heavily today as the housing bust is taking its toll. Worst of all, after causing divergence and the build-up of intra-area imbalances, Germany's wage deflation has left Euroland saddled with the formidable challenge of *restoring* intra-area competitiveness positions without the possibility of recourse to parity realignments. There is a clear lesson here: to substitute national wage deflation for union-wide macro policy does not help to regain equilibrium, but greatly destabilizes the union.

Before moving on to investigate Europe's response to the global crisis of 2008–09, it is appropriate to comment briefly on ECB policy during Euroland's characteristically *brief* boom of 2006–07. Euroland's belated participation in the record global boom that had started in 2002 was of course, once again, sponsored from abroad, although the euro's strong appreciation since 2002 had complicated freeloading this time round. Figure 10.3 above revealed the ECB's extraordinarily slow response to the 2001 slowdown, which followed the bank's aggressive tightening binge in 1999–2000. The ECB immediately started tightening in December 2005, as recovery was barely taking hold, habitually treating lost output (years of negative output gaps) as bygones. While hiking somewhat less aggressively this time round, the ECB's policy rate quickly raced ahead of domestic demand, the growth contribution of which barely and only briefly exceeded 2 percent. A conspicuous contrast was then seen again when it came to easing stance as the economy stalled: the ECB actually still *hiked* rates in July 2008 – almost a year after the start of the global crisis. Ignoring the clear message sent by benign core inflation, the ECB got carried away by the commodity price boom of 2008 that briefly pushed headline inflation well above 2 percent.[8] When headline inflation predictably reversed course a little later and then even turned negative in the summer of 2009, the ECB was quick to dismiss deflation threats by pointing to more stable core inflation. The ECB's conspicuously asymmetric policies – both words and deeds – are bound to keep Euroland's upswings brief while making protracted periods of domestic demand stagnation likely. This is especially true when the supposedly stability and growth-enhancing effects of Euroland's fiscal regime are thereby triggered as well. Euroland is laboring under a policy regime featuring an unmistakable anti-(domestic demand) growth bias.

Summing up, our analysis of Euroland's (mal)performance confirms what could be expected on the basis of the regime critique offered beforehand. Essentially, Maastricht meant spreading the "German disease" of mercantilistic export reliance paired with gross negligence regarding domestic demand stabilization. The regime designers' presumption was that exporting the German model would make it work even better, both for Germany and for everyone else too. In actual fact, however, for Euroland, emulating the German model means asymmetric "management" of domestic demand and an anti-growth bias. Ironically, and to Germany's surprise, exporting the Bundesbank "success story" has undermined its working at home too, which, in turn, led to severe intra-area divergences and imbalances as Germany adopted a wage deflation strategy. Seen from a global perspective the Maastricht regime has created a rudderless economic giant that is drifting along hoping for strong enough export currents to pull it along on a sponsored growth course. Jean-Claude Trichet said as much in 2004 when Euroland was last hoping for external sponsors of recovery: "Growth starts with exports, then passes on to investment and then to consumption. That is the normal sequence for Europe in this phase of the cycle" (*Financial Times*, 2004). Needless to say, this policy approach was unlikely to make Euroland a constructive player in fostering recovery from the current global crisis.

5 TENTH ANNIVERSARY TURMOIL IN EUROPE'S "ZONE OF STABILITY", AND POLICY RESPONSES

The above performance record was set before the perfect storm hit. The global crisis and subsequent developments have not provided any evidence of a more favorable verdict on the euro and its guardians. On the contrary, on the surface the euro, at first, seemed to have brought stability to Euroland as global financial market turmoil could no longer infect intra-Euroland nominal exchange rates. While this factor merely deflected tensions to sovereign debt markets (see below) and may well have enhanced regional currency instability between Euroland members and also non-members, European integration and unity was certainly dealt a heavy blow when national policy makers resorted to nationally focused and mostly uncoordinated policies. Overall, experiences since the global crisis have confirmed previously diagnosed regime deficiencies: disregard of any need for systematic demand management, ECB asymmetry (inflation phobia paired with deflation complacency), lack of a euro Treasury or shared funding facilities or even fiscal policy coordination, lack of a coherent EU financial system policy, and lack of instruments to deal with intra-area imbalances and regional instabilities.

Apparently in full belief of their long-cherished illusion that Euroland was no party in global imbalances, as stability-oriented macro policies had kept Euroland's own house in order, key policy makers ignored the unfolding global financial crisis until the European economy came crashing in on them. Commenting on US rescue measures in response to the Lehman failure, German finance minister Peer Steinbrück declared that "this crisis originated in the US and is mainly hitting the US . . . [In Europe and Germany, such a package would be] neither sensible nor necessary" (FT.com 2008c). The core of Europe had entered recession in the spring, but Steinbrück and his EU partners remained in complete denial until the fall.[9] Of course, protracted domestic demand stagnation in Euroland during much of the 1990s and again between 2001 and 2005 contributed to the build-up of global current account imbalances (see Bibow, 2007b and sources quoted there). And European banks – in search of higher yields outside depressed Euroland – had built up large exposures to US "toxic assets" too.

A popular idea has it that purchases of US Treasury securities by Asian central banks artificially depressed US and global interest rates and were therefore responsible for creating the US housing bubble – and bust. Bibow (2009b) debunks the "global saving glut hypothesis" as being based on *flawed* loanable funds theory. Instead, the alternative liquidity-preference-theoretical "global dollar glut hypothesis" proposed there emphasizes the role of the US dollar as the key global reserve currency. Neo-mercantilist pursuits in the rest of the world created deflationary pressures in US product and labor markets, prompting sufficiently easy US monetary conditions to nourish the excess US spending needed to sustain global growth. This is not to deny that large positions taken by certain official investors may affect *relative* yields and asset prices. But in this context it seems far more relevant to consider the role of European banks in determining US and global financial conditions. In particular, given the euro area's overall fairly balanced current account position and floating euro exchange rate there was no natural need to find some outlet in US dollar assets – in contrast to certain Asian official investors. But whereas official investors generally favored Treasuries as reserves for their safety and liquidity, more yield-oriented European banks and other private investors focused on the US mortgage credit segment. Either directly or indirectly through their financing of other players, European banks built up highly leveraged exposures to US mortgage-related credit risks thereby no doubt contributing to the compression of credit risk spreads during the winding phase of their engagements – allowing the US housing bubble to continue as long as it did. In this way, European banks were also left with a sizable US dollar funding gap that later came to haunt them and the ECB.

So as global imbalances and underlying credit structures started to implode, Euroland was actually hit by a triple whammy. First, although the US subprime mortgage sector may be identified as the initial epicenter of eruptions, through its banking exposures Europe found itself right at the center of the emerging global financial crisis right away. In other words, the crisis did not hit Europe as an external shock, but unfolded as an internal banking crisis right from the start. Moreover, given its lack of domestic defenses Europe quickly acted as amplifier of the global collapse through both trade and finance channels. Second, intra-Euroland imbalances too began to implode as interbank seizures unraveled credit structures and sent risky asset prices spiraling downward across Euroland. Third, new EU member countries as well as other countries in the region, especially those with large current account deficits that were the legacy of earlier "convergence play", saw their economies massively destabilized by sudden reversals in international capital flows on top of the collapse of key EU export markets. Given Europe's very high regional interconnectedness, negative feedback loops from cross-border linkages quickly spread and amplified troubles throughout Europe. World export champion Germany was among the most severely hit European countries as its sole growth engine – exports – plunged in line with the collapse in global trade. Other countries such as Spain and Ireland (and outside Euroland the UK) were badly hit by bursting housing market bubbles, crushing domestic demand. Crashing currencies and severe economic wreckage in the Eastern European periphery also highlighted old EU members' high exposures to banking system risks in the region, among other things.

Money markets in key global financial centers slid into turmoil on 9 August 2007.[10] From the beginning pressures for liquidity support on the ECB were greatest among leading central banks, arising as spillovers from

US dollar funding markets and reflecting euro area banks' dollar funding gap and heavy exposure to US mortgage market risks, largely through conduits and structured investment vehicles (SIVs) that had used asset-backed commercial paper markets as their source of (short-term!) finance until those seized up. As money market rates spiked well above policy target rates, the ECB responded by use of large-scale emergency liquidity injections. While the ECB proved flexible in delivering its emergency liquidity-boosting operations, the bank kept up its intentions of another rate hike, having just increased its policy rates shortly before the start of the credit market rout in June 2007, and – after some delay – then actually followed through with it in July 2008. The ECB never saw any conflict between its extensive lender-of-last-resort activities under the umbrella of financial stability policy and its exclusive monetary policy focus on perceived inflation risks.[11]

The ECB's first rate cut only occurred on 8 October 2008 as part of an internationally coordinated policy easing by key central banks (see *Wall Street Journal*, 2008b). Easing its stance more timidly than other central banks, the ECB's key policy target rate eventually reached 1 percent by May 2009. The bank then also adapted its operating procedures to fine-tune liquidity injections and to more effectively counter continued money market tensions. Measures in the ECB's "enhanced credit support approach" included: a switch to "fixed rate full allotment" tender procedures in its repo operations; an increased share of longer-term refinancing operations (up to 12 months), extensions in acceptable collateral ("qualitative easing"); inclusion of the European Investment Bank among eligible counterparties; and the decision (announced on 7 May 2009) to purchase up to €60 billion in covered bonds by *private* issuers (see ECB, 2009a).

These measures have shown some effect. Starting in the spring of 2009, financial conditions have eased significantly, with rates up to one year maturity effectively pegged at the ECB's tender rate and very short rates closer to its lower deposit rate. Interbank lending, securities issuance and especially covered bond markets have seen a revival since the ECB's announcement of support. However, while banks were facing strong incentives to recapitalize through the "carry" available on purchasing government bonds (that would later come to haunt them), bank lending to the private sector has virtually stalled as banks tightened their lending standards. Overall, the ECB has expanded its balance significantly in this period, though less than the Federal Reserve and the Bank of England, while following its incentive to play safe through diversified lending to large numbers of counterparties and making sure that money markets as a whole do not falter. From the ECB's perspective it is clearly preferable to put early pressure on governments to bail out insolvent institutions directly rather than negotiating loss coverage afterwards for whatever might have ended up on its own balance sheet. In any case, aggressive lending to markets suits the ECB better than lending of last resort to particular institutions facing doubts about their liquidity and/or solvency. As caution in a way requires the ECB to be more aggressive in its approach to financial system support, the bank has arguably been more successful in this area than in its primary domain of monetary policy. A more cautious approach in the latter domain would have required more aggressive and properly preemptive easing.[12] Restarting bank lending to the private sector was certain to pose a formidable challenge given both impaired bank capital and the tendency of member state governments to pursue national, rather than EU, objectives.

The tendency to undermine the Single Market arose even prior to the Lehman collapse when EU governments generally followed a case-by-case approach to strengthening individual bank balance sheets. But it became more of a threat in the post-Lehman period when, apart from further individual bank bailouts, governments by force of the situation increasingly turned to *national* systemwide interventions.

Bank rescues (public capital injections, guarantees for bank liabilities, and measures for relief of impaired bank assets) soared in a number of EU countries following Lehman's fall (see Ecofin, 2009). For instance, the pan-European bank Fortis was bailed out by Belgium, Luxembourg and the Netherlands, and the pan-European bank Dexia by Belgium, France and Luxembourg, while Hypo Real Estate Holding received a loan guarantee by the German government to fend off insolvency. In the UK, an emergency merger between Halifax Bank of Scotland and Lloyds TSB was brokered by the government while the Treasury directly seized Bradford & Bingley (Bloomberg, 2008b; FT.com, 2008d). While initially rapid cooperation between governments in times of crisis scored some points, nationalistic instincts quickly took over, especially as the Irish and German governments issued unilateral guarantees of all deposits in their respective banking systems and pan-European banks were effectively nationalized along national lines. An emergency summit of Euroland (plus UK) leaders in Paris on 12 October (see French EU Presidency, 2008) restarted efforts for a concerted European response.[13] Governments pledged to prevent failure of any systemically important institution and agreed on certain principles of shoring up their national financial systems. Yet, damage to the Single Market through governments' recourse to protectionist state aid measures of various forms has continued, keeping the European Commission as the guardian of the treaties and competition watchdog on high alert.

The threat of increasing market re-fragmentation has also led to a new push for writing a "single rule book" and harmonizing pan-EU financial supervision. Following a report initiated in October 2008 by the European Commission and delivered in February 2009 by the "The High-Level Group on Financial Supervision in the EU" chaired by Jacques de Larosière, EU leaders endorsed the plan to harmonize micro-prudential supervision and add a new macro-prudential supervision column to EU governance structures in June 2009. In September 2009 the European Commission (2009b) unveiled draft legislation to implement the approved changes. While day-to-day supervision of banks and financial firms would remain with national supervisors, new European supervisory authorities for banking, insurance and securities sectors (replacing the existing pan-EU coordinating committees), would be charged with developing harmonized rules and common approaches to supervision, and ensuring their consistent application. At the macro level the Commission advocated the creation of a New European Systemic Risk Board consisting of EU central bank governors and chaired by the ECB president; the proposed new board would be charged with the task of monitoring threats to financial stability in the region.

These were laudable attempts to overcome the stark contradiction between nationally segregated supervision over an area of deep (and supposedly ever deeper) financial integration, but the limitations to these endeavors are clear enough too. In the end, it is inevitably the national finance ministers who are called upon to find solutions to any problems of cross-border financial institutions that may require support from their "deep pockets". In the absence of EU budgetary resources, bailouts will remain national affairs and the national authorities will continue to stem any intrusions on their fiscal responsibilities accordingly. Therefore, it was clear that should new emergencies arise under the proposed new governance structure of pan-EU supervisors, similar nationalistic tendencies as observed in the global crisis would likely recur. So the real question remains whether increased harmonization and coordination between national and EU authorities in this area will yield improved "early warnings" and help *prevent* emergencies from arising in future; and without forgoing growth opportunities.

Inevitably, the fact that the EU is not a fiscal union also loomed large in the issue of arranging fiscal stimulus packages. Initial calls by the IMF in early 2008 were generally scoffed at. Some EU leaders, Germany's foremost among them, had a very hard time letting go their balance-the-budget ambitions when the world economy was headed for a crisis that they had no part in, in their view at least. Starting from a comfortable budget surplus position following its 15-year boom, Spain was the first EU country to implement a fiscal stimulus plan in early 2008 to counter the impact of imploding property markets. Following Lehman's fall, the European Commission proposed a "European Economic Recovery Plan" (European Commission, 2008b) featuring discretionary budgetary measures of €200 billion (1.5 percent of EU GDP) in late November 2008, which was approved at the European Council in Brussels on 11–12 December 2008. Concerning fiscal stimulus action at the union level, it was agreed that the European Investment Bank would increase its funding of immediate actions in 2009–10 by €30 billion while the bulk of €170 billion in the recovery plan would (have to) come from the member states (see European Council, 2009; IMF, 2009).

Given differing budgetary starting positions constraining countries' room for maneuver, the largest national stimulus package actually came from Germany, where leaders finally woke up to the fact of a looming general election in September 2009. Contrary to the idea that Germany was once again made EU paymaster for other countries' failures to put their fiscal houses in order during good times, Germany's more sizable fiscal stimulus in response to the crisis (1.5 percent of GDP in 2009 and 2 percent of GDP in 2010) should be seen as partial compensation for the country's notorious freeloading on exports through competitiveness gains in prior years when mindless fiscal retrenchment suffocated German domestic demand (and imports from partners). Compensation was only partial, though, because of the lingering challenge to restore competitiveness positions within Euroland and the lasting pressures on partners' budgets this has created. By comparison, it seems more than appropriate that, for instance, France enacted a somewhat smaller stimulus given that its budgetary policies had provided support to French and Euroland domestic demand in prior years. Italy was excused for its negligible stimulus in view of the country's high debt ratio. Spain enacted a series of overall sizable stimulus packages but in view of the massive turnaround in its fiscal fortunes that saw private debts plentifully amassed during boom years quickly morphing into public debts when crisis hit, Spain then headed for a very "early exit" from stimulus – a brutal awakening for the former star performer and fiscal paragon (European Commission, 2009a). Spain's announcement of VAT rate hikes in 2010 (following hikes in indirect taxes on tobacco and fuel in 2009) heralded the return of unappealing policies to Euroland in due course: fiscal retrenchment featuring "tax push inflation" (see FT.com, 2009b).

In advocating "timely, temporary, targeted, and co-ordinated" national budgetary stimulus packages the European Commission (2008c) did not tire of holding up the SGP as the "credible framework" for fiscal policies, emphasizing that the pact will be "applied judiciously ensuring credible medium-term fiscal policy strategies" with timely corrective action needed by members to avoid penalties under the EDP. The ECB too made it clear what was expected from member states at the fiscal front:

> The structural adjustment process should start, in any case, not later than the economic recovery and the consolidation efforts should be stepped up in 2011. Structural consolidation efforts will need to exceed significantly the benchmark of 0.5% of GDP per annum set in the SGP. In countries with high deficits and/ or debt ratios, the annual structural adjustment should reach at least 1% of GDP. (ECB, 2009b)[14]

If members are not sufficiently forthcoming in their consolidation efforts to meet the ECB's expectations, ECB punishment would take the form of an early monetary tightening, the ECB warned (Bini Smaghi, 2009, for instance).

Of course the SGP is not an instrument for proper coordination of policies but foremost a disciplining instrument, one of those supposed "safeguards" to protect "sound money" from fiscal profligacy. Another of those supposed safeguards – the "no bailout clause" – came to haunt Euroland in early 2009, too, with speculations about an impending euro break-up leading to soaring interest rate spreads between Euroland members. Ireland, another former star performer that has seen a sharp turnaround in its economic and fiscal fortunes with several rating downgrades on its sovereign debts since 2008, was hit especially hard (as was Greece, soon to become the focus of attack). This time around, the speculative attack hitting sovereign debt rather than currency markets was fended off as Germany's finance minister Peer Steinbrück heroically declared that "the euro-region treaties don't foresee any help for insolvent countries, but in reality the other states would have to rescue those running into difficulty" (FT.com, 2009a). The no bailout clause as an obstacle to stability – rather than safeguard – was symptomatic for experiences that highlighted just how ludicrous the design of Europe's monetary union really is. The situation was to get far worse still when, in the spring of 2010, the inevitability of either organizing bailouts or dealing with the fallout of banking and sovereign defaults focused the market's mind on a rising number of Euroland member countries.

The no bailout clause had left Euroland members even worse off than other EU members. For non-Euroland EU members in financial difficulty are at least eligible for EU financial (balance-of-payments) assistance, and the EU even agreed in May 2009 to double the lending ceiling for its support facility from €25 billion to €50 billion. Yet, this could not gloss over the fact that EU support for its new members in Eastern Europe (and the neighboring region), among the most severely hit emerging market economies in the global crisis, has proved vastly insufficient. The EU support facility was used to provide medium-term assistance to Hungary, Latvia, and Romania (Europe, 2009). However, this occurred as part of broader assistance from the IMF (as "Stand-by Arrangements", whereas Poland has an arrangement under the Fund's "Flexible Credit Line" facility). Ironically, the experience of the crisis may have both raised the willingness for new EU members to accelerate euro adoption and reduced their ability to meet the necessary criteria to be allowed in.[15] Especially in view of the stark deterioration in public finances in crisis-hit new member countries, such ambitions may have been pushed back for many years.

Once again, Euroland became the laggard in emerging from the global crisis. The Euroland economy turned the corner by mid-year 2009 but following five consecutive quarters of negative (qoq) domestic demand growth, the homemade forces for a sustainable recovery were decidedly weak.[16] All Euroland members except Cyprus, Luxembourg, and Finland had budget deficits in excess of 3 percent of GDP. Already operating under Excessive Deficit Procedures, Greece was at the time expected to squeeze its deficit below 3 percent by 2010, France and Spain by 2012, and Ireland by 2013. At least in parts of Euroland, "exit" from crisis-related stimulus measures started before any recovery. Contrary to declarations made at the G20 leaders' summit in Pittsburgh, Euroland opted for another protracted fiscal consolidation "no matter what" – in the hope that exports to the rest of the world would prove strong enough. Germany's "export-oriented growth model" stands right at the heart of Europe's problem: effectively exporting stagnation, or worse, to Euroland and beyond.

6 SUMMARY

On the occasion of the euro's tenth anniversary, Euroland and the wider Europe had little else to be cheerful about than price stability, which stands "above all else" and of which there can never be enough, of course, even as headline HICP for Euroland actually fell to *minus* 0.7 in the summer of 2009. Arguably, nothing else was to be expected, though, from a "price stability above all else" policy regime designed by German central bankers. By design there is no place within the Maastricht regime for any authority minding the domestic demand store. The peculiar ideology that price stability, fiscal austerity, and structural reform (essentially, wage compression) may be enough to generate growth overlooks the vital part that export surpluses used to play in the German "homeland of stability-oriented policy" wisdom. The point is that the world is a closed economy and the European economy too large to rely on mercantilism for its growth. Making matters worse still, Germany – as a monetary union member – supercharged its national mercantilism, thereby causing intra-area imbalances and preparing the ground for internal crises of calamitous dimensions that shook Euroland in 2010 and that are still raving in early 2012, with no resolution in sight. Ironically, beggar-thy-neighbor policies such as these were exactly what the euro was meant to ban forever. For the next 10 years of its young life the euro will have to live with the legacies of Germany's "restored" competitiveness.

Key authorities in Europe seem wholeheartedly resistant to learning, and continue to blame the rest of the world for their homemade misfortunes. In truth, the EU and particularly Euroland were very far from keeping their own house in order when the global crisis, and later the Euroland balance-of-payments crisis, struck. Europe had contributed handsomely to the build-up of global imbalances since the 1990s and come to experience their implosive unwinding as an internal crisis from the beginning. This was because of large exposures in European banks to US mortgage credit risk, engagements that had helped to finance the US housing bubble, but hit Europe with a vengeance as a severe European banking crisis as soon as the US bubble burst. In addition, having nourished its own homemade intra-Euroland and intra-EU imbalances under stability-oriented guardianship, turmoil in Europe's supposed "zone of stability" was further aggravated by the simultaneous implosion of these purely homegrown troubles: hitting as a perfect "triple whammy" storm. While more mindless fiscal austerity, rigidity waffling, and "price stability above all else" propaganda are not the solution to anything, German standard policy prescriptions are overriding any sense in Euroland today. The euro may not break, but it may make its members go broke together instead.

NOTES

*   I would like to thank the participants at the conference "The Political Economy of Central Banking/La Politique Économique et la Banque Centrale", held in Toronto, 27–28 May 2009, for their helpful comments.
1.   While Ecofin includes economics or finance ministers from all EU member countries the Euroland subgroup of such ministers is called the "Eurogroup".
2.   As with much else (see next section), the historical background to the ECB's "monetary pillar" is to be seen in the Bundesbank's "monetary targeting" strategy. In both cases, and contrary to its apparent monetarist inspiration, the primary purpose was to increase central bankers' discretion. More recently the ECB started to justify its monetary analysis as an early warning system for the build-up of financial fragility, and in view of the global crisis the ECB has added some spin to these claims. Politics and public relations aside, this is begging the question why the ECB failed to identify the

systemic risks stemming from soaring internal imbalances in Euroland and the EU (see Bibow, 2005).

3. Keynes analyzed the consequences of inflation and deflation in his Tract, concluding that "both are evils to be shunned" (Keynes, 1923[1971], JMK 4: 36). Following his visit to Germany in early 1932, Keynes (1932[1978]; JMK 18: 366) observed: "Germany today is in the grip of the most terrible deflation that any nation had experienced. A visitor to that country is offered an extraordinary example of what the effects of such a policy can be, carried out *à outrance*. . . . Nearly a third of the population is out of work. The standards of life of those still employed have been cruelly curtailed. There is scarcely a manufacturer or a merchant in the country who is not suffering pecuniary losses which must soon bring his business to a standstill. . . . Too many people in Germany have nothing to look forward to – nothing except a 'change', something wholly vague and wholly undefined, but a *change*. . . . Hamburg, living in a stupor, many miles of ships laid up silent in its harbor, with the elaborate traffic control of a great city but no traffic to be seen, is a symbol of Germany under the great deflation – a worse visitation, if it is to be continued, than even the great inflation was a few years ago".

4. For instance, former Bundesbank President Hans Tietmeyer (1991: 182) declared: "The reasons for the success of German monetary policy in defending price stability are in part historical. The experience gained twice with hyperinflation in the first half of this century has helped to develop a special sensitivity to inflation and has caused the wider public to believe in the critical importance of monetary stability in Germany. For this reason, the strong position of the Bundesbank is widely accepted by the general public – questioning its independence even seems to be a national taboo. This social consensus has yielded strong support for the policy of the Bundesbank". See also Giersch and Lehment (1981). Wolfgang Schäuble, Germany's finance minister since 2009, provided a telling example of German monetary mythology that has erased any memories of deflation when he identified "two different approaches to economic policymaking on each side of the Atlantic. While US policymakers like to focus on short-term corrective measures, we take the longer view and are, therefore, more preoccupied with the implications of excessive deficits and the dangers of high inflation. So are German consumers. This aversion to deficits and inflationary fears, which have their roots in Germany's history in the past century, may appear peculiar to our American friends, whose economic culture is, in part, shaped by deflationary episodes. Yet these fears are among the most potent factors of consumption and saving rates in our country. Seeking to engineer more domestic demand by raising government borrowing even further would, here at least, be counterproductive. On the contrary, restoring confidence in our ability to cut the deficit is a prerequisite for balanced and sustainable growth" (Schäuble, 2010).

5. See Henning (1994), Kenen (1995) and Dyson and Featherstone (1999) on the route to Maastricht. For regime analyzes, see also Allsopp and Vines (1998) and Arestis and Sawyer (2001).

6. See Bibow (2002, 2007c) on the "time inconsistency hypothesis of the euro's plunge". The European Commission (2000: 71) correctly foresaw actual outcomes: "To the extent that the depreciation in the euro is due to cyclical divergence between the euro area and the United States, a rise in interest rates in an attempt to support the currency could even backfire if it was perceived as stifling the euro-area recovery. The risk of creating an even more unbalanced growth pattern with weak domestic demand and higher export growth would be serious."

7. The European Commission's (2008a) analysis of competitiveness versus real interest rate channels is also confused and self-contradictory as a case for more structural reforms of labor markets. Supposedly the expectation is that more flexibility leads to greater wage responsiveness to cyclical positions and thus to accelerated wage divergences between members. This is missing the crucial point that wage divergences can be the *cause* of cyclical divergence in the first place, while in the absence of any *proper* asymmetric shock diverging wage trends are wholly unwarranted as they can only drive the system *away from equilibrium* and inevitably end with a bust.

8. In the fall of 2005 the ECB argued that low core inflation was about to converge to higher headline inflation, referring to the 2001–02 experience. The argument that core inflation might converge upwards assumes cyclical strength, ignoring that the earlier episode of rising core inflation was actually one of cyclical weakness, as well as a changeover to euro notes and coins (see Bibow, 2007c).

9. Quite uncharacteristically, the International Monetary Fund had urged its members to set stimulus plans in early 2008, around the time when the US launched its first stimulus package. EU authorities and particularly euro area central bankers strongly resisted any such calls, arguing that they would risk undermining the credibility of the SGP (see *Wall Street Journal*, 2008a).

10. Market stress had built up since June and was at this stage clearly focused on subprime-related losses incurred by investment funds and banks, including Germany's IKB and France's BNP Paribas, for instance.

11. Throughout the ECB continued to signal its tightening ambitions. See *Wall Street Journal* (2007); FT.com (2007); Bloomberg (2008a); FT.com (2008b). With the US Fed aggressively easing since January 2008 the euro appreciated strongly during this phase.

12. Apart from the (Wim Duisenberg) argument that a liquidity trap is best avoided by not easing interest rates in the first place, the ECB again proved itself inventive in justifying delays in policy easing. For instance, Board member Lorenzo Bini Smaghi asserted that "a stabler and less-fluctuating monetary policy" would make monetary policy more effective (see *Wall Street Journal*, 2008c), and that cutting rates sharply now makes it more difficult to raise them back to the right level once recovery takes hold as: "The lower rates are brought, the more likely the central bank will find itself behind the curve" (*Wall Street Journal*, 2009).

13. Inviting the British Prime Minister Gordon Brown acknowledged London's role as Europe's (and Euroland's) leading financial center. Through this avenue, Brown's proposal for a global summit on reforming the global financial system also provided a key impetus to the G20 summits held in Washington on 20 November 2008 and London on 2 April 2009. Brown's recommendable leadership provoked sharp attacks from Germany's Peer Steinbrueck, intellectually challenged in keeping up with the speed of events at the time, it seems, who accused the British prime minister of pursuing "crass Keynesianism", with the revealing comment: "The switch from decades of supply-side politics all the way to a crass Keynesianism is breathtaking" (FT.com, 2008e).

14. And this time round the ECB even anticipates that "increases in indirect taxation and administered prices may be stronger than currently expected owing to the need for fiscal consolidation in the coming years" (ECB, 2009b).

15. And at least in the case of Iceland, the crisis has given rise to the crisis-hit country seeking EU membership.

16. Germany recorded positive (qoq) growth already in the second quarter, once again driven by a massive net exports contribution (with imports dropping more sharply than exports).

REFERENCES

Allsopp, C. and D. Vines (1998), "The assessment: macroeconomic policy after EMU", *Oxford Review of Economic Policy*, **14** (3): 1–23.
Almunia, J. (2008), "Foreword" in European Commission, 2008a.
Arestis, P. and M. Sawyer (2001), *The Euro: Evolution and Prospects*, Cheltenham, UK and Northampton, MA, USA: Edward Elgar.
Bibow, J. (1998), "Geldpolitik als Inflationsursache?", in A. Vilks and B.P. Priddat (eds), *Wirtschaftswissenschaften und Wirtschaftswirklichkeit*, Marburg: Metropolis, pp. 15–78.

Bibow, J. (2001), "Making EMU work: some lessons from the 1990s", *International Review of Applied Economics*, **15** (3): 233–59.

Bibow, J. (2002), "The markets versus the ECB, and the euro's plunge", *Eastern Economic Journal*, **28** (1): 45–57.

Bibow, J. (2004), "Assessing the ECB's performance since the global slowdown: a structural policy bias coming home to roost?", Working Paper 409, Annandale-on-Hudson, NY: The Levy Economics Institute.

Bibow, J. (2005), "Issing fails to justify claims that ECB policy flagged up likely threats", *Financial Times*, Letter to the editor, 19 December.

Bibow, J. (2006), "Inflation persistence and tax-push inflation in Germany and the euro area: a symptom of macroeconomic mismanagement?", IMK Studies 1/2006, Duesseldorf.

Bibow, J. (2007a), "How the Maastricht regime fosters divergence as well as fragility", in P. Arestis, E. Hein and E. Le Heron (eds), *Monetary Policies: Modern Approaches*, Basingstoke: Palgrave, pp. 197–222. (Working Paper 460, Annandale-on-Hudson, NY: The Levy Economics Institute.)

Bibow, J. (2007b), "Global imbalances, Bretton Woods II, and Euroland's role in all this", in J. Bibow and A. Terzi (eds), *Euroland and the World Economy: Global Player or Global Drag?*, Basingstoke: Palgrave Macmillan. (Working Paper 486. Annandale-on-Hudson, NY: Levy Economics Institute.)

Bibow, J. (2007c), "The ECB – How much of a success story, really?", in E. Hein, J. Priewe and A. Truger (eds), *European Integration in Crisis*, Marburg: Metropolis, pp. 301–29.

Bibow, J. (2009a), "On the origin and rise of central bank independence in West Germany", *European Journal of the History of Economic Thought*, **16** (1): 155–90.

Bibow, J. (2009b), *Keynes on Monetary Policy, Finance and Uncertainty: Liquidity Preference Theory and the Global Financial Crisis*, London: Routledge.

Bini Smaghi, L. (2009), "An ocean apart? Comparing transatlantic responses to the financial crisis", speech, Rome, 10–11 September.

Center for Economic Policy and Research (CEPR) (2002), "Surviving the slowdown", Monitoring the ECB No. 4, D. Begg, F. Canova, P. De Grauwe, A. Fatás and P.R. Lane.

Duisenberg, W. (2001), Quotes from the European Parliament's Committee on Economic and Monetary Affairs Monetary Dialogue, March, available at: http://www.europarl.europa.eu/comparl/econ/pdf/emu/speeches/20010305/duisenberg/fulltxt/default_en.pdf (accessed 5 October 2009).

Dyson, K. and K. Featherstone (1999), *The Road to Maastricht: Negotiating EMU*, New York: Oxford University Press.

Ecofin (Council of the European Union) (2009), Annex to the Council (Ecofin) Report to the 18–19 June European Council on the effectiveness of financial support schemes: Report of the Task Force on reviewing the effectiveness of financial support measures, Brussels, 9 June.

European Central Bank (ECB) (2009a), "The implementation of monetary policy since August 2007", *Monthly Bulletin*, July, 75–89.

European Central Bank (ECB) (2009b), Editorial, *Monthly Bulletin*, September.

European Central Bank (ECB) (various), *Monthly Bulletin* (MB).

Europe (2009), Joint statement by the Presidency of the Ecofin Council and the Commission on providing EU medium-term financial assistance to Romania, Brussels, 25 March, available at: http://europa.eu/rapid/pressReleases

Action.do?reference=IP/09/475&format=HTML&aged=0&language=EN&gui Language=en (accessed 5 October 2009).

European Commission (2000), "The EU economy: 2000 review", *European Economy*, 71, Brussels.

European Commission (2008a), *EMU@10: Successes and Challenges after Ten Years of Economic and Monetary Union*, DC ECFIN, Brussels.

European Commission (2008b), "Labour market and wage developments in 2007", *European Economy*, 5, DG Economic and Financial Affairs, Brussels.

European Commission (2008c), "A European Economic Recovery Plan", Communication, Brussels, 16 November.

European Commission (2009a), "Public finances in EMU – 2009", *European Economy*, 5/2009, Brussels.

European Commission (2009b), "Commission adopts legislative proposals to strengthen financial supervision in Europe", Brussels, 23 September, available at: http://europa.eu/rapid/pressReleasesAction.do?reference=IP/09/1347& format=HTML&aged=0&language=EN&guiLanguage=en (accessed 5 October 2009).

European Council (2009), Presidency Conclusions, Brussels European Council 11 and 12 December 2008, 13 February 2009, Brussels.

French EU Presidency (2008), Summit of the euro area countries: declaration on a concerted European action plan of the euro area countries, Paris, 12 October, available at: http://www.eu2008.fr/PFUE/lang/en/accueil/PFUE-10_2008/PFUE-12.10.2008/sommet_pays_zone_euro_declaration_plan_action_concertee.html (accessed 5 October 2009).

Girsch, H. and H. Lehment (1981), "Monetary policy: does independence make a difference? The German experience", *ORDO*, **32**: 3–16.

Goodhart, C.A.E. (1998), "The two concepts of money: implications for the analysis of optimal currency areas", *European Journal of Political Economy*, **14**: 407–32.

Henning, C.R. (1994), *Cooperating with Europe's Monetary Union*, Washington, DC: Institute for International Economics.

International Monetary Fund (IMF) (2009), "Update on fiscal stimulus and financial sector measures", Washington, DC, 26 April.

Issing, O. (2003), "Europe and the US: partners and competitors – new paths for the future", speech given at the German British Forum, London, 28 October, available at: http://www.ecb.int/key/03/sp031028.htm (accessed 5 October 2009).

Johnson, P.A. (1998), *The Government of Money: Monetarism in Germany and the United States*, Ithaca, NY and London: Cornell University Press.

Katzenstein, P.J. (1987), *Policy and Politics in West Germany: The Growth of a Semisovereign State*, Philadelphia, PA: Temple University Press.

Kenen, P. (1995), *Economic and Monetary Union in Europe: Moving beyond Maastricht*, Cambridge: Cambridge University Press.

Keynes, J.M. (1923 [1971]) *A Tract on Monetary Reform*, Collected Writings of John Maynard Keynes, vol. 4, London: Macmillan.

Keynes, J.M. (1932 [1978]), *An End of Reparations?*, The Collected Writings of John Maynard Keynes, vol. 4, Cambridge: Cambridge University Press.

Kregel, J. (1999), "Can EMU combine price stability with employment and income growth?", *Eastern Economic Journal*, **25** (1): 35–47.

Marsh, D. (1992), *The Bundesbank: The Bank that Rules Europe*, London: Mandarin.

Mundell, R.A. (1961), "A theory of optimum currency areas", *American Economic Review*, **51**: 657–75.
Schäuble, W. (2010), "Maligned Germany is right to cut spending", *Financial Times*, 23 June.
Tietmeyer, H. (1991), "The role of an independent central bank in Europe", in P. Downes and R. Vaez-Zadeh (eds), *The Evolving Role of Central Banks*, Washington, DC: IMF, pp. 176–89.
Vocke, W. (1973), *Memoiren*, Stuttgart: Deutsche Verlags-Anstalt.
Wolf, M. (2007), "The pain in Spain will follow years of rapid economic gain", *Financial Times*, March 27.

Media

Bloomberg (2008a), "ECB vows to fight inflation even as economy contracts", 14 August (Gabi Thesing).
Bloomberg (2008b), "European lenders get bailouts as U.S. crisis spreads", 29 September (Simon Kennedy).
Financial Times (2004), "Reforms good for growth with Europe on track for recovery", interview with J.-C. Trichet, 23 April (Andreas Krosta and Tony Major).
FT.com (2007), "ECB still pursuing rate rise policy", 8 September (Ralph Atkins and John Thornhill).
FT.com (2008a), "Europe looks for allies against inflation", 9 September (Guy Dinmore and John Thornhill).
FT.com (2008b), "ECB reaffirms inflation stance", 16 September (Ralph Atkins).
FT.com (2008c), "Germany sees an end to U.S. hegemony", 26 September (Bertrand Benoit).
FT.com (2008d), "Dexia receives euro 6.4bn capital injection", 30 September.
FT.com (2008e), "Berlin hits out at 'crass' UK strategy", 10 December (George Parker and Bertrand Benoit).
FT.com (2009a), "Germany ready to help eurozone members", 18 February (Bertrand Benoit).
FT.com (2009b), "Spain raises taxes to tackle deficit", 28 September.
Reuters (2008), "ECB's Trichet holds the line on rates, inflation", 24 January (Mike Dolan and Natsuko Waki).
Wall Street Journal (2007), "ECB signals rate increase is still likely", 23 August (Joellen Perry).
Wall Street Journal (2008a), "Trichet: No fiscal stimulus here, please", 7 September (David Wessel).
Wall Street Journal (2008b), "Central banks cut rates world-wide", 8 October (Sudeep Ready and Joellen Perry).
Wall Street Journal (2008c), "ECB Stays Course on Pace of Easing", 19 November (Joellen Perry).
Wall Street Journal (2009), "ECB explains reasons for caution on rates: no deflation threat, fear of a new bubble guide policy", 22 January (Joellen Perry).

11. Quantitative easing in the United States after the crisis: conflicting views

Domenica Tropeano

1 INTRODUCTION

This chapter deals with the conflicting interpretations of the monetary policy carried out by the Federal Reserve during the current financial crisis. This policy has been referred to as "quantitative easing", because after interest rates have been lowered near the zero bound, the policy has consisted in the purchase of various types of assets from financial institutions, thereby greatly increasing banks' excess reserves and overall liquidity in the system. With interest rates unable to go any lower, the Fed has returned to a policy focused on quantities (see Adrian and Shin, 2009). This time, however, unlike during the monetarist era, the problem is not to control some money aggregate but to expand as much as possible the supply of money and credit.

Section 2 will present an overview of the main facts on the monetary policy carried out by the Federal Reserve during the 2007–08 financial crisis.

In Section 3, the liquidity trap view of the current depression will be explained and the monetary policy of the central bank will be introduced within this framework. The main thesis is that the central bank will continue to flood the market with money to cause inflation or at least inflationary expectations. A depreciation would eventually do the same job too.

In Section 4 an interpretation of the Fed's monetary policy according to Minsky is presented. An easy monetary policy carried out beyond the lender-of-last-resort intervention might have the aim of sustaining the price of investment and validating firms' plans. In other words, it would be complementary to fiscal policy with the aim of sustaining profits and investment. The problem is that the Kaleckian model Minsky was using hardly corresponds to the present situation of the US economy.

In Section 5 I shall argue that, if this model is modified in order to take into account the evolution of the economy, another possible explanation arises. The Federal Reserve and the government are simply sustaining financial profits earned by both financial and non-financial corporations. However, if no change in the economy occurs, this will set the conditions for another crisis. To date, no mechanism exists that would restore lending after the collapse of the originate and distribute system. In the originate and distribute system, banks did not lend any more and held the loans on their balance sheets but instead were just selling the loans to other intermediaries which in turn were selling to finance themselves assets whose yield was linked to the loans interest revenue. Since most of these intermediaries have not survived the current financial crisis, the originate and distribute system is no longer viable. While the few big banks which emerged after the US government interventions are enjoying huge profits on their trading desks, most local and small banks, whose main business is lending, are in trouble and often are compelled to go into bankruptcy. Section 6 concludes.

2 THE FEDERAL RESERVE'S MONETARY POLICY DURING THE CRISIS

The monetary policy carried out by the Federal Reserve during the financial crisis has consisted initially of very gradual decreases in the Fed Funds target rate. This rate has been lowered from 5.25 to 0.25 percent. These massive cuts notwithstanding, the situation in the interbank market has not improved at all and the market was virtually frozen for about a year. The reasons behind this failure of monetary policy are many. The problem from which financial institutions were suffering was one of insolvency rather than simply liquidity, thus institutions would not trust each other and would therefore not lend to each other, unless in the very short term. Moreover the interbank market had changed, becoming a market in which non-bank financial institutions were exchanging funds on the basis of repurchase agreements. The significance of the interest rate as a benchmark for the market had therefore been limited. Even traditional banks were preferring other tools for financing rather than interbank loans, where cost was linked to the Federal Funds rate (see IMF, 2008).

Although the monetary policy response by the Federal Reserve has been quicker than that of other European banks (such as the Bank of England and the European Central Bank: ECB), the sequencing of interventions seems to indicate that the central bank had hardly understood the extent and difficulty of the problem. The rate cuts, as we can see Table 11.1,

Table 11.1   Chronology of monetary policy measures by the Fed

Date	Policy measure
7 August 2007	Fed maintains target rate at 5.25%
18 September 2007	Fed lowers target funds rate at 4.75%
31 October 2007	Fed lowers target funds rate at 4.50%
11 December 2008	Fed lowers target funds rate at 4.25%
22 January 2008	Fed lowers target funds rate at 3.50%
30 January 2008	Fed lowers target funds rate at 3.00%
18 March 2008	Fed lowers target funds rate at 2.25%
30 April 2008	Fed lowers target funds rate at 2.00%
16 September 2008	Fed target rate is maintained at 2.00%
8 October 2008	In conjunction with cuts by other central banks Fed target rate lowered to 1.50%
29 October 2008	Fed lowers target funds rate at 1.00%
16 December 2008	Fed lowers target funds rate to a range 0–0.25%.
28 January 2009	Fed target rate is maintained at 0.25%
18 March 2009	Fed target rate is maintained at 0.25%
Facilities	
17 December 2007	Term Auction Facility (TAF) introduced and the first auction takes place
1 February 2008	TAF auction increased to $30 bn every two weeks
11 March 2008	Term securities lending facility is introduced
16 March 2008	Primary dealers' credit facility is created
2 May 2008	Term Securities Lending Facility (TSLF) eligible collateral expands to include AAA rated asset-backed securities (ABS)
13 July 2008	Lending to Fannie Mae and Freddie Mac at the primary credit rate is authorized
30 July 2008	84-day TAF auctions are introduced and the ECB swap line is increased
14 September 2008	Eligible collateral for TSLF and Primary Dealer Credit Facility (PDCF) expanded
28 September 2008	84-day TAF allotments increased by $75 bn, two forward TAF auctions totaling $150 bn dollar introduced and total swap line doubled to $620 bn
6 October 2008	TAF increased to provide $900 bn of funding over year-end
7 October 2008.	Commercial Paper Funding Facility (CPFF) established
21 October 2008	Money Market Investor Facility (MMIFF) is established
25 November 2008	Term Asset-Backed Securities Loan Facility (TALF) established to provide loans collateralized by ABS
25 November 2008	Fed purchase of government sponsored enterprises (GSE) direct obligations begins

Table 11.1   (continued)

Date	Policy measure
2 December 2008	PDCF, Asset-Backed Commercial Paper Money Market Mutual Fund Liquidity Facility (AMLF), and TSLF are all extended through April 30.
28 January 2009	Federal Open Market Committee (FOMC) announces willingness to begin purchase of long-term Treasury securities
3 March 2009	TALF launch
18 March 2009	Announcement of a program to buy $300 bn worth of Treasuries and to increase the purchase of agency debt
19 March 2009	TALF eligible securities expanded
19 May 2009	TALF announces acceptance of legacy Commercial Mortgage-Backed Securities (CMBS)

followed one another at frequent intervals, giving the impression that the Fed did not grasp the situation that was developing on the money and short-term securities markets, which had already deteriorated by July 2007, when the main traders more or less ceased doing business. Many scholars were aware that those markets were gradually disappearing and that the consequences to the rest of the financial system, given the web of interconnections, were presumably enormous (see Dodd, 2007). The Central Bank, however, seems not to have grasped that point, since it waited until September 2007 to cut the Federal Funds rate, and then only by 0.50 percent. We had to wait until the spring of 2008 to see the introduction of some measures, which brought relief to all markets that had virtually disappeared after the breakdown of intermediaries. The primary dealers' lending facility was started in March 2008. Many other facilities that followed focused on particular markets since markets were so segmented that the injection of liquidity at one end would never reach the other end of the system. From the end of 2008 through 2009, the Fed was engaging in a policy called "quantitative easing". Since the interest rate had reached its lower zero limit, the Fed planned and implemented open market operations that potentially increased the supply of money and credit. In late 2009, it started buying long-term Treasury securities in vast quantities in order to lower long-term interest rates as well. An official of the Federal Reserve reports that the secret of the apparent success of these operations is the size (see Sack, 2009). According to the author, the Federal Reserve now has on its balance sheet a total of about $1.8 trillion of Treasury, agency, and mortgage-backed securities. These purchase programs were not aimed at providing liquidity but to keep private long-term interest rates at rates lower than they otherwise would be. First estimates find that the Fed's purchases have lowered the long-term interest rate on Treasuries by 0.50 percent while it has also lowered the rate on mortgage-backed assets by 0.1 percent (see ibid.). The secret of the success, as Sack writes, is size. The extent of the interventions has been very large with respect to the dimensions of the markets.

The monetary policy pursued by the Federal Reserve as a response to the global financial crisis has aimed at increasing the supply of money and credit. Lower interest rates on their own were ineffective in resolving the problems caused by the financial crisis, mainly the freezing up of the inter-bank market. To complement lower rates, the Federal Reserve adopted a more aggressive policy of ad hoc interventions in various money markets by purchasing assets of different types with different maturities.

The reason behind this change in policy has been given by Ben Bernanke, chairman of the Federal Reserve, in a speech in which he wrote explicitly that conventional monetary policy is no more useful to fight the crisis if interest rates touch the zero bound (see Bernanke, 2002). This was indeed what happened in the United States after one year of very lax monetary policy and thus it was necessary to change tools. The Central Bank had to be concerned with the liquidity trap that arises when interest rates are zero and thus it had to follow a policy that already in the 1990s had already been followed by the Bank of Japan in fighting the Japanese financial crisis. At that time the Japanese central bank was trying to get out of the liquidity trap by causing a rise in prices and a depreciation of the exchange rate. Now the United States is experiencing both a very lax monetary policy and a depreciating exchange rate. Some scholars argue that they are following the same strategy once recommended to the Japanese to escape the liquidity trap (see Kregel, 2009). That policy has been called "quantitative easing".

3   QUANTITATIVE EASING AND THE LIQUIDITY TRAP

The situation in which the US economy has found itself after the financial crisis has been defined as a liquidity trap. The same expression had been used with reference to Japan's position in the 1990s after the financial crisis. In particular, Krugman (1998, 2008) has on various occasions underlined that the liquidity trap is not an obsolete concept, but that it had been revived after the great crisis of 1929, namely in Japan in the 1990s and in the United States in 2007–08. He argues in his first article on the liquidity trap that monetary policy is not ineffective during a liquidity trap situation as might be, and in fact commonly is, assumed. He argues that there is no reason to switch to fiscal policy as the only available tool. Monetary policy may indeed turn out to be effective if people believe that increase in money supply will continue in the future and that as a consequence of this policy the price level in the long run will increase with respect to the current period. They must believe that the central bank is committed to generate inflation. If the central bank is not reliable in this purpose, for instance because it has a strong anti-inflationary reputation, this policy will not work (see Krugman, 1998: 4). The theory behind this assertion is not related to the Keynesian liquidity trap. Krugman states clearly that the liquidity trap concept stands by itself in any type of model. He addresses the question in an intertemporal neoclassical rational expectations model in which the allocation of consumption between two periods depends on the time preference, on the nominal interest rates and on the price level in the current and in the future period respectively. In a model with fixed prices the main variable is the nominal interest rate. Thus, if the interest rate has reached the zero level and no negative interest rate is possible, monetary policy is ineffective. If, however, prices are flexible, then monetary policy may affect the intertemporal allocation of consumption over the two periods by changing the actual and the expected inflation rates in future periods. Basically, if future inflation is expected to rise then people will prefer to consume more in the present period than in the next one and this will stimulate the economy.

Krugman argues that a liquidity trap can occur even in a flexible price economy and that it will not cause unemployment. In order to get intertemporal equilibrium in such an economy a negative real interest rate is needed. This, however, can be reached by getting deflation in the current period. This in turn makes people think, on the basis of unchanged price-level expectations in the long run, that in the next period the price level will increase again. Krugman writes explicitly:

> Of course, in a flexible-price economy even the necessity of a negative interest rate does not cause unemployment. This conclusion may surprise economists who recall the tortured historical debate about the liquidity trap, much of which focussed on the question of whether wage and price flexibility were effective as a way of restoring full employment. In this model the problem does not arise – but the reason is a bit peculiar. What happens is that the economy deflates now in order to provide inflation later. That is, if the current money supply is so large compared with the future supply that the nominal rate is zero, but the real rate needs to be negative, P falls below P*; the public then expects the price level to rise, and this provides the necessary negative real interest rate. And to repeat, this fall in the price level occurs regardless of the current money supply, because any excess money will simply be hoarded without adding to spending. At this point we have a version of the liquidity trap: money becomes irrelevant at the margin. (Ibid.: 13–14)

The important case is that of a Hicksian liquidity trap. Here output depends on consumption and insufficient consumption may constrain output. A liquidity trap may occur because people expect either that the price level will fall in the future or that the next period's income will be lower than the current one. In both cases, to make people spend now may require a negative real interest rate, which is impossible to achieve with downward inflexible prices (see ibid.: 15). This simple model may be extended to take into account investment, the state, and the open economy. The main conclusions, however, can be drawn just from the first simple model. Monetary policy becomes effective even when the nominal rate of interest is zero if the real interest rate can fall and indeed falls. Krugman (p. 33) stresses this point:

> Second, whatever the specifics of the situation, a liquidity trap is always a product of a credibility problem – the belief by the public that current monetary expansion will not be sustained. Structural factors can explain why an economy "needs" expected inflation; they can never imply that credibly sustained monetary expansion is ineffective.

The argument above can hardly be considered Keynesian. It is an extension of intertemporal neoclassical theory of consumption allocation. Krugman (2008) confirms that his previous analysis of the liquidity trap may also be applied to the current situation in the United States. Yet, the claim that the Federal Reserve is committed to raising inflation in the long run cannot be taken seriously:

> It's a curious thing that even now, when we are clearly in a liquidity trap, we still have a lot of economists denying that such a thing is possible. The argument seems to go like this: creating inflation is easy – birds do it, bees do it, Zimbabwe does it. So it can't really be a problem for competent countries like Japan or the United States. This misses a key point that I and others tried to make for Japan in the 90s and are trying to make again now: creating inflation is easy if you're an irresponsible country. It may not be easy at all if you aren't.
>
> What's the answer? Huge fiscal stimulus, to fill the hole. More aggressive GSE lending. Maybe a "pre-commitment" by the Fed to keep rates low for an extended period – that's a more genteel version of my "credibly promise to be irresponsible." And maybe large-scale purchases of risky assets. The main thing to realize is that for the time being we really are in an alternative universe, in which nothing would be more dangerous than an attempt by policy makers to play it safe.

The solution the central bank has at its disposal in order to get out of the liquidity trap then is to commit itself in a credible way to an inflationary policy in the long run. It seems from the last quotation by Krugman that all the measures taken by the Federal Reserve could be useful to pursue this goal.

The liquidity trap view has also been explained in a modern fashion by Krugman and Obstfeld (2003) in their *International Economics* textbook. The starting point is that, when the rate of interest is zero, the central bank can no longer use monetary policy to stimulate the economy. This happens because even if the central bank tries to increase the money supply through open market operations this will not make interest rates fall. If interest rates are already at zero, people will be indifferent between holding money and holding bonds. Thus they prefer to hold money rather than bonds and thus there will be an excess supply of bonds. Thus even if the central bank increases the money supply in order to depreciate the currency the exchange rate cannot increase if the rate of interest is zero. Thus this policy will not succeed in increasing output and relieve a depression. Indeed, the right policy would be to make the market believe that the long-run future exchange rate will depreciate. This can be done either by expanding the supply of money permanently or by anchoring the currency at a higher level. Only in this case can monetary policy be effective in increasing output.

The idea is that monetary policy can no longer stimulate the economy because it cannot lower the interest rate beyond zero. Then the only way to act on the real side of the economy and revive aggregate demand is through the trade balance channel. A depreciation will increase the foreign demand for domestic output if Marshall–Lerner conditions hold, and it will raise output thereby bringing us closer to full employment. Then the next question is how to get a depreciation. If the market believes that the exchange rate in the long run is a monetary phenomenon then it is sufficient to increase the money supply and announce that it will be a long-lasting policy. If this is not believed, it is necessary to intervene in the market and cause a depreciation. In both cases the effectiveness of monetary policy will be resumed. This last case, however, is not well suited to the United States, which is a big open economy and in which the domestic demand is far bigger than the external demand for domestic goods.

The policy pursued by the central bank may be criticized for different reasons. Krugman is arguing that it is right insofar as it creates inflation. Others may argue that it is wrong even if creates inflation. For example, Kregel (2009) raises another question. The policy of getting lower and lower interest rates even at long maturities would not fulfill the main task that authorities have now, that of warranting some income to banks. Kregel recalls that the same reflation policy had been attempted after the 1929 world crisis and that it was abandoned for the same reason, that banks' income fell because of the low interest rates. He distinguishes Alan

Greenspan's policy from that pursued by Ben Bernanke in that Greenspan paid attention to maintaining a spread between short and long maturities interest rates, thus making it possible for banks to gain from the spread. Indeed, Bernanke did the opposite in the two years before the crisis, slowly but constantly raising the short-term interest rate while the long-term rate did not follow. This then caused an erosion of the banks' profit margin, since they had long-term assets and short-term liabilities. The interventions of the Fed in short-term money markets in 2008 and the large purchases of mortgage-backed securities and long-term government bonds in 2009–10 were aimed at lowering both short- and long-term interest rates. However, in Kregel's opinion this policy would not restore banks' profits since it does not increase their profit margin. The extension to longer maturities may benefit households, who have to repay their debt, but this effect may be offset by the fall in interest earned on deposits (see ibid.:).

Kregel's article was written in April 2009. The latest news on bank accounting shows that banks are gaining mainly from their trading desks rather from their borrowing activity. This may be due to the ever-flourishing speculation and to the prolonged use of the same derivatives that were used before the financial crisis. An interpretation of what happened until now might be that the central bank is not particularly interested in restoring the normal operations of banks and their profitability resulting from that part of their activity, but it is satisfied with the return of their balance sheets from red to black, whatever the means to reach this result. Even speculation may help in this! This would be confirmed by the fact that the same products, which were responsible for the financial chaos that has led to the crisis, collateralized debt obligations (CDOs) and creadit default swaps (CDS), have not been banned or restricted. They are still present as part of the portfolio of financial institutions. The markets for derivatives linked to the securitization of mortgage loans have indeed dried up because of the crisis in that sector; the industry, however, has now planned to open other business perspectives by employing tools such as CDS in the insurance industry (see Auerback and Wray, 2009).

4   QUANTITATIVE EASING AS A POLICY TO STABILIZE PROFITS: A MINSKYAN ANALYSIS

In this section we shall deal with another possible interpretation of the quantitative easing policy, this time drawing on a very different theoretical background, the Minskyan analysis of financial crises and his considerations on the task of policy during the crises. His starting point, on which the analysis of the effectiveness of policy is built, is the macroeconomic model inherited by Michal Kalecki. In the following we shall briefly describe this model, using equations and discuss the policy considerations that can be derived from it and whether it could be applied to the current crisis.

Equation (11.1) defines consumption as the sum of wages earned in the consumption goods and investment sectors. Profits in the consumption sector are equal to the price of consumption goods multiplied by the quantity minus wages multiplied by the number of employed workers (see equation (11.2)). Profits in the consumption sector are equal to wages multiplied by the number of workers in the investment goods sector. Profits in the investment sector are calculated in the same way (see equation (11.3)). By rearranging, we get the equation that shows that total profits are equal to investment. By introducing in this simple model, the state, consumption out of profits and the foreign sector one can rewrite the equation for profits. Profits would then depend on investment plus state deficit plus consumption out of profits minus saving out of wages and plus the surplus in the balance of payments (see equation (11.9)).

$$C = W_c N_c + W_I N_I \tag{11.1}$$

$$\pi_c = P_c Q_c - W_c N_c = W_I N_I \tag{11.2}$$

$$\pi_I = P_I Q_I - W_I N_I = \pi_I \tag{11.3}$$

$$\pi_I = \pi \tag{11.4}$$

$$P_I Q_I = I \tag{11.5}$$

$$\pi = W_I N_I + \pi_I = I \tag{11.6}$$

$$\pi = I + Df \tag{11.7}$$

$$\pi = I + Df + C\pi - sW \tag{11.8}$$

$$\pi = I + Df + C\pi - sW + BPS. \tag{11.9}$$

The last equation (11.9) is a more realistic step in order to take into account how stabilization policy might work. In the present environment, the state is an important economic agent and workers save, while capitalists consume part of their savings rather than investing all of them.

Minsky concentrates on fiscal policy as the main stabilization tool in order to avoid a depression. Fiscal policy would stabilize profits through a double effect. The first is the obvious one whereby increased demand by the state sustains sales and thus in the above equation prevents quantities from falling; the other is through the effect on mark-ups. An increase in state expenditure should increase the mark-up (see Minsky, 1982: 85, foot-note 2, 88–9). The total effect will be stagflation. Prices will be increasing even if demand is falling. Inflation is how a big recession was avoided in the 1970s. Every increase in expenditures on consumption goods financed by transfer expenses or profit income is inflationary. Inflation is one way to mitigate the payments on past debt. In the aggregate the unwise and risky behavior of bankers and businesspeople is repaired through an economic policy that convalidates profits. Public deficits lead to profits that convalidate past aggregate investment and the total liabilities of enterprises, but the price to be paid for this result is growing inflation and inefficient management techniques.

The current situation is such that, if one wants to use Minsky's theory to show the results of current policy, the effects of projected fiscal deficit on demand depend on the items on which state expenditures are used. Most of the current and future debt by the state stem from measures that aim at supporting the financial system. It is difficult to assess their weight even simply from the accounting perspective (see IMF, 2009). Now there is the proposal to stimulate the economy through various tools, mainly tax cuts rather than increases in state expenditure. In that sense it cannot be argued that the several measures that have been taken and that are being registered as negative items in the state balance sheet will sustain the economy because they support aggregate demand and thus firms' profits.

While in the traditional closed-economy version of the above equations it is simply investment that causes profits as underlined by Minsky himself, in contemporary capitalism other items such as fall in the savings ratio, state deficit and others appear to be more important in performing that task (see Toporowski, 2008). Minsky's model, however, could be saved by arguing that all the monetary and fiscal measures undertaken until now amount to supporting or increasing the price of capital P_I. This would help to avoid a depression which would be triggered by the fall of the demand price of capital below its supply price in Minskyan terms. The relevance of this strategy, however, would be weakened in an environment where investment does not play a big role in supporting aggregate demand. In the last decades, consumption, mainly financed by debt, has been the major impetus supporting the expansion of aggregate demand. One could imagine that this growth model must be definitely abandoned and that the crisis might offer an occasion to change and to switch to an investment-driven expansion. In that case the most appropriate candidate to sustain the expansion would be public investment, perhaps in an infrastructure according to the Keynesian public works tradition. So far, however, the only plans of the government are directed toward cutting taxes, not only for richer people but also for poorer ones, which would in any case support consumption by increasing disposable income.

As Toporowski (ibid.) argues, in the current financialized environment, the decline in the savings ratio becomes an important factor in sustaining profits. Another important point is that consumption remains the main item in aggregate demand, the fall of which triggers the downturn of the cycle. In particular, inflation in asset prices allows wealthy families to consume out of capital gains or by using the proceeds of selling inflated assets. Thus, while some families were suffering from low wages and high expenses for insurance and housing, others, the most wealthy ones, were enjoying the gain of high asset prices and using them as a means to finance consumption.

Therefore, since asset prices were an important way to finance consumption and to increase aggregate demand, any policy that aims at raising these prices further, after the fall experienced during the crisis, will in fact sustain profits. Among asset prices, a distinction must be made between the price of durable goods, such as housing, and the price of financial assets. Statistical data on housing prices show that it takes a long time before their price reverts to pre-crisis levels. It is easier instead to make financial asset prices rise again. In the United States, those households able to purchase a house in the 10 years preceding the financial crisis were mostly poor ones, toward which the so-called "subprime loans" were directed. In contrast, households investing in financial assets were wealthy. Lowering all interest rates, even long-term ones, may help homeowners pay less interest on variable rate mortgages if their income is sufficient to repay the debt, but the loss due to the fall in the value of the asset in comparison to the amount of the loan contracted may even induce them to voluntarily default.

However, homeowners overall will have little interest in financial assets, provided they invested their savings in housing. For wealthier families, the story is vastly different. While suffering real estate losses, they will enjoy a rise in asset prices, both bonds and shares. In this way the poor households who have contracted loans to buy a house will lose, being left in debt, while the households whose net wealth is positive (assets minus debt) will gain both because of the return of asset values to higher levels and of a lower cost of debt.

5 QUANTITATIVE EASING AS A WAY TO RESTORE ASSET PRICES AND CONSUMPTION OUT OF WEALTH

A third and more credible hypothesis is that the central bank does not simply want to make reflation and depreciation its only objective. Nor does it want to support an investment-led growth or recovery, even less a public investment program. Rather, it wants only to restore the asset values, particularly bonds and shares, in order to save the balance sheets of financial institutions of all types, including pension funds and at the same time protect the wealth of most citizens. However, since the wealth is unevenly distributed this policy will perpetuate the current unequal distribution of wealth. Thus the unequal-consumption-based growth model would be perpetuated and the crucial role of finance in the economy would be perpetuated as well. The financialization model would not be challenged.

We can also look at the data on the recovery of stock and house prices, as well as on the wealth distribution to confirm the idea that the current strategy of the Federal Reserve is perpetuating the existing inequality in wealth distribution. Wolff (2007) defines marketable wealth (or net worth) as the current value of all marketable or fungible assets less the current value of debts. It is defined as the difference between assets and liabilities. In turn, assets are defined as the sum of gross value of owner-occupied housing, real estate, cash and demand deposits, other deposits and money market accounts, all types of bonds and other financial securities, cash surrender value of life insurance, corporate stocks and mutual funds, net equity in unincorporated business, and equity in trust funds. Total liabilities in turn are defined as the sum of mortgage, consumer and other debts (see ibid.: 5–6). Further Wolff calculates non-home wealth as net worth minus net equity in owner-occupied housing.

Wolff finds that non-home wealth is more concentrated than net worth, with the richest 1 percent (as ranked by non-home wealth) owning 42 percent of total household non-home wealth in 2004 and the top 20 percent owning 93 percent (see Table 11.2). Wolff stresses another point, which is relevant for the interpretation of the Fed's current monetary policy: wealth inequality is positively correlated to the ratio of stock prices to house prices (p. 13).

Given the trends in housing and stock prices registered in 2009 one should expect a rise in inequality as a consequence of the monetary policy currently undertaken. In fact we can see that the major stock indexes show a recovery of almost 50 percent with respect to the pre-crisis level, while the index of house prices shows a much weaker recovery rate.

Table 11.2   Distribution of net worth and non-home wealth (top 20%)

Year	Non-home wealth Gini coefficient	Net worth Top 20%	Non-home wealth Top 20%
1983	0.893	81.3	91.3
1989	0.926	83.5	93.4
1992	0.903	83.8	92.3
1995	0.914	83.9	93.0
1998	0.893	83.4	90.9
2001	0.888	84.4	91.3
2004	0.902	84.7	92.5

Source: Wolff (2007).

This view seems confirmed by Weller and Lynch (2009), who calculate losses to households as a consequence of the financial crisis. They find that total net worth as a percentage of after-tax income was more than 30 percentage points lower on average in 2008 than during the period from March 2001 to December 2007. Moreover, they argue that two-thirds of this loss was due to declines in housing wealth and the rest was caused by financial market losses (ibid.; see also Weller and Helburn, 2009). Given the different distribution that we have seen between net worth and non-home wealth, this should enforce the conclusion that the more damaged by the crisis were those who on average own only a house and have some debt.

The recovery of stock prices, which is the major result of all the massive interventions in the market by the Federal Reserve, would worsen wealth inequality. In fact, it would help the financial institutions that do not lend but only gain from speculating on their trading desks and richest households, who may restore the value of their wealth. However, it does not improve the situation of middle-income and poor households, who have only home wealth, and a debt that is much higher than the current value of the house. The lowering of the interest rate would not help substantially in reducing net debt.

6   CONCLUSIONS

Current monetary policy has evolved from traditional interest rate cuts to the so-called "quantitative easing", that is, an increase in quantities through open market operations after the interest rate has reached the zero bound. It has evolved further, now comprising open market operations on long-term maturities to lower long-term interest rates as well.

In this chapter we have examined two possible interpretations of this policy according to different theories. The first one is the renewed version of the liquidity trap in the version given by Krugman and already applied to the Japanese crisis. This interpretation is mainly focused on an intertemporal consumption model with rational expectations or perfect foresight. Its main insight is that monetary policy can be effective even if interest rates are zero if it succeeds in governing long-term expectations on inflation. In particular, the central bank, contrary to any wise purpose, should make people believe that it is and will be committed to an inflationary policy. Furthermore, a depreciation that produces inflation in the future will do the job as well. Thus the liquidity trap ceases to be an old-fashioned concept. In the present context one could argue that all the quantity interventions by the central bank are aimed at creating inflation expectations.

The second interpretation is taken from Minsky's model. In this context a very accommodative monetary policy beyond the initial lender of last resort may be useful in sustaining the price of shares and thus firms' expected profits. This interpretation, though plausible, is in contrast to the current shape of business cycles. In recent business cycles, the booms and busts are characterized not by investment fluctuations but rather by consumption fluctuations. Minsky's theory of financial instability is still valid but the version of this theory based on a business cycle that depends on investment fluctuations does not fit current events. So did we have a minsky moment? Did "it" happen again?

Another interpretation is suggested here, that the aim of monetary policy is the recovery of financial assets to sustain bank profits and to restore the value of household wealth and, eventually, consumption. This design might be considered as successful if we look at the recent data. But those signals are not encouraging if we look at the long-term sustainability of policies. The recovery of stock prices has encouraged speculation on anything possible by the big banks and profits related to it. Moreover the recovery of asset prices in contrast to the slow motion of house prices has increased the already high inequality in wealth distribution.

REFERENCES

Adrian, T. and H.S. Shin (2009), "Prices and Quantities in the Monetary Policy Transmission Mechanism", Federal Reserve Bank of New York Staff Report 396, October.

Auerback, M. and R. Wray (2009), "Banks running wild: the subversion of insurance by 'life settlements' and credit default swaps", Levy Economics Institute Policy Note 2009/9, Bard College, Annandale-on-Hudson, NY.

Bernanke, B. (2002), "Deflation: making sure 'it' doesn't happen here", Remarks before the National Economists Club, Washington, DC, November 21, Federal Reserve website (accessed February 2012).

Dodd, R. (2007), "Subprime: tentacles of a crisis", *Finance and Development*, December: 15–19.

International Monetary Fund (IMF) (2008), "Stress in bank funding markets and implications for monetary policy", ch. 2 in *Financial Stability Report*, Washington, DC, October.

International Monetary Fund (IMF) (2009), "Crisis-related measures in the financial system and sovereign balance sheet risks", IMF Working Paper, Washington, DC, July.

Kregel J. (2009), "It's that 'vision' thing. Why the bailouts aren't working, and why a new financial system is needed", Public Policy Brief 100, Levy Economics Institute, Bard College, Annandale-on-Hudson, NY.

Krugman, P. (1998), "It's baack! Japan's slump and the return of the liquidity trap", available at: http://web.mit.edu/krugman/www/; also published in *Brookings Papers on Economic Activity*, **29** (1998–2): 137–206.

Krugman, P. (2008), "Macro policy in a liquidity trap (wonkish)", Paul Krugman Blog, November, available at: http://krugman.blogs.nytimes.com/2008/11/15/macro-policy-in-a-liquidity-trap-wonkish/ (accessed February 2011).

Krugman P. and M. Obstfeld (2003), *International Economics Theory and Policy*, 6th edn, Boston, MA: Addison Wesley.

Minsky, H. (1982), *Can "It" Happen Again? Essays on Instability and Finance*, New York: Sharpe.

Sack, B.P. (2009), "The Fed's expanded balance sheet", speech available at: www.ny.frb.org/speeches/2009/sac091202.html (accessed January 2010).

Toporowski, J. (2008), "The economics and culture of financialization", paper presented at the Workshop on Credit and Debt in Present Day Capitalism, University of Manchester, 14 March.

Weller, C. and A. Helburn (2009), "Public policy options to build wealth for America's middle class", Working Paper 210 Political Economy Research Institute, University of Massachusetts at Amherst, November.

Weller, C. and J. Lynch (2009), "Fraying the private safety net: household wealth in freefall", Center for American Progress, Washington, DC.

Wolff, E.N. (2007), "Recent trends in household wealth in the United States: rising debt and the middle-class squeeze", Working Paper 502, Levy Economics Institute, Bard College, Annandale-on-Hudson, NY, June.

Index

Aargau 116
ABCP (asset-backed commercial
    paper) 115, 123, 135, 166–7
ABS (asset-backed securities) 133, 152,
    157, 229
activist rules 4, 7
Adenauer, Konrad 199
aggregate demand, support proposals
    59–60
AIG 136, 140, 141, 151, 153, 159, 168
Almunia, Joaquín 190, 198
AMLF (Asset-Backed Commercial
    Paper Money Market Mutual
    Fund Liquidity Facility) 150, 154,
    230
animal spirits 87
The Annals of Gullibility 114
anti-depression credit expansion 123
anti-growth bias 200
ARMs (adjustable rate mortgages) 116
Asian crisis 205
asset prices 26, 238, 239–40
asset-purchase programs 153
asymmetric shocks 194, 205, 210
Atesoglu, H.S. 5, 44

bad debt 14, 15, 66
bad money 14
Bagehot principle 119
Banco de México 67–8, 69, 72–7, 145
Bank of America 136, 140, 147
Bank of Canada 113, 114, 120, 123–4,
    125, 145, 166–87
    and credit easing 179–86
    and inflation 169–72
    and quantitative easing 176–9
    and zero interest rate policy 173–6
bank credit issuance 61
bank credit rationing 64, 74, 76
Bank of England 113, 119, 120, 121–2,
    145, 155, 158, 178, 196, 215, 228

Bank of Japan 143, 145, 146, 155, 158,
    179, 231
bank rescues 216
bank reserve interest 158
bank-based financial structure 67–70
banks
    capital injection into 56–7
    central *see* central banks
    commercial *see* commercial banks
    development (public) 67, 73
    Fed lending limits to 58
    and market discipline 54
    political power in Latin America 66
    private 87–90, 97
    proposals/restrictions for 54–6
    taxation on 56
Barclays 140, 147
baseline new consensus model 21, 22–4
BdL (Bank deutscher Lander) 198–9,
    200
Bear Stearns 115, 135, 140, 148, 149,
    153, 159
Bernanke, B. 113, 117–20, 121, 122,
    124, 125, 138–9, 145–6, 153, 158,
    159, 160, 231, 235
Bibow, J. 213
BIS (Bank for International
    Settlements) 145, 161
Blinder, A. 63, 120
BNP Paribas 119, 134, 147
borrower risk 95
Bradford & Bingley 216
Bretton Woods system 48, 67, 72, 201
Bundesbank 113, 114, 122–3, 198–203,
    204, 212

C–S (Carlin–Soskice) model 22–5,
    27–33
Caisse de Depots 115
Cantor Fitzgerald 148
capital assets 87, 88